Macroeconomic Linkages between Hong Kong and Mainland China

T0289445

Macroeconomic Linkages between Hong Kong and Mainland China

Hans GENBERG

Dong HE

 HONG KONG MONETARY AUTHORITY    City University of Hong Kong Press

First published 2008

ISBN: 978-962-937-161-6

Front cover photo courtesy: Highways Department, HKSAR, with kind assistance of the Transport and Housing Bureau, HKSAR.

Published by
        City University of Hong Kong Press
        Tat Chee Avenue
        Kowloon, Hong Kong
        Website: www.cityu.edu.hk/upress
        E-mail: upress@cityu.edu.hk

Printed in Hong Kong

Table of Contents

— Detailed Chapter Contents —

6.   How Much of Hong Kong's Import from Mainland China Is Retained for Domestic Use?

Frank LEUNG and Kevin CHOW

7.   Cross-Border Fund Flows and Hong Kong Banks' External Transactions vis-à-vis Mainland China

Joanna SHI and Andrew TSANG

Foreword

In discharging its responsibilities of maintaining monetary and financial stability in Hong Kong, the Hong Kong Monetary Authority (HKMA) relies on timely and accurate information about matters such as the flows of funds in the Hong Kong dollar market, current macroeconomic developments and outlook and the health of the banking sector. To obtain this information the staff of the HKMA continuously analyses incoming data on economic growth, price inflation, interest rates, and asset prices; maintains close contacts with actors in financial markets; and examines the activities of the financial institutions over which it has regulatory responsibility.

One of the functions of our economic research is to provide background analysis that allows us to interpret the data we receive in a manner that is informative for an assessment of the state of monetary and financial stability. The results of this analysis are presented in research papers intended both for internal consumption and to inform the general public and researchers elsewhere about our views on the forces that determine the evolution of Hong Kong's economy.

The papers collected in this volume are representative of the kind of analysis that is produced by our research staff. They examine the economic integration between Hong Kong and the Mainland and its impact on our economy through both trade and financial market channels. As our economic relations with the Mainland intensify, it is important to understand the possible implications for the stability of our linked exchange rate system, for our growth prospects, and for the development and stability of our financial markets.

The conclusions that can be drawn from this research help clarify a number of issues that have received considerable interest in Hong Kong. For example, it is often suggested that the strengthening of the renminbi relative to the Hong Kong dollar we have witnessed during the past two to three years will bring about significant inflationary pressures in Hong Kong due to higher prices of imports from the Mainland. One of the papers in the volume concludes that the impact is significantly weaker than commonly believed, because imports from the Mainland for domestic use are much smaller than is frequently alleged. In addition, as I have had occasion to point out in one of my Viewpoint articles, the pass-through of exchange rate changes to domestic prices is much less than one-for-one.*

Another example where thorough analysis calls into question widely held perceptions relates to the synchronisation of business cycle fluctuations in Hong Kong and the Mainland. In the chapter entitled "Hong Kong's Economic Integration and Business Cycle Synchronisation with Mainland China and the US" the authors document that while it is indeed true that co-movements of business cycles in Hong Kong and the Mainland have increased steadily since the 1990s, this is mostly due to the common influence of the US on both economies. It follows that the link of the Hong Kong dollar with the US dollar continues to be well supported by economic fundamentals.

Other chapters in the volume deal with the increasingly important financial linkages between the Mainland and Hong Kong, showing, among other things, the potential importance of our market for portfolio capital outflows from the Mainland once restrictions on these movements are reduced further, and that Mainland-related factors have an impact on the deviations of our short-term interest rates from the corresponding US dollar rates.

As I noted at the outset, the availability of in-depth analysis exemplified by the papers included in this volume is important for the Hong Kong Monetary Authority in carrying out its mandate to preserve monetary and financial stability in Hong Kong. I hope that readers will find the papers useful also as a guide to how the HKMA views the relationships and forces that determine the evolution of the Hong Kong economy, and that this volume will encourage other researchers to carry out similar studies thus contributing to a healthy discussion of the important economic issues that affect us all.

Joseph YAM
Chief Executive
Hong Kong Monetary Authority

* Exchange rate pass-through to domestic inflation. 3 April, 2008.
www.info.gov.hk/hkma/eng/viewpt/index.htm

———— List of Illustrations ————

Tables

— Acronyms and Abbreviations —

Acronyms	Name in full	Appear First on Page
ADF	Augmented Dickey-Fuller	222
ASEAN	Association of Southeast Asian Nations	233
BEA	Bureau of Economic Analysis	124
BoP	Balance of Payments	182
BP	Band-pass	58
C&SD	Census and Statistics Department	47
CAPM	Capital Asset Pricing Model	238
CEPA	Closer Economic Partnership Arrangement	10
CPI	Consumer Price Indexes	34
CPIS	Coordinated Portfolio Investment Survey	239
ETF	Exchange Traded Funds	313
EU	European Union	47
FDI	Foreign Direct Investment	15
GDP	Gross Domestic Product	4
GDPC	per capital GDP	241
GMM	Generalised Method of Moment	281
HIBOR	Hong Kong Interbank Offered Rate	6
HKMA	Hong Kong Monetary Authority	2
HKTB	Hong Kong Tourism Board	130
HKTDC	Hong Kong Trade Development Council	136
HNWIs	High Net Worth Individuals	143
IMF	International Monetary Fund	58
IPO(s)	Initial Public Offering(s)	56
IRF	Impulse Response Function	223
IT	Information Technology	124
IVS	Individual Visit Scheme	10
LERS	Linked Exchange Rate system	6
LIBOR	London Interbank Offered Rate	6

Macroeconomic Linkages
between
Hong Kong and Mainland China

Chapter 1

Introduction

Dong HE

In addition to conducting analysis of macroeconomic developments and outlook in Hong Kong, economists in the Hong Kong Monetary Authority (HKMA) also carry out research projects to study the structural forces that shape current and future developments of major macroeconomic variables. One such important structural force has been the increasing economic integration between Hong Kong and Mainland China. The research papers collected in this volume, which were completed by HKMA economists in the past two years, study the macroeconomic linkages between Hong Kong and the Mainland through both the trade and financial market channels.

The analysis of the papers is rigorous and in line with the professional standards set by researchers in the major central banks, yet the style is not overly technical, and should be accessible to readers with a general background in economics, social and political sciences. The papers shed light on important policy issues such as how resilient the Hong Kong economy is against external shocks, what is the relative importance of Mainland shocks and US shocks in influencing output and inflation in Hong Kong, how large portfolio capital outflows from China will be once its capital account is liberalised and what share of such flows will be routed through Hong Kong, and in what ways fund flows between Hong Kong and the Mainland affect Hong Kong's monetary and financial conditions.

Broadly speaking, the first part of the book is comprised of papers that focus on the "real" linkages between Hong Kong and the Mainland, and the second part of the book is comprised of papers that focus on the financial linkages. A common message coming out of the analysis is that Hong Kong has primarily served as a gateway of trade and financial flows between the Mainland and the rest of the world, and Hong Kong's cyclical conditions are very much tied to fluctuations in the volume of flows of goods, services and capital between the Mainland and its major trading partners. Such a "bridge" role is likely to remain important for Hong Kong's economic future, even though trade and financial flows that are more closely linked to developments in the domestic demand on the Mainland will gain increasing significance.

The observation that the Hong Kong economy has been more closely associated with external demand than with domestic demand for Mainland-produced goods and services is clearly demonstrated in

Chapter 2 "The Macroeconomic Impact on Hong Kong of Hypothetical Mainland Shocks". In this Chapter, the authors use an econometric model to quantify the impact on Hong Kong of a range of Mainland macroeconomic shocks. Seven hypothetical scenarios are considered: external shocks include a large renminbi (RMB) revaluation, a significant US economic slowdown, a trade war, and an oil price hike; domestic shocks include an investment retrenchment, a credit crunch, and financial instability. The magnitudes of the shocks are deliberately set to be large—typically taken as two standard deviations of the shock variable based on historical observations over a ten year period. The simulation analysis indicates that Hong Kong would be most affected if a major trade war broke out between the Mainland and its trading partners, reflecting the critical role of trade flows between the Mainland and its trading partners in influencing the cyclical conditions of the Hong Kong economy. Nevertheless, in all the shock scenarios, the size of output losses pales in comparison with that experienced by Hong Kong during the Asian crisis.

The role that Hong Kong plays in intermediating trade flows between the Mainland and its trading partners has important implications for the relationship of economic cycles in Hong Kong and on the Mainland. In Chapter 3 "Hong Kong's Economic Integration and Business Cycle Synchronisation with Mainland China and the US", the authors analyse what factors drive the co-movements of business cycles among the three economies. Their structural vector auto-regression analysis suggests that over the medium to long run, about 60% and 45% of variations in output and prices in Hong Kong respectively can be explained by US shocks, while the impact of Mainland shocks mostly concentrates on Hong Kong's price movements. They estimate that Mainland shocks explain over one-third of Hong Kong's price developments. Using a methodology to distinguish between the effects of common US shocks and idiosyncratic domestic shocks, they find little correlation between the business cycles in Hong Kong and the Mainland in the absence of the common US influences, whereas the influence of the US shocks on these two economies leads to a high degree of synchronisation. In other words, the business cycle co-movements of Hong Kong and the Mainland are largely due to the common influence of economic conditions in the Unites States.

The common influence on both Hong Kong and the Mainland of economic conditions in the US will be better understood with a closer look at the structure of trade flows between Hong Kong and its trade partners. In Chapter 4 "Hong Kong's Trade Patterns and Trade Elasticities", the authors provide a detailed description of Hong Kong's trade structure. As a service-based economy, Hong Kong's domestic exports of goods accounted for only 5% of total exports of goods and services, or equivalent to about 10% of GDP. In contrast, re-exports of goods accounted for 77% of total exports of goods and services, or equivalent to 1.5 times of GDP. Most of Hong Kong's imports are for re-exports to other economies. Specifically, imports of goods for re-exports accounted for almost 70% of total imports of goods and services, or equivalent to 1.3 times of GDP, in 2005.

With such a complicated trade structure, how would exchange rate movements affect the volume of trade flows? In order to answer this question, the authors use an error-correction model to examine Hong Kong's long-run trade elasticities as well as their short-run dynamics. Their estimates indicate that the sum of the absolute values of the estimated price elasticities of Hong Kong's direct imports and exports is greater than one, thus implying that the Marshall-Lerner condition hold for Hong Kong. Moreover, changes in re-exports and the re-export earnings are found to be sensitive to the change in the real effective exchange rate (REER) of the renminbi and income growth of the Mainland's trading partners.

While it is true that Hong Kong has played an important "bridge" role between the Mainland and the rest of the world, wouldn't this role diminish over time as the Mainland updates its own port facilities and becomes more efficient in handling the flow of goods to such an extent that the flows will bypass Hong Kong? In Chapter 5 "Service Exports: The Next Engine of Growth for Hong Kong?" the authors document that service exports have become an increasingly important source of income growth for the Hong Kong economy. Mainland China is the largest buyer of services produced in Hong Kong, and its rising service demand has played a key role in driving the strong performance of Hong Kong's service exports in recent years. The authors argue that while trade-related service exports are expected to retain strong growth, financial service exports have the highest growth potential. In other words, Hong Kong has been and will continue diversifying its entrepôt role for Mainland produced goods and services, from a heavy reliance on

4

traditional re-exports of manufactured goods toward offshore trade and services that cater to capital flows into and out of the Mainland.

Given that the Mainland is Hong Kong's largest trading partner, does this imply that the movement of the renminbi exchange rate significantly affect Hong Kong's inflation rate? As the renminbi continues to appreciate against the US dollar and the Hong Kong dollar, there has been public concern about the impact of this trend on consumer price inflation in Hong Kong. In Chapter 6 "How Much of Hong Kong's Imports from Mainland China is Retained for Domestic Use?" the authors argue that the Mainland is actually a much smaller trading partner for Hong Kong than commonly thought in terms of imports retained for domestic use. Casual observation shows that the shops that populate most of the shopping malls in Hong Kong sell international brand name goods. Even though many of these goods are made and assembled in China, as final products, they are not necessarily considered imports of Mainland origin, and the Mainland' s contribution to the value added of these international goods is a small part of their overall costs.

Unfortunately, data on retained imports are not directly available and have to be estimated using figures of total imports, re-exports and re-export margins compiled by the Census and Statistics Department. However, while the data on imports and re-exports, compiled on the basis of trade declarations, should have a low margin of statistical error, estimation of the re-export margins is a difficult task and so the margin of error there may be significantly higher. Further, the re-export margin may vary between different goods imported from different economies, being influenced, for example, by different degrees of competition among producers and also among importers. The authors of Chapter 6 carefully analyse the sensitivity of re-export margins to different assumptions, and estimate that retained imports of China origin as a percentage of total retained imports would range from 9% to 17%. Even at these levels, the dependence of Hong Kong's retained imports on the Mainland as a source, and therefore the impact of the appreciation of the renminbi exchange rate on consumer prices in Hong Kong, seems to be much smaller than commonly perceived.

In contrast to analysis of trade linkages, analysis of fund flows between Hong Kong and the Mainland suffers more from data constraints, as balance of payments data are not available on a bilateral basis. In Chapter 7 "Cross-border Fund Flows and Hong Kong Banks' External Transactions *vis-à-vis* Mainland China", the authors extract information on cross-border fund flows between Hong Kong and the Mainland from statistics on banking transactions. Assuming that all transactions are effected through the banking system, the authors find that Hong Kong was a net investor in the Mainland in terms of direct investment and portfolio investment, implying an increase in liability of Hong Kong banks *vis-à-vis* the Mainland. The authors also find that, although net Hong Kong dollar liabilities *vis-à-vis* the Mainland have remained a small proportion of total Hong Kong dollar funding in the banking system, they accounted for a significant part of the incremental movements of the latter. Thus cross-border fund flows can be an important influence on Hong Kong's interest rates and hence monetary conditions.

Under the Linked Exchange Rate system (LERS), Hong Kong dollar interest rates should track US interest rates closely. But increasing cross-border fund flows between Hong Kong and Mainland China has raised the possibility that Mainland-related factors might exert greater influence. In Chapter 8 "How Do Macroeconomic Developments in Mainland China Affect Hong Kong's Short-term Interest Rates?" the authors examine the significance of Mainland factors in determining Hong Kong's interest rates after controlling for the influences of US factors. Using a vector auto-regression model, they find that an unexpected rise in the Mainland policy interest rate, or a higher-than-expected growth in Mainland output or money supply, have had tangible influence on the three-month HIBOR. Their analysis shows that US shocks still dominate, but Mainland shocks have become more important in accounting for the unexpected fluctuations in HIBOR in recent years. For example, from autumn 2003 to spring 2005 the large negative spread between HIBOR and LIBOR was mainly due to a Mainland-related factor—strong market expectation of a large renminbi revaluation. Thus, while the HIBOR-LIBOR spread is expected to be bounded inside a band that reflects the width of the Convertibility Zone of the Linked Exchange Rate system, Mainland-related shocks could exert a significant influence on the actual size of the spread.

As the Mainland progressively liberalises its capital account restrictions, particularly on portfolio outflows by Mainland residents, how large would be such flows and what would be their impact on international financial markets? This is an important question, and there is no shortage of answers in the popular press and investment bank reports; but most of those answers are pure guesswork. In Chapter 9 "Outward Portfolio Investment from Mainland China: How Much Do We Expect and How Large a Share Can Hong Kong Expect to Capture?" the authors provide an analytical framework for a more educated guess of the potential volume of outward portfolio investment from the Mainland and how large a share Hong Kong can capture, assuming that the Mainland's capital account is as open as any other developed economies. The authors estimate that, in the counterfactual scenario that the capital account on the Mainland is as liberalised as in an average OECD country, total outward portfolio investment from Mainland China would increase from the current 5% of GDP to 15% of GDP. They also project that the amount could eventually reach 23% to 54% of GDP, and Hong Kong could capture around 10% of such investment. These scenarios appear reasonable when compared with outward portfolio investment position of major economies and past liberalisation experience in Japan.

The authors' findings suggest that while Hong Kong's comparative advantage lies mainly in its proximity and cultural affinity with the Mainland, according to their model estimates, the most important determinant of bilateral portfolio investment is the domestic share of world stock market capitalisation. An increase in Hong Kong's stock market size to that of Japan would almost double the share captured by Hong Kong. It is therefore important for Hong Kong to further strengthen the sophistication and competitiveness of its stock market in order to maintain its attractiveness as a major avenue to invest in assets of Mainland enterprises by both Mainland investors and other overseas investors.

In this regard, it is important to improve the efficiency of the price discovery mechanism, particularly for companies that issue both A shares on the Mainland and H shares in Hong Kong. Dual-listed A and H shares now account for 10 % of the Mainland (tradable) and Hong Kong stock market capitalisation. Large and persistent price differentials between A and H share prices have been observed, raising concerns about market segmentation within China and its implication for the efficiency of price discovery. In Chapter 10 "Share Price Disparity in Chinese Stock Markets", the authors study the determinants of

A-H share price disparity and find that, apart from micro market structure factors, macroeconomic factors such as renminbi appreciation expectations and monetary expansion, have also contributed to the share price disparity.

In Chapter 11 "Price Convergence between Dual-listed A and H Shares", the authors examine the impact of price gaps on the dynamics of the corresponding A and H share prices and the wider stock markets. Their findings suggest relative price convergence but not absolute price convergence (i.e. price equalisation). The A share premium tended to reduce the corresponding A share price but raise the H share price, other things being equal. However, the relationship is found to be a nonlinear one: beyond a threshold of 100%, a larger price gap would have a diminishing dampening effect on A share prices but an increasing pulling-up effect on H share prices. The authors argue that the evidence of relative price convergence suggests some degree of arbitrage on the price gaps, and points to illicit cross-border capital flows given the restrictions on the formal channels. However, such arbitrage is partial and incomplete, and the market segmentation may induce speculative activities that exacerbate market volatility. Both concerns are likely to increase as the number of dual-listed companies rises over time. Thus, it is important to increase the linkages between the two markets by improving investor access. This would enhance the price convergence process and promote the healthy development of the financial market of the whole country.

The papers collected in this volume should be seen as a first step towards an understanding of the macroeconomic linkages between Hong Kong and Mainland China. In addition to analysing such linkages from a demand perspective, which is a focus of the papers in this volume, it is also necessary to understand better the impact of increasing economic and financial integration on Hong Kong's long-run productivity and competitiveness—an area of further research by the Research Department of the HKMA.

Chapter 2

The Macroeconomic Impact on Hong Kong of Hypothetical Mainland Shocks

Dong HE

Chang SHU

Raymond YIP

Wendy CHENG

1. INTRODUCTION

Hong Kong has enjoyed an economic boom in the past four years, registering growth of 7.2% on average during 2004–07. Apart from a generally conducive global economic environment, the Mainland factor has played an important role. Hong Kong's external trade has grown strongly as the Mainland steadily expands its export market, while growing financial linkages between the two economies have opened up business opportunities in other sectors. Supportive policies to Hong Kong such as the "individual visit" scheme (IVS) and the Closer Economic Partnership Arrangement (CEPA) not only directly bring in tangible economic benefits, but also boost confidence of Hong Kong residents and the international investor community.

However, the increasing links between the two economies also raise concerns about how Hong Kong will fare if the Mainland is hit by economic shocks, which could cause the economy to deviate from its envisaged strong medium-term growth path. In the case of a positive shock, Hong Kong can expect even stronger growth. But the economy is likely to be adversely affected if there are unfavourable developments in Mainland China. Risks originated from the external sector include a possible further renminbi revaluation, an economic slowdown in the US, trade wars and further oil price hikes, while an investment retrenchment and financial instability are risk factors from the domestic economy.

This study uses a model to describe macroeconomic linkages between the two economies and assesses the impact on Hong Kong of shocks emanated from the Mainland economy. The remainder of the Chapter is arranged as follows. Section 2 documents the Mainland's contributions to Hong Kong's growth, and outlines a medium-term outlook for the Mainland economy as a baseline scenario for examining downside risks. Section 3 suggests some scenarios of macroeconomic shocks on the Mainland, while Section 4 briefly explains the modelling approach to quantifying the impact of these risks. Sections 5 and 6 discuss the shock transmission mechanisms in the Mainland and Hong Kong, and present the simulation results on assessing the impact on the two economies respectively. Section 7 puts the simulation results in historical perspective by comparing them with a few episodes of severe economic downturns in the past. Section 8 concludes.

2. THE MAINLAND FACTOR IN HONG KONG'S ECONOMIC GROWTH

The Mainland has a dominant status in Hong Kong's external trade arising from Hong Kong's status as an entrepôt intermediating goods between the Mainland and the rest of the world. In merchandise trade, the Mainland is Hong Kong's largest partner, accounting for close to 50% of the total. About 60% of Hong Kong's imports for re-exports are sourced in the Mainland, and about half of the re-exports go to the Mainland market. Connected with the merchandise trade, Hong Kong provides a range of trade-related services to the Mainland including transportation, merchanting and merchandising.[1] The Mainland is the largest destination for goods sold through offshore trade in Hong Kong, amounting to around 40% of the total value. Mainland China is also the key factor driving a boom in Hong Kong's inbound tourism. The number of Mainland tourists has been rising particularly fast since the introduction of the "individual visit" scheme in 2003, generating around half of the tourist earnings in 2004.

In terms of financial linkages, Hong Kong is a major source of investment funding for the Mainland, with the cumulative direct investment accounting for around 40% of the total at end-June 2005. In return, Hong Kong derives HK$80 billion from these investments, or about 6.3% of the Gross National Product. At the same time, the Mainland is Hong Kong's largest source of direct investment, investing close to 30% of the total. Hong Kong also helps channelling foreign funds efficiently into China. Activities related to arrangements of syndicated loans and issuances of securities for Mainland entities generate strong demand for Hong Kong's financial, legal, accounting and other professional services.

With ongoing economic reforms and liberalisation of the Mainland economy, as well as the further impetus provided by the Mainland's entry into the World Trade Organisation (WTO) and the implementation of the CEPA, the economic relations between the two economies will

---

1. Offshore trade comprises merchanting and merchandising services which intermediate trade flows without the goods involved passing through Hong Kong. In the former case, Hong Kong companies take ownership of the goods involved, while in the latter, purchases/sales of goods are arranged on behalf of buyers/sellers outside Hong Kong.

Table 2.1

Economic Developments in Mainland China and Hong Kong:

Historical Performance vs. Medium-term Projections

	Mainland		Hong Kong	
	Historical	Projection	Historical	Projection
GDP (%, yoy)	8.6	8.1	3.6	5.7
Consumption (%, yoy)	6.9	10.4	2.1	4.8
Investment (%, yoy)	12.3	10.3	2.3	7.4
Exports (%, yoy)	17.7	13.9	7.3	9.2
Imports (%, yoy)	17.5	14.8	6.5	9.3
Inflation (%, yoy)	3.1	2.8	1.0	2.1
Unemployment rate (%, per annum)	3.4	4.0	5.1	5.2
Current account (% of GDP)	2.4	2.2	3.2	9.3
Fiscal balance (% of GDP)	-2.2	-1.1	-0.4	1.3

Note: The figures are year-on-year changes unless stated otherwise. The historical performance refers to the averages for the period of 1995–2004, while the projection are averages of the forecasts made by the Oxford Economic Forecasting for 2006–10.

grow ever closer and stronger. The close linkages between the two imply that developments in the Mainland economy will have increasingly significant impacts on Hong Kong.

Both economies are envisaged to grow strongly in the medium term. Among the factors supporting potential growth in the Mainland economy, capital accumulation is occuring at a rapid speed, and labour supply continues to be plentiful, with projected increases in the working age population and continuing substantial migration from rural to urban areas. More importantly, ongoing structural reforms should help maintain fast productivity growth. Hong Kong has increasingly become a service-based economy offering a range of high value-added services to the Mainland. As such, Hong Kong can maintain robust growth by taking full advantages of the fast rising Mainland economy.

Overall, the Mainland economy is envisaged to grow at a speed of around 7.5% to 8.5% a year in the medium term, while vigilant demand management by the central bank should be able to keep inflation stable at low levels. There could also be positive shocks to the economy such as faster-than-expected productivity growth. Strong and stable economic developments in the Mainland will provide a conducive environment for Hong Kong's economic growth. Table 2.1 provides historical data of a

Table 2.2

Shock Scenarios

Scenarios	Assumption
External shocks	
1. Renminbi revaluation	10% renminbi revaluation in one step
2. Trade war	Export growth declines by 20ppt for 1 year
3. US economic slowdown	US private consumption growth declines by 2ppt for 1 year
4. Oil price hike	Oil price rises permanently by US$20 per barrel
Domestic shocks	
5. Investment retrenchment	Investment growth declines by 15ppt for 1 year
6. Credit crunch	Credit growth declines by 20ppt for 1 year
7. Banking and currency instability	Interest rate rises by 10ppt, exchange rate depreciates by 50% and credit growth declines by 20ppt for 1 year

set of key macroeconomic variables as well as a baseline medium-term projection for the two economies by the Oxford Economic Forecasting Model, which will be discussed further in Section 4.

3. SHOCK SCENARIOS

There exist, however, risks to this benign picture, which have low probabilities of occurring but could cause short-term deviations from the baseline medium-term projection. As Mainland China becomes increasingly integrated into the world economy, its economic growth is more closely aligned with global trade cycles, and thus can be affected by adverse external developments such as unfavourable exchange rate movements, a surge in protectionism, a weakening in world demand and oil price volatility. Risks of a domestic origin also exist, including swings in investment spending and instability in the financial system.

To assess how these risk factors will affect the Mainland and Hong Kong economies, we run simulations on a global macroeconomic model developed by the Oxford Economic Forecasting. (Table 2.2) The types of risks suggested above are based on the economic characteristics of the Mainland and uncertainties present in the global economy. In quantifying the shocks, the magnitudes of the shocks are deliberately set to be large—typically taken as two standard deviations of the shock variable based on historical observations over a ten year period—in order to assess Hong Kong's resilience even under unusual circumstances.[2] It needs to be emphasised that these risk scenarios are highly hypothetical. Given the Mainland's continued strong economic performance and sustained structural reforms, they are unlikely to occur, particularly in the magnitudes assumed for the simulations in this study.

3.1   External shocks

Renminbi revaluation

Despite the revaluation in July 2005 and a move to a managed float, the renminbi may continue to face upward pressures. Domestic problems of overheating may deteriorate, constituting macroeconomic imperatives for further appreciation from a domestic viewpoint. Externally, should the Mainland continue to run large current account surpluses, trade frictions will rise again, and political pressures from the trading partner countries will periodically intensify. The combined forces of domestic and external needs may lead to a re-run of the situation before the latest exchange rate reform took place. In assessing the impact of a possible further move, we assume that the renminbi will be revalued by a further 10% in one step, which is likely to be larger than what the authorities would like to see. This magnitude of revaluation is close to two standard deviations of changes in the renminbi nominal effective exchange rate in the past decade.

Trade shocks

Merchandise trade has become an increasingly significant part of the Mainland economy in recent years with exports quadrupling in the last decade and continuing to expand at a year-on-year rate around of 30% (in value terms) on a monthly basis in the last couple of years. However, the heavy reliance on external trade has made the economy more vulnerable to external shocks such as an economic slowdown in major trading partner countries and other shocks to exports such as a rise in trade frictions. Among the major trading partners, the US can have a

---

2.   Under the assumption of a normal distribution, a two-standard-deviation shock has a small probability of occurring (less than 5%).

particularly large influence as it is the Mainland's biggest market as well as a key engine driving global growth. Separately, trade frictions with a number of major trading partners have risen considerably this year as the Mainland's strong trade performance triggered a rise in protectionist sentiment in those regions.

In this light, we consider two specific trade shocks. In the first case, Mainland China's export growth is trimmed by 20 percentage points (in volume terms) due to, for example, a rise in protectionism and ensuing trade wars. The second scenario assumes that there is a setback in the US economic growth caused by a decline of 2 percentage points in the US private consumption growth for one year, which averaged at 3.7% in the past 10 years.

Oil price hike

Oil prices have been climbing steadily in the past several years. Amidst strong energy demand and concerns over disruptions to supply, oil prices are expected to remain high and volatile in the near term. In our later assessments, we assume a further $20 increase in oil prices.

3.2 Domestic shocks

Investment retrenchment

With a share of 45% in GDP, investment spending has been a key driver of the Mainland's recent business cycles. In the downswing of the cycle, developments in investment will also be crucial in determining the pace of an economic slowdown. Here we assess the impact of a decline of 15 percentage points in real investment growth as a result of, for example, a sharp reduction in FDI, a fall in firms' profitability, or lower expected returns on investment.

Credit crunch

Although progress has been made in the Mainland's banking reforms, the banking sector remains weak. Nonperforming loans remain a long-standing issue within the system. While it is generally expected that the situation will improve, there could be a new spout of bad loans which might trigger a large reduction in bank liquidity. The most immediate risk is that banks cut back lending sharply over a short period of time. We consider a case of 20 percentage point reduction in real credit growth.

Banking and currency instability

Another major shock could be a system-wide problem of financial instability, particularly when the capital account is being increasingly liberalised. This could result in capital flight, large currency devaluations and higher domestic interest rates. In simulating this risk scenario, we assume that credit growth will fall by 20 percentage points, interest rates will rise by 10 percentage points and the renminbi will depreciate by 50%—a set of conditions close to those faced by Korea at the height of the Asian financial crisis in 1997–98.

4. MODELLING APPROACH

In order to assess the impacts of these scenarios, we run simulations on a global macroeconomic model developed by the Oxford Economic Forecasting. This model is widely used for a range of purposes by central banks, international organisations such as the International Monetary Fund, other policy-making institutions and analysts in the financial markets. The model contains detailed specifications for eight most important economies including Mainland China with more than 250 equations for each. Another 36 economies are also modelled with varying degrees of details. There are also blocks of equations to describe variables for the world as a whole, as well as for different geographic regions and different types of economies such as the OECD and emerging markets.

Each country model follows a similar structure, which has neoclassical long-run properties, but exhibits "Keynesian" features in the short to medium term. On the supply side, an individual country block is modelled as a one-sector economy with a Cobb-Douglas production function in the long run. The economies have a natural growth rate, which is determined by population and productivity growth. As to the price behaviour, the Phillips curve is vertical, and inflation is a monetary phenomenon in the long run. The employment, wage and price equations can jointly solve for the equilibrium levels of real unit labour costs and unemployment consistent with the given labour's share in the production function. In the short run, there are nominal and real wage rigidities, which result in "involuntary" unemployment and monetary effects on the real economy.

The demand side is modelled based on the income-expenditure accounting framework. Consumption is a function of real income, financial wealth and interest rates, while investment is determined by funding costs. Exports are a function of world demand and competitiveness, and real domestic demand and competitiveness are the key determinants of imports. Most of the behavioural equations for the demand side are estimated using the error correction model.

While the country blocks have many shared features, individual characteristics are also reflected. For example, parameters are different across countries for the same equations, bearing out differences in countries' responses to shocks. Coverage of non-core variables, such as disaggregated expenditure components, important indicator variables such as retail sales, also depends on data availability and features of individual economies.[3]

5. MACROECONOMIC IMPACTS ON THE MAINLAND

Assessing the macroeconomic impacts of the shocks described above is a challenging task, since the transmission of these shocks involves multiple channels and interactions among the channels. The use of a macroeconomic model allows such channels to be simplified and tractable. This section discusses the transmission channels based on the structure of the Oxford Economic Forecasting model.

---

3. See the Technical Appendix (p. 31) for details of the Mainland China and Hong Kong blocks of the model.

5.1 Shock transmission channels

The most direct impact of external shocks is a reduction in the growth rate of exports from the Mainland. Export growth slows due to weaker growth in foreign income and/or a loss of competitiveness. The terms of trade may also change. These developments spill over the domestic economy through a reduction in earnings and changes in prices. In the case of a renminbi revaluation, slower activity and a fall in import prices exert downward pressures on domestic prices. Real interest rates rise due to lower inflation, and, combined with reduced earnings from the export sector, dampen investment and consumption. Imports often fall, partly reflecting weak domestic demand, and partly reflecting the 40% share of imports relating to processing trade.

The impulses of domestic shocks, such as an investment retrenchment and a credit crunch, run from the domestic economy to the external sector. The sharp slowdown in investment growth will result in a marked contraction in aggregate demand, and a fall in prices. Real interest rates rise as the decline in nominal interest rates is smaller than the fall in prices. Consumption will be restrained by the resulting decline in earnings and higher real interest rates. The drop in domestic demand leads to a marked fall in imports, but exports will be largely unaffected.

A permanent oil price hike depresses both domestic and foreign demand. It pushes up import prices which will lead to higher production costs and consumer prices. However, as utility and petrol prices are controlled by the Mainland authorities, headline inflation will probably not rise significantly. Although domestic demand is somewhat dampened by higher prices, the more significant impact is still on exports as higher oil prices lead to a global slowdown, reducing demand for Mainland goods. Such a fall in export demand will also lower domestic demand through the multiplier effect.

Financial instability will cause a sharp reduction in domestic demand, but provide a boost to external competitiveness. Investment spending, which is sensitive to funding costs and credit availability, will fall. Consumption spending, although less affected, will be weak as a result of job losses and lower earnings. Higher import prices brought about by the sharp exchange rate depreciation will lead to some increases in prices. The pick-up in inflation will be relatively mild, however, in large part reflecting the weakness of domestic demand. As the increase in inflation cannot fully offset that in nominal interest rates, real interest rates rise and depress domestic demand even further.

In the meantime, although the exchange rate depreciation leads to significant gains in competitiveness, exports may not expand immediately, reflecting the disruption on economic activity brought about by the credit crunch. Even when exports start to accelerate, the support from export earnings is not sufficient to offset the contractionary effect of the credit crunch and interest rate rises on consumption and investment. Imports slow significantly initially partly due to sluggish domestic demand, and partly due to higher import prices, but pick up subsequently along with buoyant processing trade. The current account improves, first because imports contract more sharply than exports, and later because growth of exports outpaces that of imports.

5.2   Magnitudes of impacts

In order to gauge the magnitude of impacts as described above, this subsection presents simulation results, showing the quantitative effects of the specified shocks on Mainland GDP and its components, inflation, unemployment rate, the current account balance, and the fiscal balance. The effects are described as deviations from the baseline scenarios in the two years following a shock (Tables 2.3–2.5).

In terms of the overall impact on GDP growth, the most severe shocks are the investment retrenchment, the trade war, and financial instability scenarios where overall growth declines by 7.9, 8.9 and 11.0 percentage points accumulatively in the first two years. By comparison, the renminbi revaluation and the US slowdown have the smallest impact. The effect of an oil price hike and a credit crunch is in the middle range, lowering GDP growth by around two percentage points cumulatively in two years after the shocks.

Among the components of GDP, investment spending always reacts more strongly than consumption spending. The financial instability shock has the most drastic impact on domestic demand, driving investment growth down by as much as 28 percentage points in two years. In the more contained situation of a credit crunch, investment growth slows by a cumulative 4.7 percentage points in the first two years. While external shocks tend to have only a small effect on domestic demand, the strong negative impact of trade wars on the trade sector reduces investment by around 10 percentage points in the second year after a relatively modest decline in the first. The contraction of consumption growth is milder, mostly around 3 percentage points in two years.

In terms of the impact on exports, a two-percentage-point slowdown in the US consumption growth has the biggest effect, resulting in a fall of export growth by 2.3 percentage points in a year. A 10% renminbi appreciation does not have as severe an impact as many feared as export growth slows by a cumulative 2.1 percentage points in the first two years following the currency move, reflecting low price elasticity of export demand.

Import growth declines in all the cases due to weaker domestic demand and/or a fall in processing trade as the result of a slowdown in exports. The largest declines are seen in the scenarios of financial instability, investment retrenchment, and trade wars. The trade balance changes little in many cases. However, the trade surplus narrows by 3% of GDP when export growth slows by 20 percentage points due to trade wars, while widening by around 10% of GDP in the scenarios of an investment retrenchment and financial instability, since domestic demand is severely dented.

Inflation falls as a result of weak aggregate demand in the majority of the shock scenarios. In the investment retrenchment and trade war scenarios, the inflation rate declines by more than two percentage points in two years. It falls by 1.7 percentage points in the event of a 10% renminbi revaluation, reflecting the combined effect of weak demand and lower import prices. A credit crunch and a US slowdown result in small reductions in inflation.

Inflation rises in the cases of an oil price hike and financial instability. Oil prices push up inflation, but only mildly, by less than one percentage point over two years. In the financial instability scenario, the effect of the sharp depreciation more than offsets that of weak demand, resulting in a 2.2-percentage-point rise in inflation in the first year, but a decline in the second.

The impact on the unemployment rate is small for most of the shock scenarios. Nevertheless, when a trade war breaks out, the unemployment rate will increase by 1.7 percentage points in the first two years. If investment spending experiences a sharp retrenchment, the unemployment rate rises by a cumulative 1.3 percentage points in two years.

Among the different scenarios, the trade war has the largest impact on the fiscal position, leading to a cumulative rise of 1.0 percentage point in fiscal deficits as a proportion of GDP over two years. Fiscal deficits also rise by 0.4 percentage point of GDP in the investment retrenchment case, but narrow subsequently as the economy improves. The fiscal position is largely little affected in other cases. One exception is the financial instability scenario where fiscal deficits are shown to decline by 1% of GDP in the first year of the shock. This is due to marked increases from two revenue sources. The sharp depreciation of the exchange rate will lead to a significant rise in exports and imports in the renminbi terms, and the interest rate hike will result in a surge in interest earnings. If taxes on trade and on interest earnings are maintained as, for example, the authorities are constrained to take any stimulative measures, the two enlarged tax bases will lead to a significant increase in government revenues. This more than offsets the rises in government expenditure due to higher social transfers and interest payments on government debt, resulting in an improvement in the fiscal position.

6. MACROECONOMIC IMPACTS ON HONG KONG

6.1   Shock transmission channels

The Hong Kong economy will be affected by Mainland shocks through two main channels. First, re-exports originated from the Mainland through Hong Kong to the rest of the world, re-exports via Hong Kong from the rest of the world to the Mainland and offshore trade organised by Hong Kong firms are likely to be affected by Mainland shocks. Reduced export earnings and changes in terms of trade will then spill over to the domestic economy. Second, monetary and financial conditions in Hong Kong may be altered by changes in investor confidence and in fund flows. The resulting change in Hong Kong dollar interest rates will impact asset prices and domestic demand.

Comparing the two transmission mechanisms, the trade channel is more direct and easier to quantify. As Hong Kong is the major entrepôt for the Mainland's trade, the territory's trade performance will be affected by shocks that have a large impact on the Mainland's external sector. Conversely, shocks that have limited impacts on the Mainland's exports will have little influence on Hong Kong's trade. Furthermore, since shocks to the Mainland economy are transmitted to Hong Kong mainly from the external sector to the domestic economy, those that do not have much of an impact on trade also tend to have limited effects on domestic demand.

Among the external shock scenarios, the trade channel transmission is particularly interesting in the case of a further renminbi revaluation where there are offsetting trade flows. Because of Hong Kong's position as an entrepôt, a renminbi appreciation does not mean a gain in the territory's external competitiveness. Re-exports originated from Mainland China to the rest of the world will fall along with the Mainland's exports. Nevertheless, a positive terms-of-trade effect for the Mainland will stimulate re-exports via Hong Kong from the rest of the world. Although not modelled explicitly, inbound tourism might increase as the renminbi appreciation boosts the purchasing power of Mainland visitors. The largely offsetting movements in different types of trade result in relatively minor impacts on Hong Kong's external sector initially. However, when the Mainland's imports begin to decline along with falling exports, Hong Kong's trade will also be negatively affected.

Shocks emanated from the Mainland also impinge on Hong Kong's domestic demand through the financial market linkages. Hong Kong's interest rates equal to their US counterparts plus a risk premium. Under the Linked Exchange Rate system, local interest rates are expected to follow the movements of the US rates, which can alleviate or exacerbate the impact of the original shocks. In the case of the oil shock, for example, local interest rates will rise following their US counterparts if the Federal Reserve is compelled to raise policy rates in order to keep inflation in check, imparting a further contractionary impulse on the domestic economy.

Hong Kong's risk premium are affected by the current account and fiscal positions, levels of foreign reserves as well as the Mainland's growth prospect and general emerging market risk. Shocks to the Mainland economy may lead to a sharp rise in the risk premium for emerging markets in general, and that for Hong Kong in particular due to its close geographical proximity and economic linkages with the Mainland. The resulting rate hike will severely depress domestic demand. Property prices in Hong Kong are particularly procyclical and sensitive to interest rate movements. As housing wealth accounts for a large part of wealth in Hong Kong, a decline in property prices will severely impact private consumption directly through the wealth effect as well as by undermining consumer sentiment. Higher interest rates and falling property prices also deter investment, particularly spending on buildings and constructions.

6.2   Magnitudes of impacts

In terms of the overall impact on GDP, the trade war would inflict the largest loss on the Hong Kong economy, by 6.2 percentage points over two years, amidst an abrupt shrinkage in the trade volume of the Mainland. In the investment retrenchment and financial instability scenarios, Hong Kong's growth will decline by a cumulative 3.3 and 4.4 percentage points respectively in the two years following the shocks. Specifically, in the case of financial instability, growth will fall by around 4.1 percentage points in the first year, but the decline will moderate in the second year as the trade sector starts to recover.

In contrast, a renminbi revaluation has little impact on Hong Kong's GDP growth. Upon a US slowdown, the rate of economic expansion will slow by close to 1 percentage point, but the economy will quickly return to its baseline growth path. The declines in growth caused by a credit crunch on the Mainland and an oil price hike are around 1.5 percentage points over two years.

On Hong Kong's exports, the trade war shock will have the largest impact, reducing its growth by around 16 percentage points over two years. An investment retrenchment will also lead to a relatively large decline in Hong Kong's export growth, by a cumulative 6 percentage points. In the majority of the other shock scenarios, the decline in export growth is in the order of 1–2 percentage points. Imports usually decline by a similar magnitude as exports, reflecting the large weight of Mainland-related re-exports.

Table 2.3
External Shocks

Scenario 1: Renminbi revaluation

Assumption: 10% renminbi revaluation in one step

	Mainland		Hong Kong	
	Year 1	Year 2	Year 1	Year 2
GDP (%, yoy)	-0.9	-0.9	0.0	-0.2
Consumption (%, yoy)	-0.1	-0.3	0.0	0.0
Investment (%, yoy)	-0.6	-1.1	0.0	-0.1
Exports (%, yoy)	-0.7	-1.4	0.0	-0.8
Imports (%, yoy)	0.8	-1.2	0.0	-0.8
Inflation (%, yoy)	-0.7	-1.0	0.0	0.0
Unemployment rate (%, per annum)	0.0	0.2	0.0	0.0
Current account (% of GDP)	-0.5	-0.4	0.2	0.0
Fiscal balance (% of GDP)	-0.2	-0.1	0.0	0.0

Note: Figures are deviations in percentage points from the baseline.

Scenario 2: Trade war

Assumption: Export growth declines by 20ppt for 1 year

	Mainland		Hong Kong	
	Year 1	Year 2	Year 1	Year 2
GDP (%, yoy)	-5.8	-3.1	-3.2	-3.0
Consumption (%, yoy)	-1.3	-1.9	-1.6	-2.6
Investment (%, yoy)	-2.8	-9.9	-1.7	-2.4
Exports (%, yoy)	-20.0	0.0	-10.4	-5.7
Imports (%, yoy)	-12.2	-9.5	-10.3	-5.6
Inflation (%, yoy)	-0.6	-1.9	-0.5	-1.5
Unemployment rate (%, per annum)	0.8	0.9	0.8	2.0
Current account (% of GDP)	-3.1	0.1	-3.7	-5.0
Fiscal balance (% of GDP)	-0.6	-0.4	-0.1	-0.8

Note: Figures are deviations in percentage points from the baseline.

Reflecting the impact on exports and imports, the trade war shock will slash Hong Kong's trade surplus by 8.7% of GDP. The oil price hike also has a large impact on the current account, reducing the surplus by 4.1% of GDP. In other shock scenarios, the trade balance is not much affected, and there is a small improvement in the current account position in some cases, e.g. financial instability.

The largest impact on domestic demand in Hong Kong comes from

Table 2.3

External Shocks

(continued)

Scenario 3: US economic slowdown

Assumption: US private consumption growth declines by 2ppt for 1 year

	Mainland		Hong Kong	
	Year 1	Year 2	Year 1	Year 2
GDP (%, yoy)	-0.6	0.2	-0.9	0.2
Consumption (%, yoy)	-0.1	-0.1	-0.8	-0.1
Investment (%, yoy)	-0.3	-1.1	-1.0	0.0
Exports (%, yoy)	-2.3	3.0	-1.3	1.1
Imports (%, yoy)	-1.5	1.1	-1.3	1.0
Inflation (%, yoy)	-0.1	-0.1	-0.1	-0.1
Unemployment rate (%, per annum)	0.1	0.0	0.2	0.3
Current account (% of GDP)	-0.3	0.4	-0.2	0.4
Fiscal balance (% of GDP)	-0.1	0.0	0.0	-0.1

Note: Figures are deviations in percentage points from the baseline.

Scenario 4: Oil price hike

Assumption: Oil price rises permanently by US$20 per barrel

	Mainland		Hong Kong	
	Year 1	Year 2	Year 1	Year 2
GDP (%, yoy)	-0.9	-1.4	-0.6	-0.9
Consumption (%, yoy)	-0.6	-0.8	-0.5	-1.1
Investment (%, yoy)	-0.8	-3.0	-0.3	-0.3
Exports (%, yoy)	-1.7	-0.1	-0.9	-1.1
Imports (%, yoy)	-1.4	-1.9	-0.9	-1.1
Inflation (%, yoy)	0.3	0.4	0.1	-0.1
Unemployment rate (%, per annum)	0.1	0.2	0.1	0.3
Current account (% of GDP)	-1.3	-0.6	-2.0	-2.1
Fiscal balance (% of GDP)	-0.1	-0.1	0.0	-0.3

Note: Figures are deviations in percentage points from the baseline.

financial instability on the Mainland, with both consumption and investment growth falling by 5–6 percentage points in the first year before stabilising in the second, reflecting a sharp increase in interest rates of 9 percentage points brought about by a surge in risk premium. In the trade war and the investment retrenchment scenarios, interest rates rise by around 2 percentage points. Consequently the impacts on the

Table 2.4
Domestic Shocks

Scenario 5: Investment retrenchment

Assumption: Investment growth declines by 15ppt for 1 year

	Mainland		Hong Kong	
	Year 1	Year 2	Year 1	Year 2
GDP (%, yoy)	-5.6	-2.3	-1.9	-1.4
Consumption (%, yoy)	-1.4	-1.7	-1.4	-1.1
Investment (%, yoy)	-15.0	-5.8	-1.7	-1.1
Exports (%, yoy)	-0.9	0.9	-3.5	-2.4
Imports (%, yoy)	-11.3	-5.1	-3.4	-2.3
Inflation (%, yoy)	-0.6	-1.7	-0.3	-0.8
Unemployment rate (%, per annum)	0.7	0.6	0.5	1.1
Current account (% of GDP)	3.7	6.3	-0.8	-1.2
Fiscal balance (% of GDP)	-0.4	-0.1	0.0	-0.3

Note: Figures are deviations in percentage points from the baseline.

Scenario 6: Credit crunch

Assumption: Credit growth declines by 20ppt for 1 year

	Mainland		Hong Kong	
	Year 1	Year 2	Year 1	Year 2
GDP (%, yoy)	-1.8	-0.3	-0.9	-0.5
Consumption (%, yoy)	-0.5	-0.4	-1.1	-0.7
Investment (%, yoy)	-3.8	-0.9	-1.4	-0.7
Exports (%, yoy)	-0.1	0.3	-0.5	-0.4
Imports (%, yoy)	-1.5	-0.9	-0.5	-0.4
Inflation (%, yoy)	-0.1	-0.4	-0.1	-0.2
Unemployment rate (%, per annum)	0.2	0.1	0.2	0.5
Current account (% of GDP)	0.5	0.9	0.3	0.5
Fiscal balance (% of GDP)	-0.1	0.0	0.0	-0.1

Note: Figures are deviations in percentage points from the baseline.

domestic economy are milder, with consumption and investment growth declining by 2–4 percentage points in the first two years.

Hong Kong's inflation will be significantly affected by the trade war and financial instability, declining by 1.5–2 percentage points in two years. Other shocks have little effects on inflation in Hong Kong.

Reflecting their impacts on economic growth, the trade war and financial instability shocks will raise the unemployment rate by 2–

Table 2.4

Domestic Shocks

(continued)

Scenario 7: Banking and currency instability

Assumption: Interest rate rises by 10ppt, exchange rate depreciates by 50% and credit growth declines by 20ppt for 1 year

	Mainland		Hong Kong	
	Year 1	Year 2	Year 1	Year 2
GDP (%, yoy)	-4.7	-6.3	-4.1	-0.3
Consumption (%, yoy)	-2.1	-1.9	-5.0	-0.3
Investment (%, yoy)	-12.8	-14.8	-5.8	0.1
Exports (%, yoy)	-0.1	3.5	-2.9	-0.9
Imports (%, yoy)	-9.8	-1.9	-3.2	-0.8
Inflation (%, yoy)	2.2	-1.4	-0.7	-1.2
Unemployment rate (%, per annum)	0.6	0.6	1.1	1.7
Current account (% of GDP)	5.0	5.1	0.8	0.7
Fiscal balance (% of GDP)	1.0	-0.8	0.0	-0.5

Note: Figures are deviations in percentage points from the baseline.

3 percentage points in two years. Other shocks have milder effects on unemployment in Hong Kong.

Government deficits will rise by close to 1% of GDP in two years in the case of the trade war, and around 0.3–0.5% in the financial instability and oil price hikes scenarios as declines in government revenues from taxes on income and profits were larger than declines in government consumption and investment. The fiscal position is not much affected in other cases.

6.3   Caveats

A note of caution is in order when interpreting the simulation results. Given the complexity of economic transmission mechanisms, model simulation typically only provides an incomplete account of what would happen in the shock scenarios. Many other factors might affect the outcomes, but are difficult to be fully captured by a model.

The analysis so far, for example, has not assumed any policy response on the part of the Mainland authorities. Authorities often take measures to support the economy when deemed necessary. For example, when the full depth of the Asian crisis became apparent, monetary policy was loosened on the Mainland and a steady stream of fiscal packages, geared to infrastructure projects, were undertaken. During 2001–02, fiscal stimulus was injected to counter the large negative shock brought about by the global economic slowdown in the wake of the 9/11 event. If monetary and fiscal stimuli are considered in those risk scenarios, the economic downturns will be shallower than envisaged earlier. In Hong Kong, the government's large net asset position allows the use of fiscal policy to help cushion the impact on domestic demand if and when necessary.

As also indicated in earlier discussions, the outcomes in some of the shock scenarios can be critically affected by expectation effects. The way Hong Kong's risk premium is modelled captures in many important ways expectation effects through financial linkages, but still may not reflect their full impacts. For example, if further appreciation of the renminbi is expected, there can be large capital inflows into Hong Kong, partly because of its close proximity and economic links to the Mainland economy, and partly because the Hong Kong dollar is used as a proxy in the absence of full convertibility of the renminbi. The resulting large liquidity can help hold down interest rates. Some funds may enter equity and stock markets, pushing up asset prices. Given the wealth effect in Hong Kong, higher asset prices, especially property prices, can significantly boost consumption and residential investment. Developments in the domestic economy can cushion the negative impact of a renminbi appreciation, leading to a milder slowdown or even higher overall growth. On the downside, though, large speculative capital flows may be withdrawn from Hong Kong if renminbi appreciation expectations cease, thus pushing the economy into a deeper downturn.

7. HISTORICAL PERSPECTIVES

To gauge the plausibility of the analysis of this study, the shock scenarios and simulation results can be usefully compared to actual historical episodes of economic downturns (Table 2.5). In general, the simulation results appear to be plausible, although the economic losses in Hong

Table 2.5

Historical Episodes

	Tiananmen incident (1989)		Macroeconomic Adjustment (1994–96)		Asian Crisis (1997–98)	
	Mainland	Hong Kong	Mainland	Hong Kong	Mainland	Hong Kong
GDP (%, yoy)	-7.2	-5.3	-3.9	-2.1	-1.8	-9.7
Consumption (%, yoy)	-7.9	-4.9	1.0	-1.8	-3.6	-12.2
Investment (%, yoy)	-26.6	-3.1	-19.2	7.1	2.9	-18.4
Exports (%, yoy)	10.0	-14.4	-2.3	-7.4	2.6	-9.4
Imports (%, yoy)	-17.5	-16.6	-25.1	-7.8	-3.2	-10.7
Inflation (%, yoy)	-0.3	2.6	+9.6 (1994) -15.9 (1995–96)	-2.5	-9.1	-3.4
Unemployment rate (%, per annum)	0.6	-0.3	0.4	0.8	0.1	1.6
Current account (% of GDP)	0.0	2.6	2.9	-8.2	2.5	2.1
Fiscal balance (% of GDP)	-0.1	-1.2	0.0	-0.2	-0.5	-1.2

Note: Figures are changes in percentage points during a historical episode.

Kong during the Tian'anmen incident and, most notably, the Asian crisis were greater than the predictions in any of our simulated scenarios.

This can be explained by the fact that historical episodes reflect the combined impact of multiple shocks, whereas our simulation exercises focus mostly on a single shock. For example, the Tian'anmen incident represented not only a large shock to domestic demand on the Mainland but also a political shock to Hong Kong. The collapse of domestic demand in Hong Kong during the Asian crisis reflected a sharp rise in interest rates as a result of the crisis in the region, as well as the bursting of the property market bubble in the local economy. Replicating the historical episodes by the model would require a careful calibration of all the shocks—some of which cannot be easily quantified—hitting the economy during that period of time.

8. CONCLUDING REMARKS

The simulation analysis of this study suggests that Hong Kong is able to withstand macroeconomic shocks that are deliberately calibrated to be of small probability events but of considerable magnitudes. In most of the scenarios we consider, Hong Kong's economic growth falls relatively moderately, by less than 1.5 percentage points cumulatively in the two years following the shock. But the financial instability and trade war shocks would have larger impacts. In the former case, growth can decline by around 4.4 percentage points. The most drastic scenario is the trade war shock, which can lower growth by a cumulative 6 percentage points in Hong Kong over two years.

Nevertheless, even in the worst cases, the size of the output losses pales in comparison with that experienced by Hong Kong during the Asian crisis. Even in that extreme case, however, the Hong Kong economy endured without major defaults by the corporate sector, the household sector, or the government. Also, the simulations have not assumed any policy response by either the Mainland or the Hong Kong government to cushion the impact of shocks. In fact, with a strong net asset position, the Hong Kong government has sufficient room for policy manoeuvre, and can use fiscal policy to provide support to the domestic economy when deemed necessary.

Overall, this study demonstrates Hong Kong's macroeconomic resilience. Flexible labour markets and strong net asset positions of both the private sector and the public sector render the Hong Kong economy considerable capacity to absorb adverse shocks.

Major Equations
in the Mainland and Hong Kong Blocks
of the Oxford Economic Forecasting Model

The Oxford Economic Forecasting (OEF) model is a global, general equilibrium model. It contains detailed specifications for eight most important economies including Mainland China with more than 250 equations for each of them. Around 36 countries are also modelled with varying degrees of detail. The country blocks have similar structures, and similar variables in key behavioural equations. There are also blocks of equations to describe the evolution of variables for the world as a whole, as well as for different geographic regions and different types of economies such as the OECD and emerging markets.

The rest of the Technical Appendix describes the major equations in the Mainland and Hong Kong blocks. A number of conventions are used in the equation listing. Lower-case letters indicate natural logarithms. Data are in quarterly frequency. The subscript t denotes the time. Δ indicates a first difference, and Δ_4 a change over four quarters ago. Most major behavioural equations are estimated in an error-correction form, and long-run relationships appear in square brackets. Seasonal dummies are not reported. A full list of variables is provides at the end of the equation listing.

The Mainland block

As one of the eight major economies in the OEF global model, Mainland China is modelled with a great deal of details. The block consists of the real economy, prices, the labour market, the banking and energy sectors.

1. Real output

GDP is modelled by the expenditure approach, breaking down to domestic demand (private consumption, government consumption and investment) and trade.

$$Y_t = DD_t + X_t - M_t$$

2. Domestic demand

(i) Domestic demand

$$DD_t = C_t + I_t + G_t$$

(ii) Private consumption

Private consumption is determined by real income, real financial wealth (mainly in the form of savings) and real interest rates. Real income has a significant role, influencing consumption directly or indirectly through the accumulation of income into financial wealth. Wealth held in the property or stock markets is not taken into account. Interest rates have relatively small effects.

$$\Delta_4 c_t = 0.306\Delta_4 y_t^d + 0.276\Delta_4(w_{t-1}^f - p_{t-1}) - 0.002((0.500)(R_{t-1}^l + R_{t-1}^s) - \Delta_4 p_{t-1})$$
$$- 0.172[c_{t-4} - 0.900 y_{t-4}^d - 0.100(w_{t-4}^p - p_{t-4})]$$

(iii) Investment

Unlike the investment equation for the OECD countries which is based on a Tobin's-Q type formulation, investment in Mainland China is modelled as the sum of funding sources, which include foreign direct investment, government funding, domestic loans and self-financing by businesses from profits and other funding sources.

$$I_t = I_t^{bud} + I_t^{fdi} + I_t^{loan} + I_t^{self}$$

Among the different sources, self-funding is the largest component. It is modelled as relating to the level of economic activity, the operating surplus as a proxy for self-financing potential, competitiveness, capacity utilisation and the lending rate.

$$\Delta_4 i_t^{self} = -0.700 + 0.500\Delta_4 i_{t-1}^{self} + 0.050\Delta_4 \log(C_{t-1} + G_{t-1} + X_{t-1}) + 0.001\sum_{i=0}^{3} capu_{t-i}$$

$$-0.005\Delta_4(R_t^l - (100.000)(\pi_{t-1}^{ppi}))$$

$$+(0.005)(100.000)(\sum_{i=0}^{3}(FFUNDS_{t-i} + NETPRO_{t-i})/\sum_{i=0}^{3}Y_{t-i})$$

$$-0.700[i_{t-4}^{self} - 0.964\log(C_{t-4} + G_{t-4} + X_{t-4}) + 0.114wcr_{t-4} + 0.021R_{t-4}^l]$$

3. External trade

(i) Exports

The export equation is similar to that for other economies in that the key determinants are a demand variable (world demand for the Mainland exports) and competitiveness. The measurement of competitiveness is based on relative unit labour costs, which are affected by changes in wages and exchange rates in Mainland China as well as those in its trading partners. There are two additional variables in the model. Capacity utilisation — measured by model estimates of the output gap — has an inverse relation with exports. FDI to the Mainland has been rising very fast in recent years as foreign companies use Mainland China as a low cost production base. An FDI variable is included to capture the impact of fast growth of FDI which tends to be export-oriented.

$$\Delta_4 x_t = -7.100 + 0.122\Delta_4 x_{t-1} + 1.559\Delta_4 wt_t - (0.003)(0.250)\sum_{i=0}^{3} capu_{t-i}$$

$$-(0.002)(0.250)\sum_{i=4}^{7} capu_{t-i}$$

$$-(0.100)(0.250)(\Delta_4 wcr_t + \Delta_4 wcr_{t-1} + \Delta_4 wcr_{t-3} + \Delta_4 wcr_{t-4})$$

$$-0.691[(x_{t-4} - wt_{t-4} - fdi_{t-4} + 0.153wcr_{t-4})]$$

(ii) Imports

Imports consist of fuel imports, non-fuel retained imports and imports for re-exports. The final imports are directly taken as the half of the export volume. The equation for retained imports is broadly similar to the export equation, but with domestic demand as the demand variable. Capacity utilisation has a positive relationship with imports to reflect the need for more imports when resources of the economy are restrained. Competitiveness is measured as the relative price between imported and domestic products, and is also affected by changes in the exchange rates of the renminbi.

$$M_t = M_t^d + M_t^f + 0.500X_t$$

$$\Delta_4 m_t^d = -0.080 + 0.398\Delta_4 m_{t-1}^d + 1.162\Delta_4 dd_t - 0.182\Delta_4 (p_{t-1}^{mg} - p_{t-1}^{ppi}) - 0.100\Delta_4 e_t$$
$$+ (0.003)(0.250)\sum_{i=0}^{3} capu_{t-i} + (0.002)(0.250)\sum_{i=4}^{7} capu_{t-i}$$
$$- 0.411[m_{t-4}^d + 1.890 - dd_{t-4} + 0.300(p_{t-4}^{mg} - p_{t-4}^{ppi}) - 0.003T_{t-4}]$$

4. Prices

(i) Consumer prices

Consumer prices are a weighted average of fuel, agricultural and retail prices. Reflecting the changing composition in private consumption, agriculture prices – mainly the food component in the CPI basket – carries a declining weighting. Retail prices have the largest, and an increasing, weighting.

$$P_t = 0.050P_t^{fu} + (0.150/T_t)P_t^{agr} + (0.950 - (0.150/T_t))P_t^{rpi}$$

(ii) Agriculture prices

Agriculture prices are affected by earnings, employment and production costs:

$$\Delta_4 p_t^{agr} = 0.500\Delta_4 p_{t-1}^{agr} + (0.200/T_t)(\Delta_4 eru_{t-1} + \Delta_4 eru_{t-2}) + (0.200/T_t)\Delta_4 etu_{t-1}$$
$$+ 0.100 p_t^{ppi} - 0.250[(p_{t-4}^{agr} - p_{t-4}^{ppi})]$$

(iii) Retail prices

Retail prices are related to a range of prices including fuel, agriculture and industrial prices.

$$\Delta_4 p_t^{rpi} = 1.550 + 0.200\Delta_4 p_{t-1}^{rpi} + 0.050\Delta_4 p_t^{fu} + 0.350\Delta_4 p_t^{agr} + 0.400\Delta_4 p_t^{ppi}$$
$$+ 0.100\Delta_4 (pop_t^u - pop_t) - 0.350[p_{t-4}^{rpi} + 0.100 p_{t-4}^{fu}$$
$$- (0.500/T_{t-4}) p_{t-4}^{agr} + (0.900 - 0.500/T_{t-4}) p_{t-4}^{ppi}]$$

(iv) Industrial prices

As a key price driver in the model, industrial prices are determined by capacity utilisation, costs for non-labour inputs and unit labour costs:

$$\Delta_4 p_t^{ppi} = -1.300 + 0.100\Delta_4 p_{t-1}^{ppi} + 0.150\Delta_4 p_{t-2}^{ppi} + 0.300\Delta_4 p_{t-3}^{ppi} + 0.250\Delta_4 p_{t-4}^{ppi}$$
$$+ 0.100(\Delta_4 er_t + \Delta_4 er_{t-1}) + 0.100(\Delta_4 (et_{t-4} - y_{t-4}) + \Delta_4 (et_{t-8} - y_{t-8}))$$
$$+ 0.100(\Delta_4 nlc_t - \Delta_4 nlc_{t-4}) + (0.003)(0.250)\sum_{i=0}^{3} capu_{t-i}$$
$$- 0.200[p_{t-4}^{ppi} - 0.750(er_{t-4} + et_{t-4} - y_{t-4}) - 0.250 nlc_{t-4}]$$

5. Interest rates

Interest rates are modelled as a mark-up over the US interest rate:

$$R_t = Max(0.500, (0.100 R_t^{FED,US} + (100.000)(0.500)(\pi_{t-1} + \pi_{t-4} - 2.000)))$$

Hong Kong block of equations

The equation block modelling the Hong Kong economy shares many features with the Mainland block, but also has its distinctive features to reflect the economy's characteristics.

1. Real output

GDP is also modelled by the expenditure approach:

$$Y_t = DD_t + X_t - M_t$$

2. Domestic demand

(i) Domestic demand

$$DD_t = C_t + I_t + G_t$$

(ii) Private consumption

Apart from disposable income, financial wealth and real interest rates, the variable of property prices is also included in the private consumption equation to reflect the importance of housing wealth in determining consumer behaviour in Hong Kong. Interest rates have a bigger economic impact in Hong Kong than in the Mainland.

$$\Delta c_t = 0.211 + 0.261\Delta(w_t^p - p_t^c) - 0.281\Delta(w_{t-1}^p - p_{t-1}^c) - 0.002\Delta R_t$$
$$- 0.092[c_{t-1} - 0.600y_{t-1}^d - 0.250(w_{t-1}^p - p_{t-1}^c) - 0.150(w_{t-1}^f - p_{t-1}^c) + 0.003RR_{t-1}]$$

(iii) Investment

Investment is split into spending on buildings and construction and business investment on machinery, equipment and computer software.

$$I_t = I_t^g + I_t^{bus} + I_t^{res}$$

(iv) Business investment

The equation for business investment follows a Q-theory where Q is defined as the marginal product of capital relative to the interest rate. Profit maximising firms invest when the marginal return is greater than replacement cost (Q>1).

$$\Delta_4 i_t^{bus} = -1.305 - 0.285(i_{t-4}^{bus} - k_{t-4}) + 0.013QR_{t-4}$$

(v) Investment on buildings and construction

Spending on buildings and construction is determined by interest rates, property prices and population:

$$\Delta_4 i_t^{res} = -5.260 + 0.500\Delta(p_{t-1}^{prop} - p_{t-1}^c) - 0.010\Delta RR_{t-1} - 0.020\Delta RR_{t-2}$$
$$-0.500[(i_{t-1}^{res} - pop_{t-1} - y_{t-1})]$$

3. External trade

(i) Exports

Reflecting Hong Kong's entrepôt status, merchandise exports are decomposed into domestic exports, re-exports and exports of services.

$$X_t = X_t^g + X_t^s$$

$$X_t^g = X_t^{dg} + X_t^{rg}$$

(ii) Domestic exports

Domestic exports are determined by competitiveness and world trade:

$$\Delta x_t^{dg} = 1.000 + 0.450\Delta wt_t + 0.254\Delta wt_{t-1} - 0.100\Delta wcr_t$$
$$-0.146[(x_{t-1}^{dg} - wt_{t-1} + 0.350 wcr_{t-1})]$$

(iii) Re-exports

In the re-exports equation, the Mainland's total trade volume (exports plus imports) is the key determinant, carrying higher coefficients both in the short and long run than the variable measuring competitiveness.

$$\Delta x_t^{rg} = 0.900 + 0.164\Delta x_{t-1}^{rg} + 0.570\Delta trade_t^{CN}$$
$$-0.160[(x_{t-1}^{rg} - trade_{t-1}^{CN} + 0.050 wcr_{t-1})]$$

$$TRADE_t^{CN} = X_t^{CN} + M_t^{CN}$$

(iv) Exports of services

Exports of services consist of trade-related exports, which grow growing along with merchandise trade, and the rest. Non-trade-related exports are affected by world demand and the relative price between export and import services.

$$X_t^s = X_t^{nts} + (X_t^g + X_{t-1}^g)/15.000$$

$$\Delta x_t^{nts} = -0.050 + 1.894 \Delta y_{t-1}^w - 1.114 \Delta (p_t^{xs} - p_t^{ms})$$
$$- 0.127[x_{t-1}^{nts} - y_{t-1}^w + 0.800(p_{t-1}^{xs} - p_{t-1}^{ms}) + 0.020T_t \ ]$$

(v) Imports

Imports are also disaggregated into imports of services, retained imports and imports for re-exports. The final component is determined by re-exports, and hence affected by the Mainland's trade performance.

$$M_t = M_t^g + M_t^s$$

$$M_t^g = M_t^{fu} + M_t^{retain} + M_t^{rg}$$

(vi) Non-fuel retained imports

Retained imports are related to domestic demand and the competitiveness variable:

$$\Delta m_t^{retain} = -1.430 + 1.437 \Delta \log(X_t^{dg} + DD_t)$$
$$- 0.565[(m_{t-1}^{retain} - \log(X_{t-1}^{dg} + DD_{t-1}) - 0.150 wcr_{t-1})]$$

(vii) Imports of services

Imports of services are determined by total demand – proxied by GDP – and the relative price between export and import services:

$$\Delta m_t^s = -1.453 - 0.108 \Delta m_{t-1}^s + 0.208 \Delta y_t$$
$$- 0.299[m_{t-1}^s - 1.200 y_{t-1} + 0.200(p_{t-1}^{ms} - p_{t-1}^{xs})]$$

4. Prices

(i) Consumer prices

Consumer prices are deposed into three components – rental costs, fuel prices, and other prices.

$$P_t = 0.025P_t^{fu} + 0.050RENT_t + 0.925P_t^{nfu}$$

(ii) Rental costs

Rental costs are determined by total earnings, property prices and population.

$$\Delta rent_t = 0.122 + 0.500\Delta p_t^{prop} + 0.250(\Delta et_t + \Delta er_t)$$
$$- 0.150[rent_{t-1} - \log((0.1)(R_{t-1}^{lt})(P_{t-1}^{prop})) + 0.500(w_{t-1}^p - pop_{t-1}) - 0.005T_t \,]$$

(iii) Prices excluding fuel and rents

Prices excluding fuel and rents are positively related to economic growth, prices of non-fuel retained imports and the domestic demand deflator:

$$\Delta p_t^{nfu} = 0.010 + 0.211\Delta p_{t-1}^{nfu} + 0.100\Delta p_t^{mrg} + 0.307\Delta p_t^{dd} + 0.100\Delta p_t^{ppi}$$
$$+ \Delta \log(TR_t + 1.000) + 0.050(g_t + g_{t-1})$$
$$- 0.154[p_{t-1}^{nfu} - 0.300p_{t-1}^{mrg} - 0.500p_{t-1}^{dd} - 0.200p_{t-1}^{ppi} - \log(TR_{t-1} + 1.000)]$$

5. Interest rates

Interest rates equal to their US counterparts plus the risk premium. The latter is measured as the sum of the premium paid for foreign debt and the probability of devaluation for the Hong Kong dollar.

$$R_t = Max(0.500, (R_t^{US} + R_t^{risk}))$$

$$R_t^{risk} = R_t^{emc} + (0.500)(100.000)(PROBDEV_t)(EERI_t /115.000 - 1.000)$$

List of Variables

Name	Description
C	Real private consumption
CA	Current account balance
CAPU	Capacity utilisation
DD	Real domestic demand
E	Bilateral exchange rate between the renminbi and US dollar
EERI	Effective exchange rate
ER	Average earnings of the whole economy
ERU	Average urban earnings per employee
ET	Total employment
ETU	Urban employment
FDI	Cumulative foreign direct investment
FFUNDS	Enterprises' self-raised funds for investment
G	Real government expenditure
I	Real total investment
I^{bud}	Real investment funded by government budget (Mainland)
Ibus	Real private sector investment on machinery and equipment
I^{fdi}	Real investment funded by foreign capital flows
I^{g}	Real government investment (Hong Kong)
I^{loan}	Real investment funded by loans
I^{res}	Real investment on buildings and construction
I^{self}	Real investment funded by all other sources
K	Real capital stock
M	Real imports (appear in the Mainland block)
M^{CN}	Mainland China's real imports (appear in the Hong Kong block)
M^{fu}	Fuel imports

M^g	Imports of goods
M^{retain}	Non-fuel retained imports of goods
M^{rg}	Real imports of goods for re-exports
M^s	Real imports of services
NETPRO	Profits net of interest payments
NLC	Cost index for non-labour inputs
P	Consumer price index
P^{agr}	Purchasing price index for agricultural products
P^c	Deflator for consumption indicator
P^{dd}	Deflator for domestic demand
P^{fu}	Fuel component of the consumer price index
P^m	Import price
P^{mrg}	Import price of non-fuel retained goods
P^{ms}	Import price of services
P^{nfu}	Consumer price index exclude fuel and rents
P^{ppi}	Producer price index
P^{prop}	Property price index
P^{rpi}	Retail price index
P^{xs}	Export price of services
π	CPI inflation
π^{ppi}	Producer price inflation
POP	Total population
POP^u	Urban population
PROBDEV	Probability of devaluation
QR	Relative returns on physical capital (Tobin's Q)
R	Key short-term interest rate
R^{emc}	Risk premium for emerging economies (excluding currency risk)
$R^{FED,US}$	US federal funds rate
R^l	Interest rate on loans or bank lending
R^{lt}	Long-term interest rate
R^{risk}	Risk premium associated with exchange rate

R^s	Interest rate on 1-year savings deposits
R^{US}	Key short-term interest rate of US
$RENT$	Property rentals
RR	Real interest rate of personal sector
T	Time trend
TR	Effective tax rate
$TRADE^{CN}$	Total trade of Mainland China (appear in the Mainland block)
W^f	Net financial wealth of personal sector
W^p	Housing wealth
WCR	Relative wage cost index
WT	World trade index
X	Real exports
X^{CN}	Real exports of Mainland China (appear in the Hong Kong block)
X^{dg}	Real domestic exports of goods
X^g	Real exports of goods
X^{nts}	Real exports of non-trade-related services
X^{rg}	Real re-exports
X^s	Real exports of services
Y	Real GDP
Y^d	Real household disposable income
Y^w	Real world GDP
YC	Year-on-year rate of change in real GDP

Chapter 3

Hong Kong's Economic Integration and Business Cycle Synchronisation with Mainland China and the US

Hans GENBERG

Li-gang LIU

Xiangrong JIN

1. INTRODUCTION

While Hong Kong's monetary policy is effectively tied to the US, its real economy is increasingly linked to the Mainland economy through trade, FDI, tourism, and financial markets. As an entrepôt and an international financial centre, Hong Kong intermediates a lion's share of Mainland's external trade, provides significant flows of foreign direct investment, and acts as the largest overseas fund raising centre for Mainland companies. Hong Kong has also become a favourite tourist destination of Mainland visitors, whose spending in Hong Kong was equivalent to 5% of Hong Kong's private consumption expenditure in 2004. Anecdotal evidence suggests that the pace of economic integration between Hong Kong and the Mainland has accelerated greatly since the return of Hong Kong to the Chinese sovereignty in 1997. It is widely expected that the pace of economic integration will increase further as the Mainland moves to make its exchange rate more flexible and its capital account more open.

Closer economic integration with the Mainland has naturally raised a question as to whether the business cycles in the two economics have become more synchronised. According to the Optimal Currency Area (OCA) theory first developed by Mundell (1961), the degree of business cycle synchronisation between two economies may have important implications for the optimal monetary arrangement between them. The OCA theory suggests that an intra-area fixed exchange rate or a common currency is the most appropriate for a group of economies that are closely integrated through the product, factor, and labour markets that have similar degree of business cycle synchronisation and are subject to common economic shocks. If the business cycles are similar and shocks are common, then a coordination of monetary policies is desirable, with a common currency as the ultimate form of policy coordination. However, if shocks are predominantly country-specific or idiosyncratic, then the ability to conduct independent monetary and fiscal policy becomes more important in helping an economy adjust to such shocks.[1]

---

1. The early OCA literature is not concerned with the possibility that the OCA criteria and the decision to form an OCA can be an endogenous process. Frankel and Rose (1998) demonstrate that as a group of countries adopts a common currency their markets may become increasingly integrated, thus resulting in increased business cycle synchronisation and more symmetrical transmissions of economic shocks.

This Chapter assesses quantitatively the current state of business cycle synchronisation between Hong Kong and the Mainland. Because the US economy continues to be one of the most important trading partners of and investors in Hong Kong and, more importantly, because Hong Kong shares a common monetary policy with the US since 1983 when Hong Kong adopted the Linked Exchange Rate System (LERS), it is useful to compare business cycle synchronisation between Hong Kong and the Mainland with that between Hong Kong and the US. This Chapter attempts to achieve three objectives: First, it provides a quantitative assessment on economic and financial integration among these three economies by constructing a number of indicators for key aspects of economic integration. Secondly, the Chapter provides an updated assessment on the current status of business cycle synchronisation between Hong Kong and the Mainland and between Hong Kong and the US. Thirdly, the Chapter examines to what extent Hong Kong's output and price developments are affected by shocks from the Mainland and the US economy and whether the business cycle co-movements with the Mainland are driven by some common shocks.

The empirical findings here suggest that economic integration between Hong Kong and the Mainland, relative to that of the US, has intensified, especially through the real economy channels such as trade, FDI, and cross-border consumption. In addition, the degree of business cycle synchronisation in recent years between Hong Kong and the Mainland has also increased significantly, following a trough in the 1990s. Hong Kong's business cycle synchronisation with the Mainland has been quite high in recent years; but its synchronisation with the US has been even higher. Given that the US is one of the most important markets for both the Mainland and Hong Kong, it is possible that Hong Kong's high business cycle correlation with both economies in recent period has been driven mainly by the US economy. Our findings confirm this observation.

In terms of transmission of economic shocks, we find that in the short run, Hong Kong's output and price changes are mostly affected by domestic shocks. However, Hong Kong is predominantly affected by US shocks in the medium and long run, while the Mainland shocks have become a prominent force affecting Hong Kong's price developments, in addition to the US's and Hong Kong's own price shocks.

The rest of the Chapter proceeds as follows. Section 2 assesses the degree of economic and financial integration between the three economies using a number of key indicators based on economic theory. Section 3 assesses the degree of business cycle co-movements between these economies over time. Section 4 examines how output and price shocks are transmitted across these three economies and to what extent Hong Kong's economic shocks can be explained by those from the Mainland and the US. Section 5 discusses policy implications and concludes.

2. ECONOMIC INTEGRATION AMONG HONG KONG, THE MAINLAND, AND THE US

Economic integration was affected by both real-economy and financial-market channels. The real-economy channel refers to economic linkages through bilateral trade, FDI, and tourism. The financial channel is mostly affected by capital flows and policy interest rates. This section quantifies the degree of economic integration achieved so far by constructing a selective set of indicators on some key aspects of real economy and financial integration.

2.1 Trade integration

Trade generally promotes economic integration. It is well documented that intra-industry trade based on economies of scale, rather than comparative advantages, will allow economies to specialise in the same sectors and thus lead to increased similarities between trading partners, which in turn help promote business cycle synchronisation. On the other hand, inter-industry trade often leads to specialisation in different industries, thus leading to less co-movement of sectors and less business cycle synchronisation.

Following Shin and Wang (2004), the intra-industry trade index ($IIT_{ij,t}$) can be defined as follows:

$$IIT_{ij,t} = 1 - \frac{\sum_k | X_{ij,t}^k - M_{ij,t}^k |}{\sum_k (X_{ij,t}^k + M_{ij,t}^k)} \qquad (1)$$

Figure 3.1
Intra-industry Trade Index

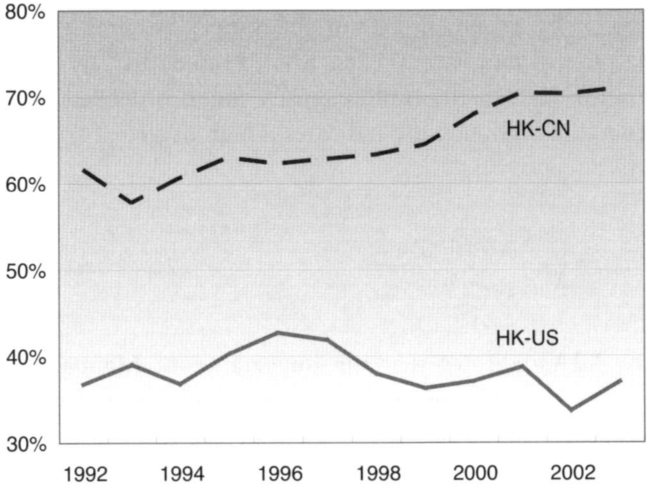

Sources: CEIC, C&SD, OECD, and authors' estimates.

where subscripts i and j denote pairs of economies; X and M represent exports and imports; and k denotes an industry sector measured by the one-digit Standard International Trade Classification (SITC) code. If an industry sector between Hong Kong and the Mainland exports and imports nearly equal amount of similar products, the numerator of equation (1) will be close to zero. As a result, the IIT index will be close to 1, suggesting a high degree of intra-industry trade. If the IIT index is close to zero, it implies a low level of intra-industry trade.

Figure 3.1 presents our calculated intra-industry trade indexes between Hong Kong and the Mainland and between Hong Kong and the US using total trade data. Intra-industry trade between Hong Kong and the Mainland has been gradually increasing from around 60% to over 70% over the past 12 years, suggesting that Hong Kong has a similar trade structure with the Mainland. On the other hand, intra-industry trade intensity between Hong Kong and the US remained fairly stable within the range of 35% to 45%, suggesting the trading pattern has not changed much over time. In fact, the level of intra-industry trade between Hong Kong and the Mainland is comparable with that among the EU economies.

47

Another trade integration measure often used is the trade intensity index. This index is similar to a bilateral trade share measure, but it controls for the relative size of an economy in the world trade. It is therefore a better measure than the simple bilateral trade shares. Following Frankel and Rose (1998), Kose, Prasad, and Terrones (2003) and Otto *et al* (2001), the trade intensity index is defined in equation (2). In general, a high measure indicates a high degree of trade intensity between two economies.

$$Trade_{HKj,t} = \frac{X_{HKj,t} + M_{HKj,t}}{X_{HKworld,t} + M_{HKworld,t}} \qquad (2)$$

Figure 3.2A indicates that the importance of Mainland trade in Hong Kong's total trade has increased significantly, rising from less than 15% in the early 1980s to close to 50% in 2004. We also observe the same pattern for re-exports. This suggests that Hong Kong has gained its importance as an intermediary between Mainland exports and the world markets since the Mainland decentralised its foreign trade regime in the 1980s. However, Hong Kong's direct trade with the Mainland for

Figure 3.2
Trade Intensity Index

A. Hong Kong and the Mainland

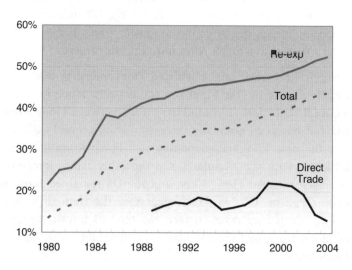

B. Hong Kong and the US

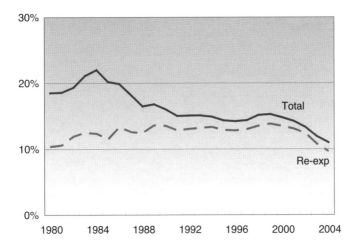

Sources: CEIC, IFS, and authors' estimates.

domestic consumption has remained at around 15% on average. Figure 3.2B shows that Hong Kong's bilateral trade with the US as a ratio in Hong Kong's total trade has declined by half from around 20% in the early 1980s to only 10% in 2004, largely reflecting the transfer of the manufacturing capacity to the Mainland. Overall, the trade intensity index presented in Figure 3.2 suggests that the Mainland accounts for increasingly larger shares in Hong Kong's trade, while Hong Kong's trade intensity with the US appears to have declined over time.

2.2 FDI exposure

FDI is another measure of integration in the real economy. Analogous to the trade measures, the FDI share measures bilateral direct investment (both inward, FDI_Inij,t, and outward, FDI_Outij,t ,) as a share of total inward and outward FDI (represented by FDI_Iniworld,t and FDI_Outiworld,t, respectively) of Hong Kong.

$$FDISH_{ij,t} = \frac{FDI\_In_{ij,t} + FDI\_Out_{ij,t}}{FDI\_In_{iworld,t} + FDI\_Out_{iworld,t}} \qquad (3)$$

Figure 3.3
FDI Exposure

A. FDI flow

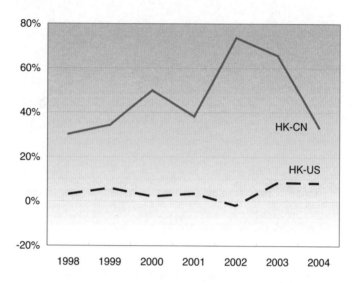

B. FDI stock

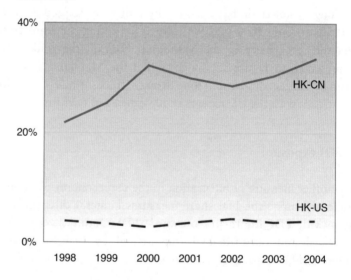

Note: The negative share in 2002 in Figure 3.3A reflects a net outflow of FDI from Hong Kong to the US.

Sources: CEIC and authors' estimates.

Figure 3.3 presents Hong Kong's FDI exposure on both a flow and a stock basis. Figure 3.3A shows that Hong Kong's FDI exposure to the Mainland by flow statistics has more than doubled from around 30% in 1998 to 66% in 2003 before it fell back to close to 30% in 2004, suggesting Hong Kong firms have taken up investment opportunities on the Mainland by directing the majority of their outward FDI to the Mainland. On the other hand, the FDI exposure of Hong Kong in the US remained negligible until 2002 before increasing to 10% in 2004. Figure 3.3B suggests that Hong Kong's FDI exposure to the Mainland measured by FDI stock has increased steadily from 22% in 1998 to 30% in 2003 while its exposure to the US has remained low and relatively flat at around 3%, largely because the US is one of the world's largest FDI recipients and investors.

2.3 Tourism related cross-border consumption

Associated with the rising cross-border tourism between Hong Kong and the Mainland, cross-border consumption has gone through a period of rapid expansion. A study by Ho *et al.* (2006) shows that

Figure 3.4
Cross Border Consumption

A. Consumption

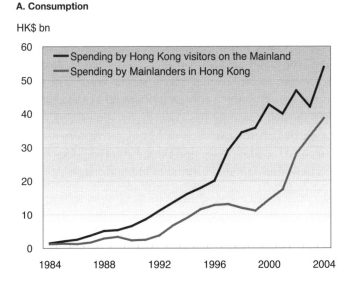

B. Consumption share

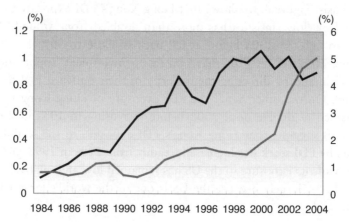

— Hong Kong visitors' spending on the Mainland as a share of Mainland household consumption (LHS)

— Mainlanders' spending in Hong Kong as a share of Hong Kong PCE (RHS)

Sources: Ho, *et al*., (2006)

visitors from both sides of the border spend much more than they did 20 years ago and Hong Kong visitors to the Mainland spend more than their Mainland counterparts in aggregate (Figure 3.4A). Figure 3.4B shows Mainland visitors' spending in Hong Kong as a share of Hong Kong's private consumption expenditure has risen particularly fast in recent years, from around 1.5% in 1999 to 5% in 2004. Meanwhile, the spending of Hong Kong residents on the Mainland as a share of its household consumption has also increased steadily, from less than 0.2% two decades ago to around 1% in recent years. The growth rate of cross-border consumption has been quite rapid as the share of private consumption of each economy has risen by five times over the past two decades. In particular, the spending of Mainland visitors in Hong Kong jumped sharply after 2000, reflecting the substantial policy shift to relax travel restrictions on Mainland visitors to Hong Kong.

2.4 Money market integration

In this section, we examine three aspects of money market integration: US dollar and renminbi deposits as ratios of total foreign currency deposits in Hong Kong, Hong Kong dollar demand on the Mainland, and correlation of benchmark policy rates.

Figure 3.5A presents the ratios of US dollar and renminbi deposits as a share of total foreign currency deposits in Hong Kong. The US dollar deposits stayed at around 70% in 2004, suggesting the dominant role of the US dollar in total foreign currency deposits in Hong Kong. However, US dollar position has experienced a sharp swing. It dropped by more than half from 85% in the mid 1980s to 40% in the early 1990s before returning to the current level. As banks in Hong Kong were allowed to take the renminbi deposits only recently, the absolute scale of renminbi deposit as a ratio to total foreign currency is still relatively small. However, the rate of growth of the renminbi deposits has been rapid, in part reflecting the expectation of the renminbi appreciation.

Figure 3.5B shows the estimated Hong Kong dollar currency holdings by the Mainland residents (Ho, *et al.*, 2006). The estimates suggest that Hong Kong dollars held by Mainland residents as a proportion of total Hong Kong dollars in circulation has risen dramatically from 5% in 1990 to close to 60% in 2004.

We next examine the correlation of monetary policy rates. We choose one-year benchmark lending rate for the Mainland, one-year HIBOR (Hong Kong Interbank Offer Rate) for Hong Kong, and the federal fund rate for the US. Figure 3.5C depicts correlation coefficients of monthly data for each year between 1991 and 2005. Indeed, notwithstanding some abnormal behaviour during the Asian financial crises in 1997–98, the high correlation of the policy rates between Hong Kong and the US is not surprising. This largely reflects Hong Kong's LERS, which links the Hong Kong dollar to the US dollar. As expected, there appears to be little similarity in the behaviour of the policy rates between Hong Kong and the Mainland, suggesting Mainland monetary policy is mainly driven by its own domestic factors. Although the policy rates of Hong Kong and the Mainland are hardly correlated, the monetary conditions indices of these two economies, which is weighted by real interest rate, real effective exchange rate, and money stock, have shared a relatively high correlation since the 1990s (Figure 3.5D).[2]

---

2. This is indeed mainly due to the movements of the real effective exchange rate (REER) of both economies because of their de-facto peg to the US dollar (until July 2005 in the Mainland's case). Hong Kong's monetary condition index is a weighted sum of Hong Kong dollar REER, renminbi REER, and real interest rate and the Mainland's monetary condition index is a weighted sum of its REER and real lending rate.

Figure 3.5
Money Market Integration

A. Foreign currency deposit ratios in HK

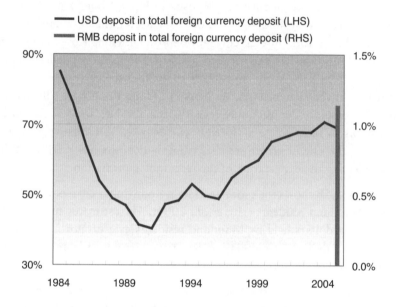

B. HKD currency holding by Mainlanders/Total HKD currency

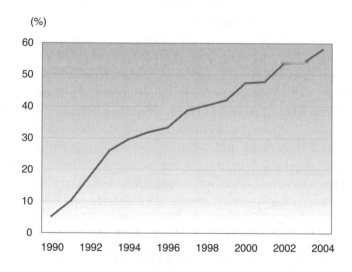

C. Correlation of interest rates

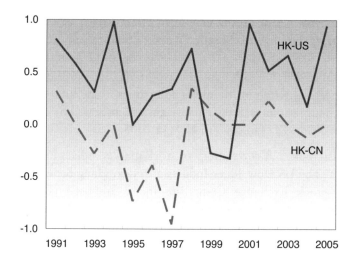

D. Evolution of monetary conditions indices

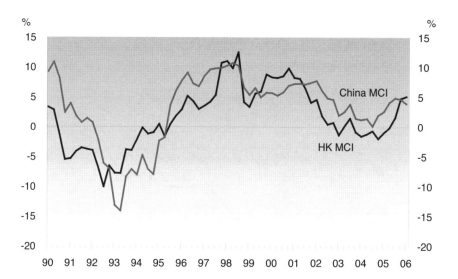

Note: The correlation between HK MCI and China MCI is 0.758

Sources: Sources: CEIC, Ho et al. (2006), and authors' estimates.

2.5   Stock market integration

Mainland firms began raising capital in Hong Kong's stock market in 1987. Largely because of Mainland firms' fund-raising activities, the Hong Kong Stock Exchange has become the third largest market in Initial Public Offering (IPO) in the world. Figure 3.6A indicates the weight of capitalisation of Mainland companies in the total Hong Kong Stock Exchange capitalisation. This weight has increased by almost eight folds from 5% in 1993 to close to 40% in 2005.

We also looked at correlations of stock market indices in these three economies. The US Dow Jones Industrial Index, Hang Seng Index, and Shanghai Stock Exchange Composite Index are used (Figure 3.6B). In terms of co-movements of the indices, Hong Kong's stock market is closely correlated with that of the US, whereas the Mainland index appears to have a pattern of its own. There is little positive correlation between the Hang Seng Index and the Shanghai Index.

In summary, despite relatively high real economy integration between Hong Kong and the Mainland as measured by trade, cross-

Figure 3.6

Stock Market Integration

A. Market capitalisation

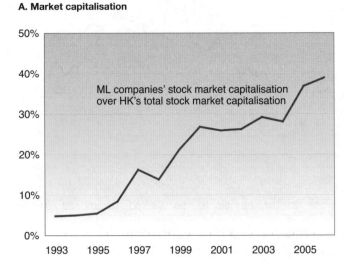

B. Correlation of market indices

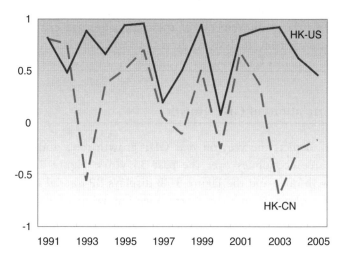

Sources: Authors' estimates.

border consumption and FDI, the Mainland appears to have little in common with Hong Kong in terms of monetary policy rates and the co-movements of the stock market indexes, notwithstanding a quite close correlation of monetary conditions. The Hong Kong dollar's peg to the US dollar and the largely closed nature of the Mainland capital account, which drives a wedge between domestic and external fund flows, may have prevented convergence of the financial market indicators. This situation may change in the future as the Mainland progressively liberalises capital account controls.

3. BUSINESS CYCLE CO-MOVEMENTS THROUGH TIME

A business cycle is usually defined as fluctuations of real GDP around some measure of its potential level. Business cycle synchronisation refers to the degree of co-movements of output fluctuations across economies and time. Following the conventions of the existing literature, we provide two measures of business cycle synchronisation: correlations of real GDP growth rates and their band-pass (BP) filtered cyclical component,[3 & 4] and correlations of output gaps and their BP filtered cyclical component., In addition, the co-movements of these measures are examined using principal component analysis to determine whether there is a common factor that explains synchronisation among the three economies.[5]

3.1 Correlations of GDP growth

Figure 3.7 depicts the year-on-year GDP growth rates and their cycles for the three economies over the past 25 years. Figure 3.7A displays GDP growth rates and the Figure 3.7B displays BP filtered GDP growth rate.[6] Two observations are worth mentioning here. First, business

Figure 3.7
GDP Growth—Hong Kong, the Mainland, and the US

A. Real GDP, year-on-year growth rates

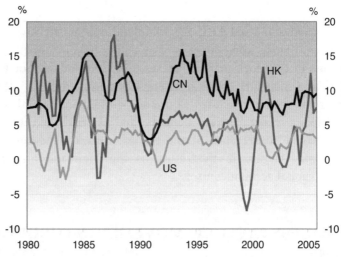

3. See Frankel and Rose (1998) and IMF Occasional Paper 152 (1997), for instance.
4. The cyclical component of quarterly real GDP is derived by using the band-pass filter proposed by Baxter and King (1999). This filter removes low-frequency trend variation (slowly evolving secular trends) and smoothes high-frequency irregular variation (rapidly varying seasonal or irregular components), while retaining the major features of business cycles.
5. See Gerlach-Kristen (2005) for example.
6. BP filter retains frequency components between 6 and 32 quarters.

B. Real GDP cycles (BP-filtered)

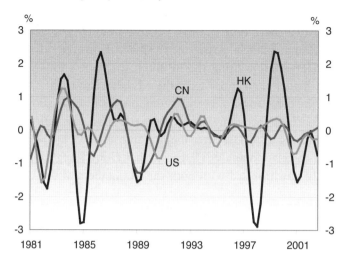

Sources: CEIC and authors' estimates.

Table 3.1

Output Correlations

HK with:	Correlation of real GDP			Correlation of GDP cycles		
	(YoY growth rates)			(band-pass filtered)		
	1979–89	1990–99	2000–05	1979–89	1990–99	2000–02
CN	0.04	0.36	0.46	0.28	0.13	0.92
US	0.09	-0.21	0.85	0.32	0.18	0.92

Sources: CEIC and authors' estimates.

cycles in Hong Kong appear to be quite volatile, compared with those in Mainland China and particularly those in the US. Secondly, the volatility of business cycles on the Mainland has declined markedly since 1995 and followed the US cycles rather closely.

Table 3.1 presents Hong Kong's output correlations with the Mainland and the US from 1979 to 2005. Two observations are in order. First, the correlation of Hong Kong's real GDP growth rates with those of the Mainland has increased markedly over time, while the correlation with the US turned negative in the 1990s before reaching the high of 0.85 during the last five years. The negative correlation in the 1990s was largely due to a sharp drop of the GDP growth in Hong Kong associated with the Asian financial crisis in 1997–98. However, after adjusting the irregular variation using the BP filter, the correlations with the US were even higher than those with the Mainland over the two periods. Secondly, the correlation of cyclical components of GDP showed similar patterns for both economy pairs. In particular, the correlation rose markedly during 2000–02 after dipping into its lows in the 1990s. The BP filtered correlation analysis suggests that Hong Kong's business cycle was equally synchronised with both the Mainland and the US in recent years.

We examine this further by analysing the correlations of the eight-year moving windows over the sample period. The rationale of using an eight-year moving window is that a full business cycle in the US usually last between six quarters and eight years (Baxter and King, 1999).

Figure 3.8 displays Hong Kong's correlation coefficients of the eight-year moving windows with the Mainland and the US. Quite remarkably, the eight-year moving correlation coefficient of GDP growth between Hong Kong and the Mainland rose from around minus 0.2 in the early 1980s to close to 0.7 in the mid-1990s. This was probably driven by rapid trade integration following the opening of the Mainland economy. However, the correlation coefficient dropped significantly from 1997 to 2002 (Figure 3.8A), a period when Hong Kong was severely affected by the Asian financial crisis in 1997–98, to which China was largely immune. The correlation coefficient has since recovered to around 0.4 in eight years up to 2004, reflecting the rapid recovery of the Hong Kong economy and continued high growth on the Mainland. While the correlation of GDP growth rates in Hong Kong and the Mainland China increased until 1998, those between Hong Kong and the US started to move into the opposite direction after 1988, reaching minus 0.3 in 1998 before a sharp recovery to 0.4 in eight years up to 2004, the same degree of correlation as between Hong Kong and the Mainland.

Compared with their counterparts in panel A, the correlations of the BP-filtered GDP growth rates in panel B demonstrate a similar but smoother pattern. While moving together in the same direction, the cyclical correlations between Hong Kong and the US have been

Figure 3.8
Growth and Cycle Correlation

A. Real GDP, year-on-year growth rates

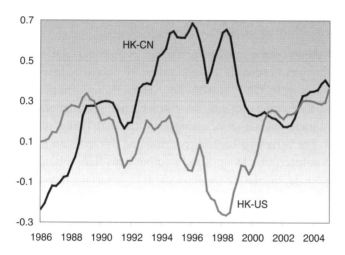

B. Real GDP cycles (BP-filtered)

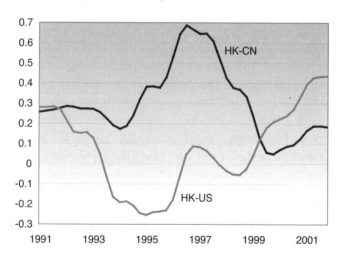

Note: For Figure A, the first correlation reported is for the period between 1979:Q1 and 1986:Q4.
For Figure B, the first correlation reported is for the period between 1982:Q1 and 1989:Q4 as
the BP filter often drops the first and the last three years of data in calculation.

Sources: CEIC and authors' estimates.

persistently higher than those between Hong Kong and the Mainland since 1999.

3.2 Correlations of output gaps

Figure 3.9 shows output gaps as a percentage of potential GDP on a quarterly basis for the three economies as well as their BP filtered components. Similar to the year-on-year GDP growth rate, Hong Kong's output gaps show the largest fluctuations among the three economies. It experienced some substantial under-utilisation of resources in the mid 1980s, the late 1990s, and 2003. The latter two occasions correspond to the Asian financial crisis and SARS respectively. Hong Kong's output gaps have rebounded sharply in recent periods, suggesting the economy is experiencing increased capacity constraint.

Table 3.2 reports the correlation of output gaps and their cyclical components for the three pairs of economies. Following the methodology used in Dodsworth, *et al.* (1997), a business cycle is identified from a trough to a trough and we calculate correlation coefficients of both output gaps and BP-filtered output gaps for the identified cycles. These correlation coefficients are reported in Table 3.2A. The correlation coefficients of output gaps and their cyclical components for Hong Kong and the Mainland were quite high in the 1990s, but they dropped substantially during 1998–99 and 2003, before rising again to similar levels in the early 1990s. The output gap correlations between Hong Kong and the US were low before the mid 1990s and were even negative from the mid 1990s to 1998–99. Since then, the correlation between these two economies increased markedly, recording a correlation coefficient of 0.98 in the latest cycle. Hong Kong's output gaps appeared to be more correlated with those of the Mainland before the Asian financial crisis in 1997–98 but more correlated with those of the US after the crisis. Table 3.2A also shows that the output gap correlation between the Mainland and the US was high before the mid 1990s, but it became negative in the second half of 1990s before rising to a relatively high level again in the latest cycle.

Table 3.2B shows the output gap correlation for longer periods. It shows that the correlation between Hong Kong and the Mainland in the new millennium rose to 0.52 from 0.32 in the 1990s. Over the same

Figure 3.9
Output Gaps and Cycles

A. Output gap

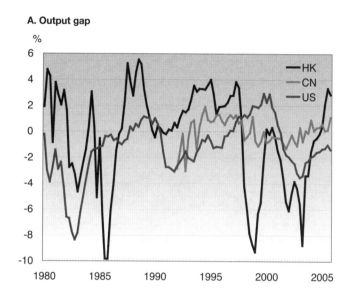

B. BP-filtered output gap

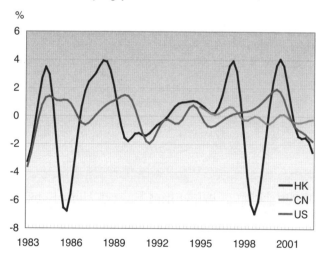

Sources: US Congressional Budget Office and authors' estimates.

Table 3.2

Output Gap and Cycle Correlation

A. Output Gap Correlation for Short Periods

	Cycle 1	Cycle 2	Cycle 3	Cycle 4	Cycle 5	Cycle 6
Based on Ygap:	1980Q1–1985Q4	1985Q4–1990Q1	1990Q1–1995Q3	1995Q3–1999Q1	1999Q1–2003Q2	2003Q2–present
HK–CN	**-0.51**	**0.07**	0.67	0.69	0.21	0.67
HK–US	0.00	0.38	0.15	-0.70	0.46	0.98
CN–US	**0.67**	**0.75**	0.59	-0.56	0.02	0.64
Based on BP-filtered Ygap:	1980Q1–1985Q4	1985Q4–1990Q1	1990Q1–1996Q1	1996Q1–1998Q4	1998Q4–2003Q2	
HK–CN			0.98	0.78	0.20	
HK–US	0.15	-0.35	0.21	-0.51	0.39	
CN–US			0.89	-0.39	0.35	

Note: Numbers in bold are from IMF(1997) study.

Sources: IMF (1997) and authors' estimates.

B. Output Gap Correlation for Longer Periods

Based on Ygap:	1980–89	1990–99	2000–present
HK–CN		0.32	0.52
HK–US	0.24	-0.57	0.51
CN–US		0.12	-0.19

Source: Authors' estimates.

period, the correlation of output gaps between Hong Kong and the US recovered even more strongly and reached 0.51 during the period from 2000 to the present, from a large negative value of -0.57 in the 1990s. The correlation coefficients of the output gaps between China and the US changed from positive in the 1990s to negative during 2000 to 2005, although the magnitudes were small.

Figure 3.10
Output Gap and Cycle Correlation

A. Output gap correlation

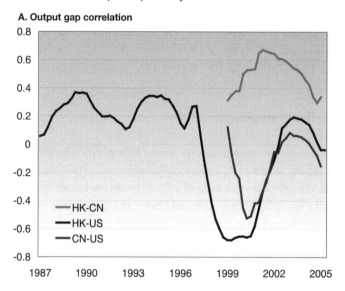

B. BP-filtered output gap correlation

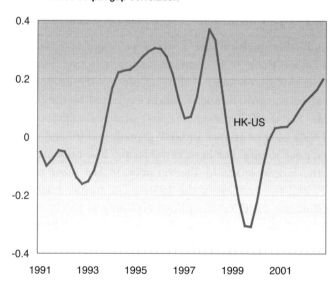

Note: For Figure A, the first correlation reported is for the period between 1980:Q1 and 1987:Q4.
For Figure B, the first correlation reported is for the period between 1984:Q1 and 1991:Q4.

Sources: Authors' estimates.

Figure 3.10 presents the time-varying correlation coefficients using the eight-year rolling windows. Figure 3.10A indicates that the output gap correlations for the Hong Kong-Mainland pair were higher than those for the Hong Kong-US pair. The correlation between Hong Kong and the US appeared to track closely with that between the Mainland and the US from 1999 to 2005.

3.3   Principal component analysis

The correlation analysis suggests that Hong Kong's business cycle synchronisation with the Mainland has increased over time. Despite the LERS, the correlation of business cycles between Hong Kong and the US in the 1990s was negative. In addition, the correlation analysis also suggests that Hong Kong was more correlated with the Mainland when there was a common external shock to both of them (for example, the Asian financial crises in 1997–98). However, the three economies tend to move closely together in 2000–05, a period when the US economy was growing strongly. Because the US is the second largest export market of both Hong Kong and the Mainland, one would wonder whether the increased correlation between Hong Kong and the Mainland was affected by a common factor, that is, the US effect.

To study this question, we apply a principal component analysis to test whether there is a common factor affecting business cycles among these three economies. Table 3.3 reports the proportions of the variance of output growth and inflation explained by the first principal component. For the full period, the first principal component explains 48% and 61% of the variance in GDP growth and inflation respectively for the three economies. For both variables the first principal component explains the largest share of the variance in the most recent period (2000–05) and the smallest in the 1990s. The former might reflect the strong US income effect on the global economy in recent years and the latter might be due to the Asian financial crisis and brief periods of deflation experienced in Hong Kong and the Mainland. Factor loadings for the full period for both GDP and CPI show that loadings for each economy are similar, suggesting they are likely to be influenced by a common factor. Whether the US is the common factor will be analysed in the next section.

Table 3.3

Principal Component Analysis

	GDP growth		CPI inflation	
	Variance explained by 1st Principal Component	Factor Loading	Variance explained by 1st Principal Component	Factor Loading
Full Period	48	US 37	61	US 32
		CN 38		CN 29
		HK 24		HK 39
1980–89	49	US 44	57	US 45
		CN 44		CN 10
		HK 12		HK 44
1990–99	46	US -20	57	US 33
		CN 56		CN 25
		HK 64		HK 42
2000–05	77	US 36	63	US 28
		CN 30		CN 35
		HK 34		HK 37

Note: The factor loadings are the normalised first eigenvector of the principal component analysis.
Sources: CEIC and authors' estimates.

4. THE TRANSMISSION OF ECONOMIC SHOCKS

The correlation analysis in the previous section reveals important information on the degree of business cycle synchronisation. However, it does not tell us how economic shocks are transmitted across the three economies, which is more appropriately handled using a structural economic model, in our case a structural vector auto regression (SVAR) model. Our analysis follows most closely the approach adopted in Genberg, Salemi, and Swoboda (1987), Cushman and Zha (1997) and, for East Asia, Genberg (2005). Because of the size of the US economy, it is reasonable to assume that the US output and price and interest rate shocks will affect both Hong Kong and the Mainland, but not vice versa. Similarly, because of the relative sizes of Hong Kong and the Mainland we assume that Mainland shocks are transmitted to Hong Kong but the economic developments in Hong Kong have no influence on the Mainland.

Our VAR system contains seven variables: CPI inflation, real GDP growth in the Unites States, the three-month US Treasury bill rate, inflation and real GDP growth in Mainland China, and finally inflation and real GDP growth in Hong Kong. As already noted, the system of equations is specified so that the Hong Kong variables have no effect on either the Mainland or US variables, Mainland variables have no effect on the United States, but they do effect Hong Kong, and US variables influence both the Mainland and Hong Kong.

The contemporaneous correlation between the error terms in each variable is assumed to obey the causal structure illustrated in equation (4):

$$
\begin{pmatrix}
\Delta y_t^{US} \\
\Delta p_t^{US} \\
TB_t^{US} \\
\Delta y_t^{CN} \\
\Delta p_t^{CN} \\
\Delta y_t^{HK} \\
\Delta p_t^{HK}
\end{pmatrix}
=
\begin{pmatrix}
1 & a_{12} & a_{13} & 0 & 0 & 0 & 0 \\
a_{21} & 1 & a_{21} & 0 & 0 & 0 & 0 \\
a_{31} & a_{31} & 1 & 0 & 0 & 0 & 0 \\
a_{41} & a_{42} & a_{43} & 1 & a_{45} & 0 & 0 \\
a_{51} & a_{52} & a_{53} & a_{54} & 1 & 0 & 0 \\
a_{61} & a_{62} & a_{63} & a_{64} & a_{65} & 1 & a_{66} \\
a_{71} & a_{72} & a_{73} & a_{74} & a_{75} & a_{76} & 1
\end{pmatrix}
\begin{pmatrix}
\varepsilon_{yt}^{US} \\
\varepsilon_{pt}^{US} \\
\varepsilon_{tbt}^{US} \\
\varepsilon_{yt}^{CN} \\
\varepsilon_{pt}^{CN} \\
\varepsilon_{yt}^{HK} \\
\varepsilon_{pt}^{HK}
\end{pmatrix}
\qquad (4)
$$

where Δy_t^* and Δp_t^* denote quarterly real GDP growth rate and CPI inflation for these three economies and TB_t^{US} represents quarterly average of three-month US treasury bills. ε_t^* represents corresponding shocks.

The equations are estimated using the Seemingly Unrelated Regression method over the sample period from the first quarter of 1990 to the last quarter of 2005 with the number of lags set to be 4.[7] To fully

---

7. The 4 lags are chosen because of sample size and the nature of quarterly data. Two lags are also used for robustness checks and they do not appear to make a difference.

Table 3.4

Variance Decomposition of Shocks

Panel A. Impact on Hong Kong					
Output			Price		
US	CN	HK	US	CN	HK
In 1 quarter	37.63	7.69	54.68	2.22	1.71	96.06
One year	56.27	7.62	36.11	21.47	10.03	68.51
5 year	57.92	8.47	33.61	41.74	34.49	23.77
10 year	60.92	8.00	31.08	44.57	35.91	19.52
Panel B. Impact on China					
In 1 quarter	19.21	80.79	0.00	0.32	99.68	0.00
One year	33.09	66.91	0.00	5.49	94.51	0.00
5 year	67.11	32.89	0.00	27.31	72.69	0.00
10 year	78.79	21.21	0.00	30.65	69.35	0.00

Source: Authors' estimates.

identify the system we set $a_{12}= a_{13}= a_{21}= a_{45}= a_{66}=0$. Although this implies a causal structure between the shocks within each economy, we do not make use of this in the analysis that follows.

Panel A of Table 3.4 presents the variance decompositions of the Hong Kong variables to see to what extent Hong Kong's output and inflation variations can be explained by US shocks, Mainland shocks, and its own shocks. A few observations emerge from this table. First, Hong Kong's output and price developments are mostly affected by its own domestic factors in the short run. Secondly, for the medium (5 years) and long run (10 years), US shocks (combining shocks from GDP, CPI, and three-month interest rates) appear to have explained 60% and 45% of Hong Kong's output and price variations respectively. Thirdly, the Mainland has only limited impact on real GDP growth in Hong Kong. However, it appears that Mainland shocks explain more than one-third of Hong Kong's inflation developments. Fourthly, Hong

Macroeconomic Linkages between Hong Kong and Mainland China

Kong's own shocks account for about 30% and 20% of its output and price variations respectively over the medium to long run.

These results appear to be consistent with our intuitions. In addition to the fact that the US is a key market for exports from both Hong Kong and the Mainland, the choice of the exchange rate regime in Hong Kong and on the Mainland may have played a role in explaining the increased business cycle synchronisation. The peg of the Hong Kong dollar and the renminbi (up to July 2005) to the US dollar could reinforce the transmission of shocks in these two pairs of economies. For example, our earlier results show that Hong Kong's integration with the US through trade and FDI channels is much weaker than that with the Mainland. The fact that US shocks are the dominant force in Hong Kong's output and price movements possibly suggests the endogenous effect through the LERS. This is also confirmed by the US effect on the Mainland economy in Panel B of Table 3.4. Over the medium to long run, the US output effect explains about 67% and 79% of Mainland output variations respectively, surprisingly higher than that in Hong Kong, although the US shocks only explain less than one-third of the variations of Mainland prices. This result appears to suggest that other than the external demand channel (as the US is currently the Mainland second largest trading partner), Mainland's de-facto US dollar pegged exchange rate regime may also help explain the large US effect. On the other hand, as the real economy channel currently dominates economic integration between Hong Kong and the Mainland, the Mainland's inflation rate exerts a big impact on Hong Kong's domestic price development, whereas on the Mainland, its own domestic factors tend to explain most of its own price developments.

To understand whether US shocks are responsible for the business cycle synchronisation between Hong Kong and the Mainland, we estimate two separate VAR specifications, one containing only the US and Mainland variables and the other only the US and Hong Kong variables.[8] The moving-average representation of these systems can be written as the follows:

---

8. The two SVARs are estimated using SUR and the same lag length for the sample period from 1990: Q1 to 2005:Q4. Another approach is to continue to use the previous seven-variable specification for Hong Kong together with the five-variable specification using only US and Mainland variables for the Mainland. Not reported here, the results are quite similar to what reported here.

$$\Delta y_t^{HK} = \sum_{i=0}^{\infty} a_i^{US} \varsigma_{t-i}^{US} + \sum_{i=0}^{\infty} a_i^{HK} \varsigma_{t-i}^{HK} \qquad (5a)$$

$$\Delta p_t^{HK} = \sum_{i=0}^{\infty} b_i^{US} \varsigma_{t-i}^{US} + \sum_{i=0}^{\infty} b_i^{HK} \varsigma_{t-i}^{HK} \qquad (5b)$$

$$\Delta y_t^{CN} = \sum_{i=0}^{\infty} c_i^{US} \varsigma_{t-i}^{US} + \sum_{i=0}^{\infty} c_i^{CN} \varsigma_{t-i}^{CN} \qquad (6a)$$

$$\Delta p_t^{CN} = \sum_{i=0}^{\infty} d_i^{US} \varsigma_{t-i}^{US} + \sum_{i=0}^{\infty} d_i^{CN} \varsigma_{t-i}^{CN} \qquad (6b)$$

The effects of US shocks on the real growth rates in Hong Kong and in the Mainland are represented by $\Delta y_t^{HK}(US) \equiv \sum_{i=0}^{\infty} a_i^{US} \varsigma_{t-i}^{US}$ and $\Delta y_t^{CN}(US) \equiv \sum_{i=0}^{\infty} c_i^{US} \varsigma_{t-i}^{US}$ respectively. Corresponding decompositions can be made for inflation in Hong Kong and the Mainland. This would give:

$\Delta y_t^{HK}(US)$ = the effect on Hong Kong's real growth of US shocks only

$\Delta p_t^{HK}(US)$ = the effect on Hong Kong's inflation rate of US shocks only

$\Delta y_t^{CN}(US)$ = the effect on the Mainland's real growth of US shocks only

$\Delta p_t^{CN}(US)$ = the effect on the Mainland's inflation rate of US shocks only

$\Delta y_t^{HK}(HK)$ = the effect on Hong Kong's real growth of Hong Kong shocks only

$\Delta p_t^{HK}(HK)$ = the effect on Hong Kong's inflation rate of Hong Kong shocks only

$\Delta y_t^{CN}(CN)$ = the effect on the Mainland's real growth of Mainland shocks only

$\Delta p_t^{CN}(CN)$ = the effect on the Mainland's inflation rate of Mainland shocks only

Table 3.5

Correlations of Domestically Generated Output Growth Rates (Row 1)
and Inflation (Row 2) between Hong Kong and the Mainland

	1994–2005	1994–1997	1998–2000	2000–2005
GDP	0.09	-0.01	0.11	0.12
CPI Inflation	0.09	0.26	-0.29	0.14

Note: Estimates calculated using historical decompositions from equations 5(a, b) and 6(a,b).
Source: Authors' estimates.

Table 3.6

Correlations of Output Growth Rates (Row 1) and Inflation (Row 2)
in Hong Kong and the Mainland Generated Exclusively by US Shocks

	1994–2005	1994–1997	1998–2000	2000–2005
GDP	0.43	0.48	0.53	0.62
CPI Inflation	0.63	0.60	-0.39	0.59

Note: Estimates calculated using historical decompositions from equations 5(a,b) and 6(a,b).
Source: Authors' estimates.

Through these two SVAR systems, we examine how synchronised the economies of Hong Kong and the Mainland would be if there were only domestic shocks, i.e., if the common effect from the United States were absent. The results are presented in Table 3.5, and they reveal a lack of co-movements between the two economies resulting from purely domestic shocks. For example, the correlation between real GDP growth rates that one would observe if there were only domestic shocks is merely 0.09 during 1994–2005. This is in sharp contrast with the much higher correlations reported in Table 3.1, which refers to the actual data. The conclusion would have to be that the high actual correlation between Hong Kong and the Mainland growth rates and inflation must have come from the effects of shocks originating in the United States. This is also what we have found out.

Table 3.6 reports the correlations between $\Delta p_t^{HK}(US)$ and $\Delta p_t^{CN}(US)$ on the one hand and $\Delta y_t^{HK}(US)$ and $\Delta y_t^{CN}(US)$ on the other, i.e., between the evolution of growth and inflation in the two economies related exclusively to US shocks. These correlations are generally much higher (except for inflation rates during 1998–2000) implying that the high business cycle and inflation co-movements between the Hong Kong and the Mainland economy after the 1990s could be mostly driven by their high correlation with the US economy.

Overall, the structural VAR analysis reveals that over the medium and long run, US shocks appear to affect both output and inflation developments in Hong Kong strongly. Mainland shocks affect Hong Kong's inflation development significantly, but its impact is still smaller than that exerted by shocks in the US. Furthermore, it appears that the components of both output growth and inflation that are domestically generated in Hong Kong and on the Mainland are hardly correlated. The generally high degree of synchronisation of output growth between Hong Kong and the Mainland presented in the previous section is therefore largely attributed to the common US factor. The common high correlation with the US leads to the high correlation between Hong Kong and the Mainland.

5. CONCLUSION AND POLICY IMPLICATIONS

This Chapter has examined various aspects of economic and financial market integration among Hong Kong, the Mainland, and the United States. We have found that economic integration between Hong Kong and the Mainland has deepened over time. This is especially prominent in the areas of trade, FDI, and tourism-related consumption. However, Hong Kong has little in common with the Mainland in terms of the movements of interest rates and stock market indices, undoubtedly reflecting the substantially closed capital account on the Mainland. We have also examined synchronisation of GDP growth among the three economies. The findings suggest that the co-movements of the business cycle in Hong Kong with those of the Mainland and the US have increased markedly since 2000, following some low and even negative correlations with the US in the 1990s. This high correlation naturally raises the question of what drives the co-movements among the three economies. Our structural VAR analysis suggests that over 60% of the variations in output shocks and over 45% of the variations in price changes in Hong Kong can be explained by US shocks, whereas

Mainland China shocks explain over one-third of Hong Kong's price movements. Using a methodology that permits us to distinguish between the effects of common US shocks and idiosyncratic domestic shocks, we conclude that there is little correlation between the component of the business cycles attributable to domestic shocks in Hong Kong and the Mainland, whereas the influence of the US shocks on the two economies leads to a high degree of synchronisation. In other words, the business cycle co-movements of Hong Kong and the Mainland are largely due to the common influence of economic conditions in the Unites States, possibly because of their US dollar-pegged exchange rate system.

Our results also show that Hong Kong's business cycles are quite volatile compared with those of the Mainland and the US. Hong Kong's price developments are strongly affected by domestic forces in the short run, although the influences from the US and the Mainland are dominant over the medium and long run. This is somewhat puzzling given that Hong Kong is a small open economy. One explanation may be that large swings of property prices are responsible for the importance of domestically generated shocks.[9] This is plausible since the rental component of the composite CPI is highly affected by property prices and has a weight of 30% in the index. Therefore, policy considerations to reduce large volatilities emanating from property prices are warranted to improve the smooth functioning of the LERS.

Our analysis also suggests that while the three economies are normally highly synchronised, they can move apart when shocks unrelated to the United States materialise. This is revealed by our findings that during the Asian financial crises in 1997–98, the co-movement of business cycle between the Mainland and Hong Kong increased sharply; but their co-movement with the US economy turned negative. This pattern suggests that both economies are sensitive to regional shocks to which the US economy is largely immune. It means that measures that help maintain regional economic stability are important even where extra-regional influences on business cycles are normally dominant.

The results of this study are mostly drawn from a time when the Mainland economy was under tight capital control and its exchange rate was largely pegged to the US dollar. As the Mainland progressively

9. See comments by Peng (2005) on Gerlach and Gerlach-Kristen (2005).

liberalises its capital account by encouraging capital outflows (for example, through the QDII scheme), economic shocks, specifically financial market shocks, from the Mainland to Hong Kong are likely to increase progressively over time. This may increase synchronisation of real growth and inflation. But because of the structural differences between the two economies, it does not necessarily mean that the domestic shocks would become more similar. Since it is the similarity of shocks that matter the most for the choice of exchange rate regime, the LERS, which links the Hong Kong dollar to the US dollar, would continue to be desirable for the foreseeable future.

REFERENCES

Andrews, Dan and Marion Kohler, 2005, "International Business Cycle Co-Movements through Time," in C. Kent and D. Norman, eds., *The Changing Nature of the Business Cycle*, Economic Group, Reserve Bank of Australia.

Baxter, Marianne, and Robert G. King, 1999, "Measuring Business Cycles: Approximate Band-Pass Filters for Economic Time Series," *The Review of Economics and Statistics* 81(4), 575-593.

Bayoumi, Tamim, and Barry Eichengreen, 1993, "Shocking Aspects of European Monetary Unification," in F. Giavazzi and F. Torres, eds., *The Transition to Economic and Monetary Union in Europe*, Cambridge University Press, New York.

Benalal, Nicholai, Juan Luis Diaz del Hoyo, Beatrice Pierluigi, and Nick Vidalis, 2006, "Output Growth Differentials across the Euro Area Countries: Some Stylized Facts," European Central Bank Occasional Paper Series No. 45.

Blanchard, Olivier Jean, and Danny Quah, 1989, "The Dynamic Effects of Aggregate Demand and Supply Disturbances," *The American Economic Review* 79(4), 655–673.

Crosby, Mark, 2003, "Business Cycle Correlations in Asia-Pacific," HKIMR Working Paper No. 4/2003.

Cushman, David O., and Tao Zha, 1997, "Identifying Monetary Policy in a Small Open Economy Under Flexible Exchange Rates," *Journal of Monetary Economics*, 39:45–65.

Darvas, Zsolt, and Gyorgy Szapary, 2004, "Business Cycle Synchronisation in the Enlarged EU," Working Paper.

Dodsworth, John, and Dubravko Mihaljek, 1997, "Hong Kong, China: Growth, Structural Change, and Economic Stability During the Transition," IMF Occasional Paper 152.

Fiess, Norbert, 2003, "Business Cycle Synchronisation and Regional Integration: A Case Study for Central America," Working Paper, World Bank.

Frankel, Jeffrey A., and Andrew K. Rose, 1998, "The Endogeneity of the Optimum Currency Area Criteria," *The Economic Journal*, 108, 1009–1025.

Garcia-Herrero, Alicia, 2006, "How Close is Asia to An Optimal Currency Area in terms of Business Cycle Co-movement?" *Mimeo*.

Genberg, Hans, Michael K. Salemi and Alexander K. Swoboda, 1987, "Foreign and Domestic Disturbances as Sources of Aggregate Economic Fluctuations: Switzerland 1964-1981," *Journal of Monetary Economics*, 19:45-67.

Genberg, Hans, 2005, "External Shocks, Transmission Mechanisms and Deflation in Asia," *Working Paper*, No. 6/2005, Hong Kong Institute of Monetary Research.

Gerlach, Stepfan and Gerlach-Kristen, Petra, 2005, "Monetary Policy Regimes and Macroeconomic Outcomes: Hong Kong and Singapore," *BIS Working Paper*, No. 204.

Gerlach-Kristen, Petra, 2005, "Business Cycle and Inflation Synchronisation in Mainland China and Hong Kong," *Working Paper*, The University of Hong Kong.

Ho, Daryl, Jimmy Shek, and Joanna Shi, 2006, "External Demand for Hong Kong Dollar Currency (Revisited)," *Hong Kong Monetary Authority Quarterly Bulletin*.

Kawai, Masahiro, and Taizo Motonishi, 2005, "Is East Asia an Optimal Currency Area? Financial Interdependence and Exchange Rate Regimes in East Asia," Institute for Policy Research, Ministry of Finance, Japan.

Kim, Sunghyun Henry, M. Ayhan Kose, and Michael G. Plummer, 2000, "Dynamics of Business Cycle in Asia: Differences and Similarities," *Working Paper*.

Kose, Ayhan, Eswar Prasad, and Marco Terrones, 2003, "How does Globalisation Affect the Synchronisation of Business Cycles?" *American Economic Review, Papers and Proceedings* 93(2), 57–62.

Otto, Glen, Graham Voss, and Luke Willard, 2001, "Understanding OECD Output Correlations," *Reserve Bank of Australia Research Discussion Paper* No 2001–05.

Peng, Wensheng, 2005, "Comments on Monetary Policy Regimes and Macroeconomic Outcomes: Hong Kong and Singapore by Stefan Gerlach and Petra Gerlach-Kristen" *Mimeo*, Hong Kong Monetary Authority.

Prasad, Eswar, *et al.*, 2004, Hong Kong SAR: Meeting the Challenges of Integration with the Mainland, *IMF Occasional Paper* 226.

Shin, Kwanho, and Yunjong Wang, 2004, "Trade Integration and Business Cycle Synchronisation in East Asia," *Asian Economic Papers* 2:3.

國家計委宏觀經濟研究院課題組，2002，促進內地與香港建立更緊密經貿關係的研究。

Chapter 4

Hong Kong's Trade Patterns
and
Trade Elasticities

Li-gang LIU
Kelvin FAN
Jimmy SHEK

1. INTRODUCTION

A salient feature of Hong Kong's external trade is its intermediation role. As the entrepôt for Mainland China, Hong Kong helps channel raw materials and semi-manufacturing products from the rest of the world to the Mainland for further processing and then helps re-export the processed goods and final products to the rest of the world. Reflecting this, total trade in goods and services represented over 3.8 times GDP in 2005. Moreover, about one-fifth of Mainland's merchandise trade transited through Hong Kong in 2005.

Economic theory suggests that the effect of a real exchange rate depreciation on an economy's trade balance can be ambiguous. This is because the real exchange rate depreciation often has two direct and, to a certain extent, offsetting effects on the trade balance, namely the volume and the value effect. On the one hand, a real depreciation improves the competitiveness of the economy's exports and discourages imports in volume terms, thus contributing to an improvement in the trade balance. On the other hand, imports in value measured in domestic currency would become more expensive, thus leading to a worsening of the trade balance. The net effect depends on whether the volume or the value effect would dominate. If the volume effect dominates, a real depreciation would in general lead to an improvement of the trade balance. This criterion, also known as the Marshall-Lerner condition, requires the sum of the price elasticities of demand in absolute term for imports and exports to exceed one.[1] Thus, whether this condition holds or not and the stability of these trade elasticities could be used to predict the potential effect of a change in the real exchange rate of an economy on its trade balance.

The Linked Exchange Rate System (LERS) implies that Hong Kong cannot use exchange rate policy to influence its external trade because the value of the Hong Kong dollar (HKD) against other major currencies is exogenously determined by the movements of the US dollar. However, this does not mean that movements in Hong Kong's

---

1. The Marshall-Lerner condition was derived based on the assumptions that supply elasticities for exports and imports are perfectly elastic, so that changes in demand volumes have no effect on prices.

Figure 4.1
Hong Kong's Trade Balance

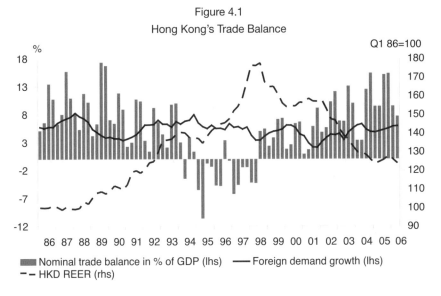

Nominal trade balance in % of GDP (lhs)   —— Foreign demand growth (lhs)
-- HKD REER (rhs)

Sources: Census & Statistics Department and authors' estimates.

real exchange rate do not matter. Although casual observation suggests that movements in Hong Kong's real effective exchange rate (REER) are negatively correlated with its trade balance (Figure 4.1), Hong Kong's trade pattern, particularly the role of re-exports, may have complicated the estimation of Hong Kong's trade elasticities. Indeed, over 70% of Hong Kong's total trade in goods and services is related to re-exports, which not only respond to the exchange rate of the HKD but also to that of other currencies involved and foreign income. Partly because of the complicated nature of re-exports, there has not been any adequate study on whether the Marshall-Lerner condition holds for an entrepôt economy such as Hong Kong.

This paper intends to fill this void by providing a careful treatment of this complication when estimating Hong Kong's trade elasticities. The objectives of this paper are twofold: first, we provide a careful analysis of the trade pattern of Hong Kong with a special emphasis on Hong Kong's re-export trade with Mainland China; second, we apply a well-established methodology to estimate both the long-run trade elasticities and their short-run dynamics for both Hong Kong's direct trade and its re-export trade with the Mainland.

The rest of the paper proceeds as follows. The next section discusses the stylised facts about Hong Kong's external trade pattern, in terms of trading partners and product composition, with a particular focus on re-export trade with the Mainland. Section 3 applies an error correction model to test whether the Marshall-Lerner conditions hold for Hong Kong's trade and presents the empirical results. Section 4 concludes.

2. FEATURES OF HONG KONG'S EXTERNAL TRADE

This section discusses the stylised facts about Hong Kong's external trade pattern, in terms of trading partners and product composition, with a particular focus on the re-export trade with the Mainland.

2.1 Trade flows by major trading partners and products

Table 4.1 summarises Hong Kong's external trade flows with its largest four trading partners, namely, the Mainland, the US, the euro area, and Japan, in 2005. Table 4.2 provides information on the major products of merchandise trade. Additional charts and more detailed statistics of trade in goods and services by main trading partner and product category are presented in Appendix 4A. Several key observations emerge as follows:

First, as a service economy, Hong Kong's domestic exports of goods accounted for only 5% of total exports of goods and services, or equivalent to about 10% of GDP.[2] The Mainland and the US are the two largest markets, with each accounting for about 30% of the total domestic exports. Among those exports to the Mainland, more than half were raw materials or semi-finished manufacturing products for further processing with a contractual arrangement for subsequent re-importation of the processed goods into Hong Kong (the so-called outward processing trade). Of the total domestic exports, over 40% were articles of apparel and clothing accessories. The second largest category was electrical machinery, apparatus and appliances, and electrical parts, which accounted for 14% of total domestic exports.

---

2. Domestic exports are the natural produce of Hong Kong or the products of a manufacturing process in Hong Kong which has changed permanently the shape, nature, form or utility of the basis materials used in manufacture.

Table 4.1
External Trade Pattern, 2005

Exports	In % of GDP	In % of total	In % of sub-total	Imports	In % of GDP	In % of total	In % of sub-total
Total exports	197.9	100.0	100.0	Total imports	185.4	100.0	100.0
Of which:				Of which:			
Mainland China	82.9	41.9	41.9	Mainland China	78.9	42.6	42.6
US	33.3	16.8	16.8	US	10.3	5.5	5.5
Euro area	19.3	9.8	9.8	Euro area	10.6	5.7	5.7
Japan	11.1	5.6	5.6	Japan	20.7	11.2	11.2
Exports of goods	162.9	82.3	100.0	Imports of goods	167.2	90.2	100.0
Of which:				Of which:			
Mainland China	73.3	37.0	45.0	Mainland China	73.9	39.9	44.2
US	26.1	13.2	16.0	US	7.6	4.1	4.5
Euro area	16.4	8.3	10.1	Euro area	9.7	5.2	5.8
Japan	8.6	4.3	5.3	Japan	19.1	10.3	11.4
Domestic exports	9.9	5.0	100.0	Retained imports	40.9	22.1	100.0
Of which:				Of which:			
Mainland China	3.2	1.6	32.8	Mainland China	1.8	0.9	4.3
US	2.7	1.4	27.8	US	3.2	1.7	7.9
Euro area	1.0	0.5	10.2	Euro area	4.6	2.5	11.2
Japan	0.3	0.2	3.2	Japan	6.6	3.6	16.2
Re-exports	153.1	77.3	100.0	Imports for re-exports	126.3	68.1	100.0
Of which:				Of which:			
Mainland China	70.1	35.4	45.8	Mainland China	72.2	38.9	57.1
US	23.4	11.8	15.3	US	4.3	2.3	3.4
Euro area	15.4	7.8	10.1	Euro area	5.1	2.7	4.0
Japan	8.3	4.2	5.4	Japan	12.5	6.7	9.9
Exports of services*	35.0	17.7	100.0	Imports of services*	18.2	9.8	100.0
Of which:				Of which:			
Mainland China	9.6	4.8	27.4	Mainland China	5.0	2.7	27.4
US	7.2	3.6	20.6	US	2.7	1.4	14.7
Euro area	2.9	1.5	8.3	Euro area	1.0	0.5	5.4
Japan	2.5	1.3	7.2	Japan	1.6	0.9	8.7

Note: * Data on breakdown of service trade by trading partner for 2005 are not yet available. Ratios are based on those in 2004.

Sources: Census & Statistics Department and authors' estimates.

Table 4.2

Product Composition of Merchandise Trade, 2005

	In % of sub-total
Domestic exports of goods	100.0
Articles of apparel and clothing accessories (84)	41.3
Electrical machinery, apparatus and appliances, and electrical parts (77)	13.8
Miscellaneous manufactured articles (89)	11.1
Office machines and automatic data processing machines (75)	10.1
Total of the above	76.3
Imports of goods	100.0
Electrical machinery, apparatus and appliances, and electrical parts (77)	22.8
Telecommunications and sound recording and reproducing apparatus and equipment (76)	12.7
Office machines and automatic data processing machines (75)	10.7
Articles of apparel and clothing accessories (84)	6.2
Total of the above	52.4
Re-exports of goods	100.0
Electrical machinery, apparatus and appliances, and electrical parts (77)	20.9
Telecommunications and sound recording and reproducing apparatus and equipment (76)	15.4
Office machines and automatic data processing machines (75)	13.0
Miscellaneous manufactured articles (89)	8.6
Total of the above	57.8

Note: Numbers in brackets are the Standard International Trade Classification (SITC) codes.

Sources: Census & Statistics Department and authors' estimates.

Secondly, re-exports of goods were the largest category, accounting for 77% of total exports of goods and services, equivalent to 1.5 times of GDP.[3] In particular, more than 60% of re-exports originated in the Mainland and most of the remaining 40% were imports from other economies for re-export to the Mainland. Within those re-exports to the Mainland, almost 40% were for further processing and most of those processed goods were ultimately re-exported to other places through Hong Kong. Of the total re-exports, over half were electrical and

---

3. Re-exports are products which have previously been imported into Hong Kong and which are re-exported without having undergone in Hong Kong a manufacturing process which has changed permanently the shape, nature, form or utility of the product.

electronic products. Electrical machinery, apparatus and appliances, and electrical parts accounted for 21% of the total, telecommunications and sound recording and reproducing apparatus and equipment accounted for 15%, and office machines and automatic data processing machines accounted for another 13%.

Thirdly, because Hong Kong is a small economy with limited natural resources and small agriculture and manufacturing sectors, most of the necessities are imported from other economies. Thus, retained imports of goods represented 41% of GDP in 2005.[4] Unlike other trade flows which concentrate on a small number of countries, retained imports are more widely split among different source economies. In particular, retained imports from the Mainland only accounted for 4% of total retained imports, while those from Japan and the Euro area accounted for 16% and 11%, respectively. This suggests that the direct impact of the appreciation of the renminbi on Hong Kong's overall domestic price level would be quite limited. Statistics of retained imports by end-use category show that about 40% were raw materials and semi-manufacturing products, while shares of both capital and consumer goods in total were about 20%, and those of both foods and fuels were roughly 10%.

Fourthly, reflecting Hong Kong's role as an entrepôt, most of its imports are for re-export to other economies, accounting for almost 70% of total imports of goods and services, equivalent to 1.3 times of GDP, in 2005. As a large proportion of re-exports of goods originated on the Mainland, imports of goods for re-export from the Mainland accounted for almost 60% of the total. Moreover, the product composition of imports for re-exports was very similar to that of re-exports of goods.

Fifthly, exports of services, which have been growing rather fast in recent years, accounted for 18% of total exports of goods and services, or 35% of GDP. Similar to exports of goods, the Mainland and the US were the two largest trading partners, accounting for 27% and 21% of total exports of services, respectively. Out of the major export service

---

4. Retained imports refer to those imported goods which are retained for use in Hong Kong. The value of retained imports is derived by subtracting the estimated import value of re-exports from the value of imports. The former is obtained by removing an estimated re-export margin from the value of re-exports. The Census and Statistics Department regularly conducts a survey of re-export trade, based on which the rates of re-export margin for different categories of goods are estimated for deriving the retained import statistics.

categories, exports of merchanting and other trade-related services was the largest group, accounting for 34% of the total.[5] It was followed by transport, travel, and financial services, which accounted for 31%, 17%, and 9%, respectively. For merchanting and other trade-related services, the Mainland and the US were the two most important destinations, with each accounting for nearly 30% of the total exports of services. For travel services, the Mainland was the largest contributor, accounting for more than half of the total. For financial services, the most important counterparts were the US and the UK, together contributing half of the total.

Finally, imports of services accounted for 10% of total imports of goods and services, equivalent to 18% of GDP. Imports of services from the Mainland and the US accounted for 27% and 15% of the total respectively. Travel was the largest major service group, accounting for over 41% of the total. It was followed by transportation and merchanting and other trade-related services, accounting for 29% and 7% of the total respectively. For travel services, the Mainland was the most important source, which accounted for 30% of the total.

In sum, the Mainland is Hong Kong's largest trading partner in both trade in goods and services. The US is the second largest destination for exports of goods and services, while Japan is the second largest source of imports of goods and services. Owing to the close trade link between Hong Kong and the Mainland, more detailed discussions on the trade flows between them are provided in the following section.

2.2 Merchandise flows between Hong Kong, the Mainland, and the rest of the world

Hong Kong, as an entrepôt for the Mainland, helps channel raw materials and semi-manufacturing products from the rest of the world to the Mainland for further processing, and then re-exports the processed goods to other economies. Moreover, as discussed above, Hong Kong's trade in goods with the Mainland is to a large extent related to outward

---

5. Merchanting and other trade-related services comprise mainly offshore trade, for which the goods involved do not enter and leave Hong Kong.

Figure 4.2

Traffic of Goods between Hong Kong, Mainland China,
and the Rest of the World, 2005

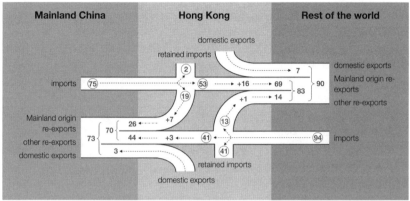

Note: Import figures are in grey circle, exports are in black, and re-export margins are those with a
    plus sign (+) beside them. All the figures are value of goods expressed in percentage of GDP.
    Figures may not add up to total due to rounding.

Sources: Census & Statistics Department and authors' estimates.

processing activities. More than 80% of Hong Kong manufacturers have established production facilities on the Mainland, which have boosted outward processing activities and thus re-exports.

Figure 4.2 illustrates the goods flows between Hong Kong, the Mainland, and the rest of the world. All figures in the chart are values of goods in 2005, expressed in percentage of GDP. Of the total imports of goods from China, 70% (53 out of 75) were for re-export to the rest of world and 25% (19 out of 75) were for re-export back to the Mainland. Among those re-exported back to the Mainland, over half were electrical and electronic products.[6] For those re-exported to the rest of the world, about half were electrical and electronic products. Clothing and textiles accounted for less than 10%. Less than 3% (2 out of 74) of the imports from the Mainland are for Hong Kong's domestic use.

---

6. One possible reason for these round tripping trade flows is to make use of the logistics facilities
    in Hong Kong. For example, shipments of raw materials and semi-manufacturing from factories
    in some northern Mainland cities to Hong Kong by sea and then transport the goods to factories
    located in southern cities by truck for further processing may be cheaper than the direct shipments of
    the goods from the northern to southern parts.

Table 4.3

Re-exports of Goods by End-use Category and Main Origin, 2005

Re-exports by end-use and origin	In % of total re-exports			In % of total end-use		
	All economies	Mainland China	Others	All economies	Mainland China	Others
Raw materials and semi-manufacturing	34.1	21.8	54.4	100.0	39.6	60.4
Consumer goods	34.7	46.5	15.4	100.0	83.2	16.8
Capital goods	30.4	31.5	28.5	100.0	64.4	35.6
Foodstuffs	0.6	0.2	1.2	100.0	19.9	80.1
Fuels	0.2	0.0	0.4	100.0	10.8	89.2
Total	100.0	100.0	100.0	100.0	62.1	37.9

Sources: Census & Statistics Department and authors' estimates.

Of the total imports of goods from places other than the Mainland, 44% (41 out of 94) were imports for re-exports to the Mainland and 14% (13 out of 94) were for re-exporting to the rest of the world. A large part of goods re-exported to the Mainland were raw materials and semi-manufacturing for further processing on the Mainland. About 44% (41 out of 94) of goods were retained in Hong Kong. Taking all imports of goods together, over 75% were for re-export. In other words, only 25% of imports were for domestic use.

Of the total re-exports to places other than the Mainland, 83% (69 out of 83) originated from the Mainland. For those re-exporting to the Mainland, 63% (44 out of 70) originated from the rest of the world. Taking all re-exports together, around 90% either originated from the Mainland or were re-exported to the Mainland from other places. These Mainland-related re-exports depend mainly upon demand conditions on the Mainland and its trading partners as well as the RMB exchange rates against currencies of these partners. Hong Kong's margins earned from re-exports were estimated to amount to 26% of GDP in 2005, of which over 80% arose from re-exports of Mainland origin.

Table 4.3 shows that 46.5% and 31.5% of the re-exports originating from the Mainland were consumer goods and capital goods, respectively, and only 21.8% were raw materials and semi-manufacturing products. By contrast, for re-exports originating from other places (of which around 75% were exported to the Mainland), about 55% were raw materials and semi-manufactured products. These statistics indicate that most of the Mainland origin re-exports are final products, while a large part of re-exports to the Mainland are raw materials and semi-manufactured products for further processing. In particular, among the total re-exports of consumer and capital goods, over 80% and 60%, respectively, originated from the Mainland. This suggests that Hong Kong plays an important role in channelling raw materials and semi-manufacturing from the rest of the world to the Mainland for further processing, and then re-exporting the processed goods to other economies.

3. EMPIRICAL ESTIMATION

This section estimates the price and income elasticities of Hong Kong's demand for foreign imports and the foreign demand for Hong Kong's exports. To get a quick gauge on the long-run elasticities, we conduct the empirical analysis using the more aggregate trade data. Following a well-established approach by Hooper, Johnson, and Marquez (2000) to estimate price and income elasticities for the G-7 industrial economies and more recently a paper by Chinn (2005) to estimate the US trade elasticities, we specify both an import and an export equation based on trade theory of imperfect substitution. By assuming log-linear function forms, these two equations can be written as follows:

$$IM_t = \alpha_0 + \alpha_1 Y_t + \alpha_2 RER_t^{IM} + \mu_{t,IM} \qquad (1)$$

$$EX_t = \beta_0 + \beta_1 FY_t + \beta_2 RER_t^{EX} + \mu_{t,EX} \qquad (2)$$

where IM_t, Y_t, and RER_t^{IM} in equation (1) are Hong Kong's real imports, real GDP, and the import-weighted real effective exchange rate, respectively. EX_t, FY_t, and RER_t^{EX} in equation (2) are Hong Kong's real exports, foreign real GDP, and the export-weighted real effective exchange rate, respectively. It is expected that both α_1 and β_1 are greater than zero. Because both RER_t^{IM} and RER_t^{EX} are measured relative to the Hong Kong dollar, we thus expect $\alpha_2 > 0$ and $\beta_2 < 0$. In addition, this specification implies that the real effective exchange rate (REER) can be considered as a composite indicator that combines both the exchange rate pass-through effect and the price effect. Thus, this approach allows one to have a direct interpretation of the response of imports to changes in the real effect exchange rate (Chinn, 2005).

Recognising the simultaneity among income, real effective exchange rate, and trade, we next test for co-integration and identify co-integration vectors using the methods proposed by Johansen (1988) and Johansen and Juselius (1990). In addition, because movements in international trade may respond differently in the short and long run to those in key determinants of trade, we use the error correction method to capture the short-run dynamics. Thus, a vector error correction model (VECM) for the import equation can be written as follows:

$$\Delta IM_{it} = \gamma_{10} + \varphi_1(IM_{t-1} - \alpha_0 - \alpha_1 Y_{t-1} - \alpha_2 RER_{t-1}^{IM}) + \gamma_{11}\Delta IM_{t-1} + \gamma_{12}\Delta RER_{t-1}^{IM} + \gamma_{13}\Delta Y_{t-1} + \xi_{1t} \quad (3)$$

$$\Delta RER_t^{IM} = \gamma_{20} + \varphi_2(IM_{t-1} - \alpha_0 - \alpha_1 Y_{t-1} - \alpha_2 RER_{t-1}^{IM}) + \gamma_{21}\Delta IM_{t-1} + \gamma_{22}\Delta RER_{t-1}^{IM} + \gamma_{23}\Delta Y_{t-1} + \xi_{2t} \quad (4)$$

$$\Delta Y_t = \gamma_{30} + \varphi_3(IM_{t-1} - \alpha_0 - \alpha_1 Y_{t-1} - \alpha_2 RER_{t-1}^{IM}) + \gamma_{31}\Delta IM_{t-1} + \gamma_{32}\Delta RER_{t-1}^{IM} + \gamma_{33}\Delta Y_{t-1} + \xi_{3t} \quad (5)$$

Similarly, a VECM for the export system can be written as:

$$\Delta EX_t = \gamma_{40} + \varphi_4(EX_{t-1} - \beta_0 - \beta_1 FY_{t-1} - \beta_2 RER_{t-1}^{EX}) + \gamma_{41}\Delta EX_{t-1} + \gamma_{42}\Delta RER_{t-1}^{EX} + \gamma_{43}\Delta FY_{t-1} + \xi_{4t} \quad (6)$$

$$\Delta RER_t^{EX} = \gamma_{50} + \varphi_5(EX_{t-1} - \beta_0 - \beta_1 FY_{t-1} - \beta_2 RER_{t-1}^{EX}) + \gamma_{51}\Delta EX_{t-1} + \gamma_{52}\Delta RER_{t-1}^{EX} + \gamma_{53}\Delta FY_{t-1} + \xi_{5t} \quad (7)$$

$$\Delta FY_t = \gamma_{60} + \varphi_6(EX_{t-1} - \beta_0 - \beta_1 FY_{t-1} - \beta_2 RER_{t-1}^{EX}) + \gamma_{61}\Delta EX_{t-1} + \gamma_{62}\Delta RER_{t-1}^{EX} + \gamma_{63}\Delta FY_{t-1} + \xi_{6t} \quad (8)$$

where Δ stands for the difference of a variable between time t and t-1. φ_i's are coefficients of error correction terms, which account for the difference between actual imports (exports) and their long-run values as predicted by the co-integration relationship among the import (export) system. It is expected that φ_1 and φ_4 are negative and statistically significant in trade equations as trade flows react to long-run disequilibria by closing the gap in the cointegration relationship. Although it can be directly tested, the error correction coefficients in those non-trade equations also indicate whether there exist weakly exogenous relationships for the exchange rate and income.

The two VECM systems are estimated using quarterly data from

1994 Q1 to 2006 Q1.[7] All variables are in logarithm and detailed descriptions of the data are provided in Appendix 4B. Different from Hong Kong's direct trade, trade flows related to re-export activity depend primarily on economic conditions outside Hong Kong. In particular, about 90% of re-exports either originate from the Mainland to the rest of the world or are re-exported to the Mainland from the rest of the world. These Mainland-related re-exports depend mainly on demand conditions on the Mainland and of its trading partners, and the real exchange rates of the renminbi against currencies of these trading partners. In estimating the price and income elasticities of Hong Kong's re-exports, we use both Hong Kong's re-export flows and re-export margins (re-exports minus imports for re-exports) in logarithms to regress on the logarithms of the renminbi REER and the Mainland's foreign demand.[8] For this purpose, a measure of the renminbi REER is computed based on the methodology presented in Peng and Fan (2005) and Peng and Leung (2005), for which the currency weights are determined by the trade pattern of the Mainland, adjusting for its trade via Hong Kong with the rest of the world. The Mainland's foreign demand is defined as the trade-weighted real GDP of its major trading partners.[9]

Before estimating the two VECM systems, we need to select lag length. The Johansen (1988) procedure was used to estimate the co-

---

7.   Before 1994, Mainland China had a dual exchange rate system for the renminbi (RMB). The official rate was set by the government at 5.8 RMB/USD and the "swap" rate was set by the market according to the supply and demand. The foreign exchange swap market was first established in early 1980's in which those who held retained foreign exchanges could sell to those who needed them. It appears that most of the trade related transactions are determined using the swap rate. Partly reflecting this, these two exchange rates were merged on 1 January 1994. The official rate was de facto devalued from 5.8 RMB/USD to 8.7 RMB/USD. Since the movement of the RMB/HKD exchange rate has a significant influence on the HKD REER given that the RMB has the largest currency weight, we use data starting from 1994 to avoid any distortions due to the unification of the official and the swap rates. In addition, Figure 4A6 in Appendix 4A shows that there appears to be a structural shift in Hong Kong's trade pattern from conventional re-exports to offshore trade since the middle of 1990's. To avoid these complications, a sample starting from 1994 may be preferable.

8.   Because most of the re-exports from the rest of world passing through Hong Kong to the Mainland are for processing on the Mainland, this implies that ultimate demand is still foreign. Thus in the re-export equation, only foreign demand is considered. That said, it may be worthwhile to estimate these re-exports of the opposite directions separately.

9.   The reason on foreign income is used in estimating trade elasticities of re-export is that a large portion of the re-exports originated from the rest of the world to the Mainland is for further processing. Thus, the ultimate demand remains foreign.

Table 4.4

Cointegration Test for Aggregate Data

Variable	↑ max	↑ trace	H_0	H_1	lags
Retained imports & import of services	23.82*	30.43*	$r = 0$	$r = 1$	5
	6.42	6.62	$r \leq 1$	$r = 2$	
Domestic exports & exports of services	22.53*	32.21*	$r = 0$	$r = 1$	5
	9.58	9.68	$r \leq 1$	$r = 2$	
Re-export volume	32.09*	43.16*	$r = 0$	$r = 1$	9
	9.32	11.07	$r \leq 1$	$r = 2$	
Re-export margins	83.84*	55.17*	$r = 0$	$r = 1$	9
	28.67*	28.48*	$r \leq 1$	$r = 2$	
	0.19	0.19	$r \leq 2$	$r = 3$	

Note: * Denote significant at the 95% level. r = 0 represents no cointegrating, vector, lags defines the length of lag in the Vector Autogression.

integrating vectors using lag lengths up to nine quarters. The optimal lag length is chosen based on the minimum of the Akaike and Schwarz information criteria, in addition to the judgement on whether the signs of the coefficients are consistent with economic theory. As such, the lag lengths for the co-integrating vectors tend to vary across trade aggregates. The estimation results are presented in Table 4.4. For retained imports and services and domestic exports and services, the optimal lag selected is 5. For re-exports and re-export margins, the lag chosen is 9. In addition, two test statistics (the trace and the maximum eigenvalue) for testing the alternative of cointegration against the null of no cointegration are also calculated as shown in Table 4.4. These tests indicate that for retained imports and imports of services, domestic exports and exports of services, and re-report volume, there is only one co-integration vector. However, for re-export margins, we cannot reject the null hypothesis of two co-integration vectors. Thus, some judgement has to be exercised in order to determine as to which price and income elasticities from the two co-integration vectors are more plausible ones according to both economic theory and intuitions.[10]

Table 4.5 presents the estimated long-run price and income elasticities and error correction coefficients. The price elasticities in absolute terms of Hong Kong's demand for imports and the foreign demand for Hong Kong's exports are found to be 0.65 and 0.52,

10. Detailed statistics are presented in Appendix 4C.

Table 4.5

Johansen MLE Estimates for Aggregate Trade Data

	RER Elasticity	Income Elasticity	Error Correction Coefficients		
			Export or Import	RER	Income
Import					
Retained import and import of services	0.65** (2.2)	1.57*** (5.9)	-0.065*** (-3.4)	0.09** (2.30)	0.08* (1.7)
	Lags: 5, Intercept and trend included				
Export					
Domestic export and export of services	-0.52*** (-5.9)	0.78*** (11.6)	-0.93*** (-2.9)	0.18 (1.7)	-0.01 (-0.2)
	Lags: 5, Intercept and trend included				
Re-export volume	-2.04*** (4.2)	4.27*** (11.2)	-0.25*** (1.99)	-0.05 (0.63)	-0.01 (-0.27)
	Lags: 9, Intercept included				
Re-export margin	-1.98*** (-4.4)	4.17*** (11.9)	-0.25* (-2.0)	-0.05 (-0.6)	-0.01 (-0.3)
	Lags: 9, Intercept and trend included				

Note: t- statistics are in parentheses; ***, **, * denotes significance at the 1%, 5%, 10% level.

respectively. This suggests that 1% depreciation in Hong Kong's real effective exchange rate will lead to an increase of Hong Kong's retained imports of goods and service by 0.65% and a decrease of Hong Kong's direct exports of goods and services by 0.52%. Adding up, the sum of these point estimates is 1.17, implying that the Marshall-Lerner condition for Hong Kong's direct trade is satisfied. This also implies that a depreciation of the HK dollar REER would help improve the balance of direct trade in goods and services holding other things constant. With respect to the income elasticity, we find that the Hong Kong's elasticity for imports of goods and services is larger than foreign income elasticity for Hong Kong's exports of goods and services. For the re-export volume, the estimated price and income elasticities are -2.02 and 4.27 respectively.[11]

---

11. An appreciation of the RMB would hurt re-exports originating from the Mainland to the rest of the world, but would help Hong Kong's re-exports to the Mainland. The estimated coefficient of the RMB REER suggests that the negative effect on re-exports originating from the Mainland outweighs the positive effect on re-exports to the Mainland. This is not surprising because the size of re-exports from the Mainland has been much larger than that of re-exports in the opposite direction. Moreover, a large part of re-exports to the Mainland is related to outward processing activities, most of them are ultimately re-exported to the rest of the world through Hong Kong.

Table 4.6
Chow Forecast Test

	Dates of Instability
Retained import and import of services	stable
Domestic export and export of services	instable for (2001Q1–2003Q2)
Re-export volume	stable
Re-export margin	stable

Similar results are also obtained for re-export margins. As both price and income elasticities are much greater than one, this suggests that Hong Kong's re-exports are quite sensitive to changes in the exchange rate and in foreign demand.

The error correction coefficients for equations (3) and (6) of the VECM system are negative and significant statistically, suggesting both imports and exports respond to disequilibria in the long-run relationship, but with exports adjusting to disequilibria faster than imports. Similarly, for equations (4) and (5) of the import VECM system, the error coefficients are both statistically significant, suggesting that movements in Hong Kong's real effective exchange rate and income also affect its imports of goods and services from overseas. However, for equations (7) and (8) in the export VECM system, the error correction coefficients are no longer statistically significant. This implies that foreign income and prices may be weakly exogenous to Hong Kong's exports, consistent to the view that Hong Kong is a small open economy where its exports are mostly determined by both foreign income and prices.

Although Hong Kong's trade does satisfy the Marshall-Lerner condition, it remains to be confirmed whether these estimated price elasticities are stable over the sample period between 1994 and 2005. We next use a one-step-ahead Chow test to examine the stability of price elasticities. This procedure is implemented by first estimating the price elasticity for the sub-period of 1994 Q1 to 2000 Q4 and obtaining the sum square of errors (SSE). The sub-sample is then extended by one quarter forward to obtain a new price elasticity estimates and a re-computed SSE. This procedure is carried out forward quarter-by-quarter until all observations are exhausted. The test results for the error

Table 4.7

Johansen MLE Estimates for Bilateral Trade Data

	RER Elasticity	Income Elasticity		RER Elasticity	Income Elasticity
HK Imports of goods			HK Exports of goods		
From Mainland China	3.26*** (6.0)	4.33*** (10.9)	To Mainland China	-2.29*** (3.3)	0.89*** (5.0)
From US	1.40*** (22.6)	1.80*** (30.1)	To US	-0.04 (0.6)	0.89*** (8.3)
From EU	-0.82*** ^ (4.9)	0.6* (1.3)	To EU	-0.75*** (12.9)	2.25*** (30.6)
From Japan	0.74*** (3.9)	1.69*** (18.0)	To Japan	-2.82** (2.3)	9.98*** (6.2)

Note: t- statistics are in parentheses; ***, **, * denotes significance at the 1%, 5%, 10% level;

^ The sign of the coefficient is opposite to that expected.

correction equation indicate that the price elasticities are mostly stable for the sample period investigated (Table 4.6). However, for domestic exports and exports of services, the price elasticities are found to be instable over the sample period between 2001 Q1 and 2003 Q2. With hindsight, this may not be surprising given this period of time is filled with large external shocks such as the US recession during 2000-01, the terrorist attack on the US on 11 September 2001, and the eruption of a pandemic, SARS, on the Mainland and in the East Asian region in early 2003.

The remainder of this section presents the estimated price and income elasticities of bilateral trade between Hong Kong and its four largest trading partners, the Mainland, the US, the EU, and Japan. Since the statistics on bilateral service trade are only available for the period of 1999–2004, the estimations are based on merchandise trade data only. The empirical results in Table 4.7 suggest that the Marshall-Lerner condition is satisfied for bilateral trade of Hong Kong with the Mainland, the US, and Japan, but it is inconclusive for trade with the EU as the price elasticity for imports has an incorrect sign. For merchandise trade between Hong Kong and the Mainland, the price elasticities for both imports and exports and the income elasticity for imports are much larger than one; but the income elasticity of the Mainland for Hong

Kong's exports is lower than one. This suggests that the real bilateral exchange rate and Hong Kong's GDP growth have significant influence on real trade flows and imports respectively, while exports to the Mainland are relatively less responsive to the Mainland's GDP growth. The latter could be explained by the fact that about 40% of exports to the Mainland are for outward processing, which are not for meeting Mainland's own domestic demand. Thus, it is unlikely to be responsive to its growth. Moreover, exports involving outward processing are sensitive to the production costs on the Mainland, which are affected by the real bilateral exchange rate between the HK dollar and the renminbi. Similar to the results for aggregate trade data, the income elasticity is, in general, larger than the price elasticity, except for exports to the Mainland.

4. CONCLUDING REMARKS

This paper starts by discussing the stylised facts about Hong Kong's external trade pattern in terms of trading partners and product composition, with a special focus on the re-export trade with the Mainland. As an entrepôt for the Mainland, Hong Kong helps channel raw materials and semi-manufactures from the rest of the world to the Mainland for further processing and then re-export the processed goods to the rest of the world.

Because of the importance of the external trade sector, it is natural to ask whether the Marshall-Lerner condition holds for Hong Kong. Our empirical analysis suggests that the Marshall-Lerner condition appears to hold for Hong Kong's direct trade, implying that a real depreciation of the HK dollar would likely lead to an improvement in the balance of trade in direct exports and imports, holding other things constant. Given that a large part of Hong Kong's export earnings comes from its role as an entrepôt for the Mainland, movements in the renminbi real effective exchange rate plays an important role in influencing Hong Kong's overall trade balance. In particular, the price elasticity of re-export margins is much greater that that of direct exports. In addition, we find that these price elasticities estimated are mostly stable over the sample period, suggesting they are quite useful tools in helping predict the effect of changes in real exchange rate on Hong Kong's trade balances.

Price and income elasticities of bilateral merchandise trades between Hong Kong and its four largest trading partners, the Mainland, the US, the EU, and Japan, are also estimated. The empirical results suggest that the Marshall-Lerner condition is satisfied for bilateral trade of Hong Kong with the Mainland, the US, and Japan, but it is inconclusive for trade with the EU. In particular, the movements in the real bilateral exchange rate between the HK dollar and the renminbi are found to have significantly affected trade flows between Hong Kong and the Mainland. This probably reflects that a large proportion of goods traded with the Mainland are related to outward processing activities, which are quite sensitive to the production costs on the Mainland. Furthermore, we find that the US income elasticity for Hong Kong's imports is much larger than Hong Kong income elasticity for US imports. The finding appears to be consistent with those using aggregated US data with respect to the rest of world.

This study can be extended by examining the Marshall-Lerner conditions with respect to disaggregated data. In addition, the re-exports can be further divided into those from and to the Mainland to better understand changes in income and prices in both Mainland China and the rest of the world on the behaviours of such trade flows. Finally, it would be of interest to separate goods from services as the services trade in Hong Kong is gaining increasing prominence over time.

REFERENCES

Bruggemann, 2002, "On the Small Sample Properties of Weak Exogeneity Tests in Cointegrated VAR models," "http://ideas.repec.org/s/wop/humbsf.html" *Sonderforschungsbereich* 373, Humboldt Universitaet Berlin.

Census and Statistics Department, *Annual Review of Hong Kong External Merchandise Trade, 2005*, Trade Analysis Section, Census and Statistics Department.

Census and Statistics Department, *Report on Hong Kong Trade in Services Statistics for 2004*, Trade in Services Statistics Section, Census and Statistics Department.

Chinn, 2005, *Doomed to Deficits? Aggregate U.S. Trade Flows Re-Examined*, Kiel Institute for World Economics.

Hooper, Peter, Karen Johnson, and Jaime Marquez, 2000, "Trade Elasticities for G-7 Countries," *Princeton Studies in International Economics*, No. 87, August.

Johansen, S., 1988, "Statistical Analysis of Cointegrating Vectors," *Journal of Economic Dynamics and Control* 12 (2–3): 231–254.

Johansen, S., and K. Juselius, 1990, "Maximum Likelihood Estimatin and Inference on Cointegration—With Applications to the Demand for Money," *Oxford Bulletin of Economic and Statisitics* 52(2): 169–210.

Peng, Wensheng and Kelvin Fan, 2005, "A Review of the Hong Kong Dollar Effective Exchange Rate," *HKMA Research Memorandum*, November 2005 (unpublished).

Peng, Wensheng and Frank Leung, 2005, "A Monetary Conditions Index for Mainland China," *HKMA Research Memorandum*, January 2005.

Yang, Jiawen, Haiyan Yin, and Hui He, 2004, "The Chinese Currency: Background and the Current Debate," School of Business, The George Washington University, The GW Center for the Study of Globalization, July 2004.

Appendix 4A

Statistics on Trade by Main Trading Partner and Product

Figure 4A1
Real Export Growth

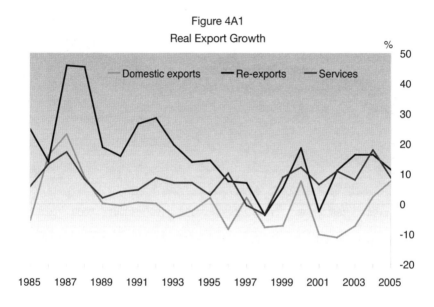

Figure 4A2
Real Import Growth

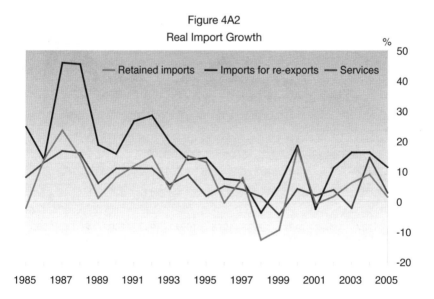

Figure 4A3
Exports of Goods by Main Destination

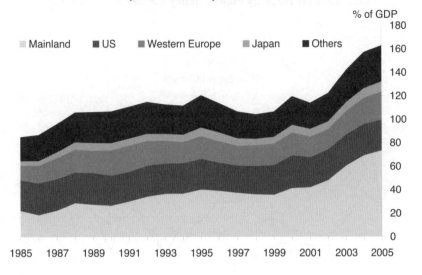

Figure 4A4
Imports of Goods by Main Supplier

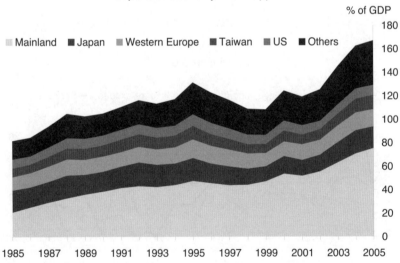

Figure 4A5
Re-exports Related to Mainland China

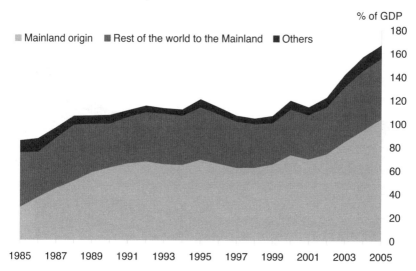

Figure 4A6
Real Growth of Re-exports and Offshore Trade

Figure 4A7
Exports of Services by Broad Category

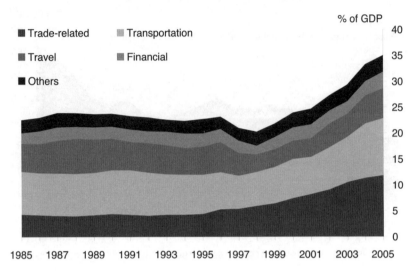

Figure 4A8
Imports of Services by Broad Category

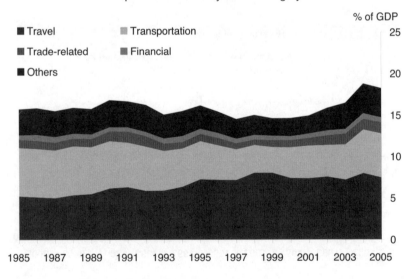

Sources: Census and Statistics Department and authors' estimates.

Table 4A1

Domestic Exports of Goods by Main Destination and Product, 2005

Domestic exports of goods by main destination and product	In % of total	In % of sub-total
To Mainland China	32.8	100.0
Articles of apparel and clothing accessories (84)	10.6	32.4
Electrical machinery, apparatus and appliances, and electrical parts (77)	5.5	16.8
Plastics in primary forms (57)	3.2	9.9
Miscellaneous manufactured articles (89)	2.0	6.0
Total of the above	21.4	65.1
To US	27.8	100.0
Articles of apparel and clothing accessories (84)	18.6	67.2
Miscellaneous manufactured articles (89)	3.6	12.9
Office machines and automatic data processing machines (75)	2.4	8.8
Electrical machinery, apparatus and appliances, and electrical parts (77)	1.8	6.3
Total of the above	26.4	95.1
To all other destinations	39.4	100.0
Articles of apparel and clothing accessories (84)	12.1	30.6
Electrical machinery, apparatus and appliances, and electrical parts (77)	6.6	16.7
Miscellaneous manufactured articles (89)	5.5	14.0
Office machines and automatic data processing machines (75)	6.8	17.3
Total of the above	31.0	78.6

Note: Numbers in brackets are the Standard International Trade Classification (SITC) codes.

Sources: Census & Statistics Department and authors' estimates.

Table 4A2

Imports of Goods by Main Supplier and Product, 2005

Imports of goods by main supplier and product	In % of total	In % of sub-total
From Mainland China	45.0	100.0
Telecommunications and sound recording and reproducing apparatus and equipment (76)	8.1	17.9
Electrical machinery, apparatus and appliances, and electrical parts (77)	7.5	16.6
Articles of apparel and clothing accessories (84)	5.6	12.5
Office machines and automatic data processing machines (75)	4.9	10.9
Total of the above	26.1	58.0
From Japan	11.0	100.0
Electrical machinery, apparatus and appliances, and electrical parts (77)	3.0	27.1
Telecommunications and sound recording and reproducing apparatus and equipment (76)	1.5	13.6
Office machines and automatic data processing machines (75)	1.1	10.3
Miscellaneous manufactured articles (89)	0.7	6.4
Total of the above	6.3	57.5
From Taiwan	7.2	100.0
Electrical machinery, apparatus and appliances, and electrical parts (77)	3.4	46.6
Office machines and automatic data processing machines (75)	0.8	11.7
Plastics in primary forms (57)	0.6	9.0
Telecommunications and sound recording and reproducing apparatus and equipment (76)	0.5	7.4
Total of the above	5.4	74.7
From all other suppliers	36.7	100.0
Electrical machinery, apparatus and appliances, and electrical parts (77)	8.9	24.3
Office machines and automatic data processing machines (75)	3.8	10.4
Telecommunications and sound recording and reproducing apparatus and equipment (76)	2.6	7.1
Total of the above	15.4	41.8

Note: Numbers in brackets are the Standard International Trade Classification (SITC) codes. The ratios in this table are slightly different from those in Table 4A1, as import data in this table are classified by suppliers while those in Table 4A1 are classified by origins.

Sources: Census & Statistics Department and authors' estimates.

Table 4A3

Re-exports of Goods by Main Origin, Destination, and Product, 2005

Re-exports of goods by main origin, destination, and product	In % of total re-exports	In % of sub-total by origin	In % of sub-total by origin and destination
Country of origin: Mainland China			
To all destinations	62.1	100.0	
Telecommunications and sound recording and reproducing apparatus and equipment (76)	11.9	19.2	
Electrical machinery, apparatus and appliances, and electrical parts (77)	9.8	15.8	
Office machines and automatic data processing machines (75)	8.4	13.5	
Miscellaneous manufactured articles (89)	7.8	12.5	
Total of the above	37.9	61.1	
To Mainland China	17.0	27.3	100.0
Electrical machinery, apparatus and appliances, and electrical parts (77)	4.0	6.5	23.8
Office machines and automatic data processing machines (75)	3.7	5.9	21.8
Telecommunications and sound recording and reproducing apparatus and equipment (76)	3.5	5.7	20.8
Textile yarn, fabrics, made-up articles, and related products (65)	1.9	3.0	11.1
Total of the above	13.1	21.2	77.5
To US	14.1	22.7	100.0
Miscellaneous manufactured articles (89)	3.2	5.1	22.6
Articles of apparel and clothing accessories (84)	2.4	3.9	17.0
Telecommunications and sound recording and reproducing apparatus and equipment (76)	2.1	3.4	14.8
Electrical machinery, apparatus and appliances, and electrical parts (7)	1.6	2.5	11.1
Total of the above	9.2	14.9	65.5
To Japan	4.8	7.7	100.0
Telecommunications and sound recording and reproducing apparatus and equipment (76)	0.9	1.5	19.5
Miscellaneous manufactured articles (89)	0.8	1.3	16.9
Electrical machinery, apparatus and appliances, and electrical parts (77)	0.8	1.3	16.3
Articles of apparel and clothing accessories (84)	0.6	1.0	13.3
Total of the above	3.2	5.1	65.9
To Germany	3.1	4.9	100.0
Telecommunications and sound recording and reproducing apparatus and equipment (76)	0.7	1.2	23.4
Articles of apparel and clothing accessories (84)	0.6	0.9	18.3
Miscellaneous manufactured articles (89)	0.5	0.8	16.7
Electrical machinery, apparatus and appliances, and electrical parts (77)	0.4	0.6	13.0
Total of the above	2.2	3.5	71.4
To all other destinations	23.2	37.3	100.0
Telecommunications and sound recording and reproducing apparatus and equipment (76)	4.7	7.5	20.1
Electrical machinery, apparatus and appliances, and electrical parts (77)	3.1	4.9	13.2
Total of the above	7.7	12.4	33.3

Note: Numbers in brackets are the Standard International Trade Classification (SITC) codes.

Sources: Census & Statistics Department and authors' estimates.

Table 4A3
Re-exports of Goods by Main Origin, Destination, and Product, 2005
(continued)

Country of origin: Japan			
To all destinations	8.8	100.0	
Electrical machinery, apparatus and appliances, and electrical parts (77)	2.2	24.6	
Telecommunications and sound recording and reproducing apparatus and equipment (76)	1.6	18.3	
Office machines and automatic data processing machines (75)	1.0	11.4	
Photographic apparatus, equipment and supplies and optical goods, watches, and clocks (88)	0.8	9.4	
Total of the above	5.6	63.7	
To Mainland China	7.3	83.1	100.0
Electrical machinery, apparatus and appliances, and electrical parts (77)	1.9	21.6	25.9
Telecommunications and sound recording and reproducing apparatus and equipment (76)	1.4	15.6	18.8
Office machines and automatic data processing machines (75)	0.9	10.6	12.8
Machinery specialised for particular industries (72)	0.5	5.6	6.8
Total of the above	4.7	53.4	64.3
To all other destinations	1.5	16.9	100.0
Electrical machinery, apparatus and appliances, and electrical parts (77)	0.3	3.0	18.0
Telecommunications and sound recording and reproducing apparatus and equipment (76)	0.2	2.7	15.9
Office machines and automatic data processing machines (75)	0.1	0.8	4.9
Total of the above	0.6	6.5	38.7
Country of origin: Taiwan			
To all destinations	7.2	100.0	
Electrical machinery, apparatus and appliances, and electrical parts (77)	3.3	46.2	
Office machines and automatic data processing machines (75)	1.1	14.6	
Telecommunications and sound recording and reproducing apparatus and equipment (76)	0.6	7.9	
Plastics in primary forms (57)	0.6	7.9	
Total of the above	5.5	76.6	
To Mainland China	6.3	87.2	100.0
Electrical machinery, apparatus and appliances, and electrical parts (77)	2.7	37.6	43.1
Office machines and automatic data processing machines (75)	1.0	13.5	15.5
Plastics in primary forms (57)	0.6	7.8	9.0
Textile yarn, fabrics, made-up articles, and related products (65)	0.5	6.7	7.7
Total of the above	4.7	65.6	75.2
To all other destinations	0.9	12.8	100.0
Electrical machinery, apparatus and appliances, and electrical parts (77)	0.6	8.7	67.9
Telecommunications and sound recording and reproducing apparatus and equipment (76)	0.1	1.6	12.9
Office machines and automatic data processing machines (75)	0.1	1.0	8.1
Total of the above	0.8	11.3	88.8

Note: Numbers in brackets are the Standard International Trade Classification (SITC) codes.

Sources: Census & Statistics Department and authors' estimates.

Table 4A4

Trade in Services by Main Group and Trading Partner, 2005

	Exports of services		Imports of services	
	In % of total	In % of sub-total	In % of total	In % of sub-total
Total	100.0			100.0
Merchanting and other trade-related	33.8	100.0	7.2	100.0
Mainland China*	9.7	28.6	3.3	45.3
US*	9.1	27.1	0.9	12.4
Japan*	1.8	5.4	0.7	9.0
Transportation	31.5	100.0	29.0	100.0
US*	5.7	18.1	2.7	9.4
Mainland China*	5.0	15.9	7.5	25.7
Japan*	3.5	11.3	2.3	8.0
Travel	16.5	100.0	41.1	100.0
Mainland China*	9.5	57.6	12.6	30.6
US*	1.1	6.8	4.7	11.4
Japan*	0.8	5.0	3.0	7.3
Financial	9.1	100.0	3.4	100.0
US*	2.7	29.8	0.8	25.0
UK*	1.7	18.4	0.6	17.2
Singapore*	0.7	7.8	0.5	14.7

Note: * Data on breakdown of service trade by trading partner for 2005 are not yet available. Ratios are based on those in 2004.

Sources: Census & Statistics Department and authors' estimates.

Appendix 4B

Data Descriptions

Trade data on a more aggregate level are obtained from the national account statistics compiled by the Census and Statistics Department. Direct exports are the sum of domestic exports of goods and exports of services at constant 2000 prices, and direct imports are the total of an estimated retained imports of goods and imports of services at constant 2000 prices. Retained imports are derived by subtracting the estimated imports for re-exports from total imports of goods. The former is obtained by removing an estimated re-export margin from the total re-exports of goods.

The real effective exchange rate (REER) for the Hong Kong dollar (HKD) is a CPI-based REER, using currency weights based on the direct trade in goods and services. It is different to the official REER which includes re-exports but excludes service trade in determining the currency weights.[13] Specifically, the export-weighted REER is based on the trade pattern of domestic exports of goods and exports of services between 2000 and 2004, while the import-weighted REER is based on retained imports of goods and imports of services during the same period. The REER for the renminbi (RMB) is computed based on the methodology presented in Peng and Leung (2005), for which the currency weights are determined based on the Mainland's merchandise trade pattern, adjusting for its trade via Hong Kong with the rest of the world. The currency weights of the HKD and RMB REERs are presented in Table 4B1 and the REERs are shown in Figure 4B1.

Table 4B1
Currency Weights of the Real Effective Exchange Rates

	HKD REER (export-weighted)	HKD REER (import-weighted)	RMB REER
Mainland China	30.6	16.7	–
US	26.8	11.7	25.9
Japan	7.2	14.9	24.9
Euro area	9.0	13.3	18.4
Taiwan	6.5	6.5	10.5
Singapore	3.0	7.7	3.5
S. Korea	2.5	8.7	10.1
UK	6.5	4.8	3.5
Malaysia	1.4	3.6	3.1
Thailand	1.1	3.3	–
Canada	1.8	1.9	–
Australia	1.5	3.1	–
Philippines	1.1	2.0	–
Switzerland	0.9	1.8	–
Total	100.0	100.0	100.0

Source: Staff estimates.

---

13. For details, see Peng and Fan (2005).

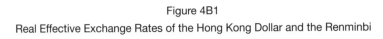

Figure 4B1

Real Effective Exchange Rates of the Hong Kong Dollar and the Renminbi

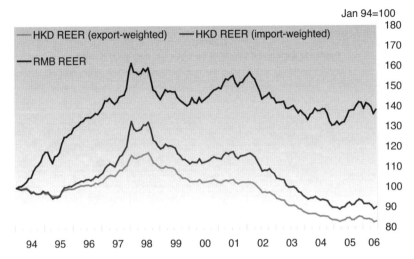

For data on bilateral merchandise trade, real exports of goods to the Mainland, the US, and Japan are computed based on the quantum indices for domestic and re-exports to these economies published by the Census and Statistics Department, while real imports of goods from the above economies are based on the respective quantum indices for imports. Real exports to and imports from the EU are estimated by deflating the nominal values of exports and imports by the corresponding export and import unit value indices with the UK. The real bilateral exchange rates are derived from adjusting the nominal exchange rates for the relative consumer price inflation.

Appendix 4C

Data Description

Table 4C1
Domestic Export and Export of Services Cointegration Results

	Number of lags Included							
	2	3	4	5*	6	7	8	9
RER elasticity	-0.75	-1.49	-0.78	-0.52	-0.03	-1.40	-16.40	-0.05
	(10.51)	(7.70)	(10.28)	(5.91)	(0.11)	(7.66)	(4.99)	(0.17)
Income elasticity	0.62	-0.15	0.63	0.78	1.14	0.22	-7.24	0.73
	(14.70)	(1.33)	(11.14)	(11.57)	(5.75)	(1.55)	(3.04)	(4.31)
intercept	✓	✓	✓	✓	✓	✓	✓	✓
trend	×	×	×	✓	×	✓	×	×
AIC	-2.96	-3.16	-3.49	-3.38	-3.46	-3.32	-3.22	-3.19
SBC	-2.65	-2.72	-2.92	-2.68	-2.63	-2.36	-2.12	-1.95

Table 4C2
Retained Import and Import of Services Cointegration Results

	Number of lags Included							
	2	3	4	5*	6	7	8	9
RER elasticity	-0.34	-0.39	-0.75	0.65	4.38	-16.78	-0.92	-0.76
	(4.59)	(4.77)	(5.69)	(-2.21)	(-3.32)	(3.50)	(14.7)	(8.37)
Income elasticity	0.57	0.54	-2.33	1.54	4.74	-16.43	-3.05	0.43
	(-9.32)	(-8.07)	(3.69)	(-6.01)	(-3.95)	(3.79)	(8.72)	(-5.38)
intercept	✓	✓	✓	✓	✓	✓	✓	✓
trend	×	×	✓	✓	×	×	×	×
AIC	-3.77	-3.73	-3.38	-3.29	-3.19	-3.27	-3.91	-5.75
SBC	-3.34	-3.21	-2.69	-2.47	-2.24	-2.18	-2.68	-4.38

Table 4C3
Re-export Volume Cointegration Results

	Number of lags Included							
	2	3	4	5	6	7	8	9*
RER elasticity	-0.64	-0.94	-14.63	-5.16	-3.50	-4.05	-9.53	-2.04
	(-2.10)	(-3.15)	(-4.83)	(- 3.81)	(- 2.52)	(- 2.79)	(- 5.11)	(4.17)
Income elasticity	3.43	3.37	-5.87	1.49	3.06	3.27	2.93	4.27
	(13.89)	(14.02)	(-2.31)	(1.54)	(3.07)	(3.21)	(2.28)	(11.16)
intercept	✓	✓	✓	✓	✓	✓	✓	✓
trend	×	×	×	×	×	×	×	×
AIC	-3.97	-3.97	-3.75	-4.02	-3.98	-3.86	-4.18	-4.8263
SBC	-3.57	-3.45	-3.10	-3.25	-3.08	-2.82	-3.01	-3.4613

Table 4C4
Re-export Margin Cointegration Results

	Number of lags Included							
	2	3	4	5	6	7	8	9*
RER elasticity	1.32	-1.61	8.91	-9.05	2.78	59.36	-7.24	-1.98
	(1.79)	(4.06)	(4.36)	(3.48)	(2.17)	(2.71)	(5.01)	(4.39)
Income elasticity	3.91	3.52	3.91	0.63	4.88	15.99	4.91	4.17
	(6.13)	(9.89)	(2.07)	(0.30)	(5.05)	(0.93)	(3.82)	(11.90)
intercept	✓	✓	✓	✓	✓	✓	✓	✓
trend	×	×	×	×	×	×	×	✓
AIC	-3.88	-3.96	-3.81	-3.94	-3.83	-3.76	-4.42	-4.82
SBC	-3.45	-3.40	-3.12	-3.12	-2.88	-2.67	-3.20	-3.45

Chapter 5

Service Exports:
The Next Engine of Growth for Hong Kong?

Frank LEUNG
Kevin CHOW
Jessica SZETO
Dickson TAM

1. INTRODUCTION

Service exports have become an important source of income growth for the Hong Kong economy. At the current pace of expansion of 10–20% per annum, service exports would be a key contributor to GDP in the coming years. In 2007, income generated from net service exports accounted for 20% of GDP, while consumer and business spending constituted 60% and 20% of GDP respectively. The growing significance of service trade to the domestic economy mainly reflects faster growth in service exports relative to imports, thanks to vibrant expansion in offshore trade, strong growth in financial service exports and rising number of inbound visitors.

A key impetus to the recent strong performance of service exports is the growing service demand from Mainland China. The implementation of the Closer Economic and Partnership Arrangement (CEPA) since 2003 has created new business opportunities for service providers in Hong Kong. Recently, the Mainland's financial sector reforms and capital account liberalisation have boosted fund-raising and asset management activities in Hong Kong. In fact, Mainland China is the largest buyer of services produced in Hong Kong followed by the US, and its significance is growing. Our projections show that, if the size of the Mainland economy doubles over the next decade, service exports would rise from the current 40% of GDP to 50% of GDP by 2016, of which about half of the increase could be attributable to the Mainland factors.

This Chapter is organised as follows: Section 2 analyses the key drivers of service exports in Hong Kong and discusses the growing importance of service exports to output growth. Section 3 identifies the opportunities and challenges ahead in the face of growing service demand from Mainland China, and discusses the possible constraints faced by service providers in Hong Kong. Section 4 measures the benefits brought about by the continued expansion of the Mainland economy to Hong Kong, and projects the medium-term growth path of service exports in Hong Kong. Section 5 concludes.

2. SERVICE EXPORTS AS A KEY DRIVER OF ECONOMIC GROWTH

The rapid expansion of Hong Kong's services trade in recent years has been a key driver of economic growth. The surplus in services trade has been growing strongly, accounting for 20% of GDP in 2007, up from 6-7% in the late 1990s. This compares with persistent merchandise trade deficits of 5–10% of GDP (Figure 5.1). The steady expansion in the service trade surplus has been driven by the strong growth in services exports relative to imports (Figure 5.2). The rise in services trade is indeed a global trend, as services increasingly take on tradeable characteristics and become more specialised, which can be seen from the rising trend of service off-shoring and growing business flows between the parent company and its affiliates overseas. Hong Kong has positioned itself well to capitalise on this trend, given its proximity to Mainland China, and its competitive advantage in trade and financial services.

Figure 5.1

Net Exports of Goods and Services in Hong Kong

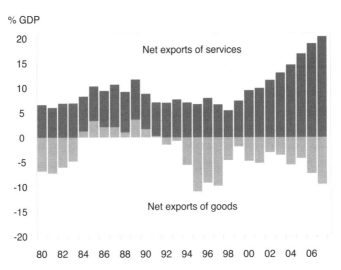

Source: C&SD.

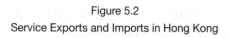

Figure 5.2
Service Exports and Imports in Hong Kong

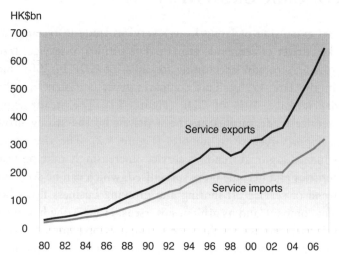

Source: C&SD.

Disaggregate data show that offshore trade is the major source of earnings in service exports, contributing to more than half of the surplus from trade in services, followed by transport and financial services. The balance of trade in travel services turned negative starting from the 1990s, but the deficit has been narrowing recently thanks to the strong growth in Mainland visitors (Figure 5.3). The rise of Mainland China as the largest exporting country in the world will continue to boost Hong Kong's offshore trade of Mainland origin.[1] At the same time, a more salient feature has been the fast-growing exports of financial services recently, in part reflecting increasing financial integration between Hong Kong and Mainland China (Figure 5.4).

For a small, open and service-oriented economy like Hong Kong, service demand from non-residents has become an important factor driving GDP growth. Over the past two decades, the sizable re-export and offshore trade of merchandise of Mainland origin increased the value-added of the import/export sector from less than one-tenth of GDP in the early 1980s to more than one-fifth of GDP in the 2000s to become

1. According to the IMF Direction of Trade Statistics, Mainland China overtook Germany as the world's largest exporting country in US dollar terms in late 2007.

Figure 5.3

Contribution to Net Service Exports by Service Group

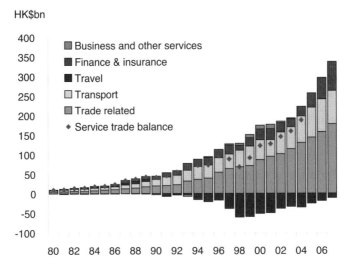

Source: C&SD.

Figure 5.4

Growth in Service Exports by Key Service Group

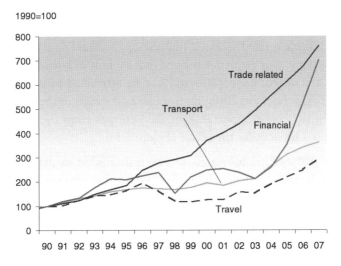

Source: C&SD.

the largest service sector in Hong Kong. Recently, financial sector liberalisation on the Mainland has boosted the external demand for financial services in Hong Kong, particularly those related to IPO and fund management services, raising the ratio of financial sector output to GDP from 9% in 1996 to 14% in 2006. The implementation of the Individual Visit Scheme by the Chinese authorities was another strong boost to the tourism industry in Hong Kong, raising its contribution to GDP from 2.3% in 2000 to 3.2% in 2006.

Given that trade in services is also the largest contributor to the current account surplus, the factors driving the growth of service exports are not only important for understanding GDP growth but also have important implications for the external payment position of Hong Kong. In the following sections, we take a closer look at the underlying driving forces of offshore trade, financial service exports and inbound tourism in recent years.

2.1   Offshore trade

Trade-related services accounted for nearly one-third of Hong Kong's total service exports in 2007, making it the largest component of service exports. Trade-related service exports refer to the provision of services to non-residents to facilitate merchandise trade that for the most part does not actually pass through the territory. In recent years, Hong Kong's traditional strength in handling re-exports is coupled with the rise in the exports of trade-related services, illustrating the evolving nature of trade in the economy. Our estimates suggest that roughly one-half of the value-added of the import-export industry can be attributed to net exports of trade-related services in 2006, up from just over 20% in the early 1990s, suggesting the rising importance of the earnings from the provision of trade-related services for the sector (Figure 5.5).

Over 90% of trade-related service earnings is made up of those from merchanting and merchandising for offshore transactions, which together are also known as offshore trade.[2] Merchanting refers to the

---

2.   Other than merchanting and merchandising for offshore transactions, trade-related services also include merchandising for onshore trade as well as other services such as the arrangement of subcontract processing services, but as these make up a small share of total trade-related services exports, they are not discussed in depth in this Chapter.

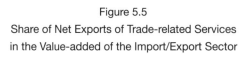

Figure 5.5
Share of Net Exports of Trade-related Services
in the Value-added of the Import/Export Sector

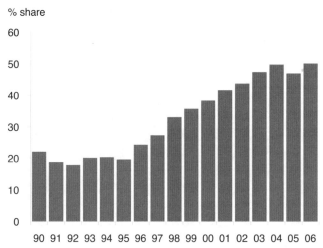

Sources: C&SD and authors' estimates.

trading of goods which are purchased from and sold to parties outside Hong Kong without the goods ever entering and leaving Hong Kong, while the one engaged in merchanting takes ownership of the goods involved. Merchandising for offshore transactions, on the other hand, refers to the case where the agent does not take ownership of the goods involved. Merchanting is the key driver of trade-related service exports in recent years, given that it makes up over 80% of Hong Kong's offshore trade and posts a higher growth rate. Merchandising, on the other hand, makes a smaller contribution to the growth of trade-related service exports (Figure 5.6).

One of the reasons for the rapid growth of merchanting trade is the increasingly complex global supply chain, which led to importers' demand for a broader range of services and more risk-sharing with its suppliers. For the importer, the outsourcing of such operations as sourcing, production, and logistics helps reduce the risks involved in working with different suppliers and coordinating from overseas. Some tasks are also less costly for the merchanting service provider than for the importer to do, such as ensuring compliance with relevant environmental and labour standards, where local knowledge and expertise are needed.

Figure 5.6

Gross Offshore Trade Earnings and Commission Rate by Service Group

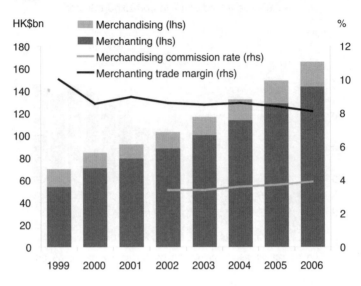

Source: C&SD.

Furthermore, given Hong Kong's robust legal system, importers may also feel more confident entering into contractual arrangements with Hong Kong service providers rather than with the manufacturers directly.

For the service provider of merchanting trade, taking ownership of the goods concerned means that they are typically more involved in the production process than are service providers of merchandising trade. For instance, merchanting service providers often help source and provide credit for raw materials and parts, and are sometimes affiliated with the production units to ensure smooth operation. Commensurate with the provision of more value-added services and the higher risk-taking, the trade margin in merchanting services is higher than the commission rate in merchandising (see Figure 5.6). In any case, both the trade margin and the commission rate have been stable in the past few years, suggesting that service providers have been able to keep their margin steady in the face of keen global competition.[3]

---

3. Merchanting and merchandising service providers may have broadened the range of products and services they provide, and diversified their sourcing markets and destination countries, and in the process kept their trade margin stable.

Figure 5.7

Gross Margin/Commission by Origin of Supplier

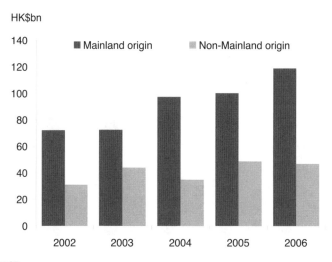

Source: C&SD.

Offshore trade by supplier country shows that the Mainland is a key factor behind the rapid rise of Hong Kong's offshore trade. Earnings from providing offshore trade services to goods of Mainland origin make up 70% of total offshore trade earnings, due to both the larger volume of goods traded as well as the higher trade margin (Figure 5.7). This is not surprising given the robust trade performance of Mainland China in recent years, the key role it plays in the global supply chain, and Hong Kong's long-standing role as an entrepot for Chinese exports. While the Mainland may have developed the requisite port facilities and the necessary logistics expertise to handle direct shipments, there still exist important gaps in the supply chain that Hong Kong service providers can fill—such as finding overseas buyers and meeting their quality standards, as well as sourcing raw materials and parts and co-ordinating work with other suppliers. Knowledge and experience of the Chinese market is likely to have allowed Hong Kong service providers to add more value and thus command a higher margin in China-originated offshore trade than in trade of other origin (Figure 5.8).

Figure 5.8
Gross Trade Margin and Commission Rate by
Service Group and Origin of Supplier

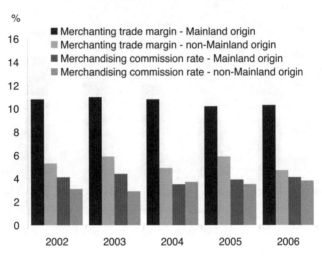

■ Merchanting trade margin - Mainland origin
■ Merchanting trade margin - non-Mainland origin
■ Merchandising commission rate - Mainland origin
■ Merchandising commission rate - non-Mainland origin

Source: C&SD.

2.2   Exports of financial services

Financial service exports have registered remarkable growth in recent years, more than tripling in value between 2003 and 2007. This is equivalent to a compound annual growth rate of 35%, faster than the 32% growth in imports of financial services (Figure 5.9). As a result, financial service exports, which are the sales of financial services to non-residents, have become an important source of income growth to the financial industry in Hong Kong. During 2003–06, net financial service exports as a share of financial sector output rose from 17% to 27%, and about 40% of output growth in the financial sector could be attributed to external demand (Figure 5.10).

Reflecting Hong Kong's status as an international financial centre, a significant portion of financial services produced in Hong Kong is consumed by non-residents. Over the past two decades, growth in net financial service exports has tracked growth in financial sector output closely (Figure 5.11). In recent years, growth in net financial service exports has become more volatile, in part reflecting the swing in

Figure 5.9
Financial Service Exports and Imports

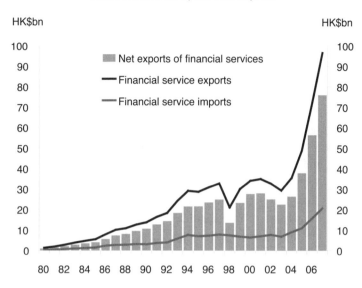

Source: C&SD.

Figure 5.10
Contribution of Financial Service Exports to Financial Sector Output

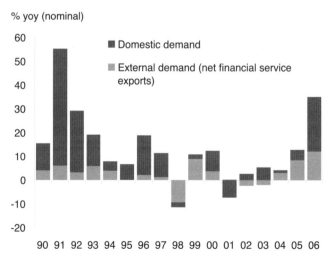

Sources: C&SD and authors' estimates.

financial market activities following the Asian financial crisis in 1998 and the burst of the global IT bubble in 2000. Recently, increased IPO and fund-raising activities of Mainland enterprises in Hong Kong have boosted the business receipts of the non-bank financial sector, mainly driven by increased activities in domestic securities markets and the asset management industry (Figure 5.12).

Like other international financial centres such as New York and London, Hong Kong has successfully attracted companies and private capital around the world, particularly within the Asian region, to use the financial services and infrastructure in Hong Kong. External demand has played an important role in boosting financial sector activities recently, especially in areas like asset management and securities transactions. In general, financial services could be broadly grouped into four key categories, namely asset management, securities transactions, financial intermediation and other financial services.[4] Based on official statistics

Figure 5.11

Net Financial Service Exports and Financial Sector Output

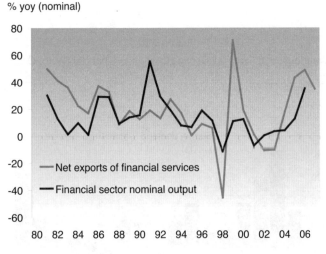

% yoy (nominal)

—— Net exports of financial services

—— Financial sector nominal output

Source: C&SD.

---

4. We follow the classification of financial services used by the U.S. Bureau of Economic Analysis (BEA). Asset management includes fund management and investment advisory (e.g., merger and acquisitions) services. Securities transactions include brokerage, underwriting and private placement services. Financial intermediation includes interbank and customer credit services. Other financial services include securities lending, clearing and other financial services.

Figure 5.12

Business Receipts of Banking and Non-bank Financial Services

2000=100

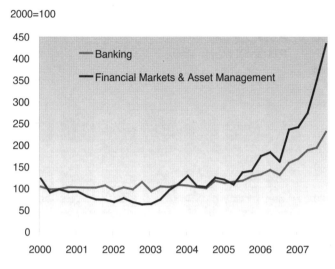

Source: C&SD.

Figure 5.13

Contribution to Growth in Financial Service Exports

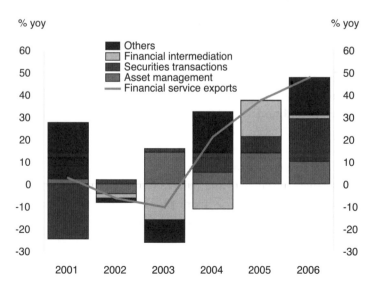

Sources: C&SD and authors' estimates.

Figure 5.14

Share of Financial Service Exports by Service Group

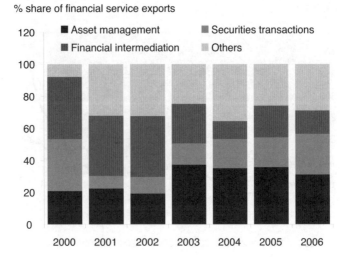

Sources: C&SD and authors' estimates.

and market sources, a crude estimate shows that asset management and securities transactions have been the two most important drivers of growth in financial service exports in recent years (Figure 5.13). Reflecting the strong growth in these two financial service areas, their combined share in financial service exports increased from 30% in 2001 to nearly 60% in 2006 (Figure 5.14).[5]

The growing significance of asset management and securities transaction services in Hong Kong's financial service exports reflects the shift from traditional banking business to areas with higher value-added, which is a natural outcome as the domestic financial industry moves up the value chain. In fact, it is a global phenomenon for financial institutions to strengthen their capacity in customised financial services like IPOs, structured finance and private wealth management, as keener competition has suppressed the interest margin of conventional banking business like trade finance and customer lending.

---

5. Please refer to the Appendix for the fee structure used to derive the composition of financial service exports by service type.

Figure 5.15

Financial Service Exports by Major Destination

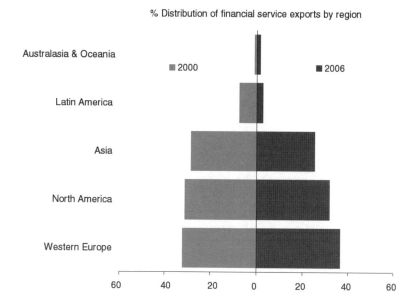

% Distribution of financial service exports by region

Source: C&SD.

Despite growing fund-raising activities by Mainland enterprises in Hong Kong, the US remains the largest destination of financial service exports in Hong Kong, followed by the UK and Singapore. Grouping by region, Western Europe and North America contributed more than two-third to export earnings of financial services in 2006, while Asia contributed a quarter to the total (Figure 5.15). The contribution from China remains tiny, at about 3% of Hong Kong's exports of financial services.

However, alternative measures point to growing importance of the Mainland factors in the recent expansion of financial service exports. To gauge the benefits derived from growing financial integration with the Mainland, four key areas of financial developments are used to measure the contribution of the Mainland factors to the financial industry in Hong Kong. These include: (1) increased number of Mainland shares listed in Hong Kong; (2) increased turnover of Mainland-related shares in the Hong Kong stock market; (3) the rise of merger and acquisition

127

Figure 5.16

Financial Service Exports Contributed by the Mainland Factors in 2006

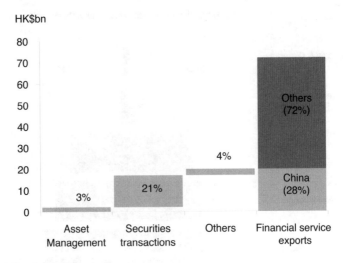

Source: Authors' estimates.

(M&A) activities in Hong Kong and Mainland China; and (4) increased inward portfolio investment (PI) from Mainland investors. Based on survey results and information on the fee structure of these financial services, a crude estimate shows that about 30% of financial service exports in 2006 could be attributable to the Mainland factors, mainly reflecting the sizable underwriting fee from IPO services and brokerage fee from trading Mainland-related shares by non-residents (Figure 5.16).[6]

---

6. Two possible reasons explain the difference between our estimates of financial service income derived from China and official estimates of financial service exports to China. First, a usual practice for the allocation of IPO underwriting fee between foreign-owned affiliates in Hong Kong and their parent companies overseas (mainly in the US and Europe) is that the former book the fee income to the latter after completing the IPOs for Mainland enterprises. In return, their parent companies will distribute a portion of the underwriting fee to their affiliates in Hong Kong. This redistribution of fee income from the US and Europe will be captured as financial service income received by their affiliates in Hong Kong in official statistics, although the underlying demand for the IPO services comes from Mainland enterprises. Secondly, we classify the brokerage fee due to trading of Mainland-related shares (e.g. H-shares and red-chips) by overseas investors in Hong Kong as service income derived from the Mainland factors, even though most of overseas investors are from places outside China.

Figure 5.17

Exports of Travel Services

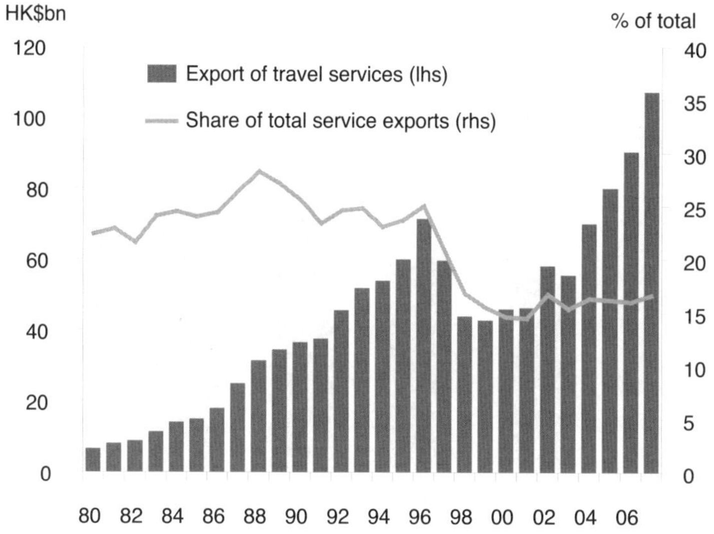

Source: C&SD.

2.3   Exports of travel services

Exports of travel services measure the expenditure on goods and services consumed by overseas visitors in Hong Kong.[7] During 1998–2007, service income from inbound tourism rose by 10% per annum, and its share in total service exports remained stable at around 16% in recent years.[8] During 1980 -1996, exports of travel services increased at an annual growth rate of 16%, with its share of total service exports moving between 22% and 28%. Exports of travel services then declined markedly during the Asian financial crisis in 1997–98, partly reflecting recessions in the regional economies and a reduction in the number of

---

7.   Visitors refer to civilian visitors, cruise passengers, service visitors, transit passengers and foreign crews. Export of travel services includes the expenditure on all goods and services (e.g. accommodations, shopping and meals) of these visitors in Hong Kong.

8.   Exports of travel services do not include the expenditure on transportation services by visitors, which is captured in the trade of transport services. If the expenses of passenger transportation were counted in travel services, exports of travel services would account for 22% of total service exports in 2006.

Figure 5.18
Total Expenditure by Type of Visitors

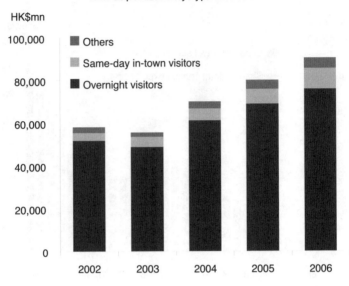

Sources: C&SD and HKTB.

Figure 5.19
Total Expenditure by Purpose of Visitors

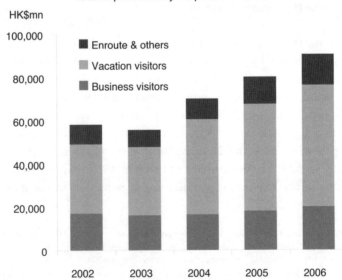

Sources: C&SD, HKTB and authors' estimates.

Notes: Vacation visitors refer to visitors going to Hong Kong for vacation and visiting friends/ relatives.

Figure 5.20
Total Travel Expenditure by Mainland Visitors

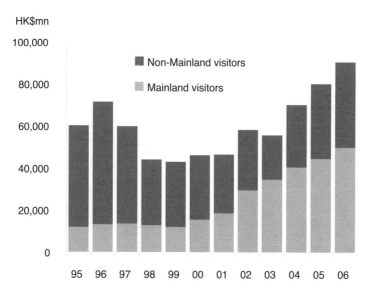

Sources: C&SD, HKTB and authors' estimates.

Figure 5.21
Contributions to Growth in Total Travel Expenditure

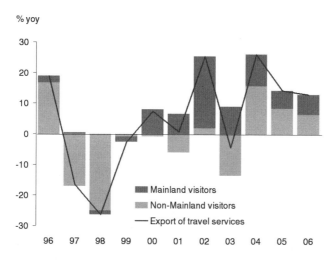

Sources: C&SD, HKTB and authors' estimates.

Figure 5.22

Per-capita Spending of Mainland and Non-mainland visitors

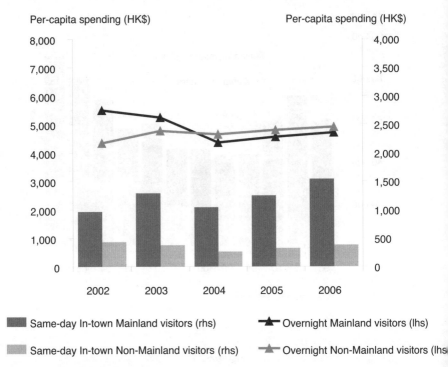

Sources: HKTB and authors' estimates.

visitors from Asia. Exports of travel services recovered starting from 2002, more than doubling in value between 2001 and 2007, despite a temporary dip during the SARS outbreak. However, its share of total service exports has not increased in recent years, reflecting the strong growth in offshore trade and exports of financial services (Figure 5.17).

According to a regular survey conducted by the Hong Kong Tourism Board (HKTB), overnight visitors have been the major contributor to tourism spending in Hong Kong, while spending by the same-day in-town visitors is growing (Figure 5.18). Most of the tourism spending comes from visitors for vacation purpose, followed by business visitors (Figure 5.19). However, on a per-capita basis, spending of the latter is higher than the former. Breakdown by sources of visitors shows that Mainland visitors have been a key source of growth to the tourism

Figure 5.23

Number of Mainland Visitors

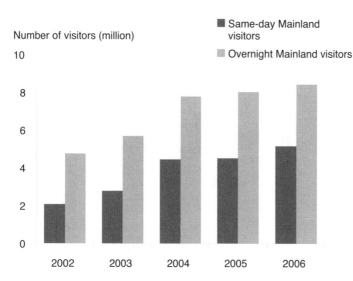

Sources: HKTB and authors' estimates.

industry in Hong Kong, thanks to the implementation of the Individual Visit Scheme (IVS) in July 2003 (Figures 5.20 and 5.21). In 2007, visitor arrivals from Mainland China rose by 14% to reach a record high of 15 million, of which more than half were under the IVS.

The number of Mainland visitors coming to Hong Kong will be boosted by the extension of IVS and their spending is expected to increase along with the income growth of Mainland residents. During 2002–06, the number of same-day in-town visitor arrivals from the Mainland grew strongly by 26% per annum while that from non-Mainland only increased slightly by 3% per annum. As per-capita spending of the former is almost four times that of the latter, Mainland visitors under the IVS have become an important source of income to the catering and retail sectors in Hong Kong (Figures 5.22 and 5.23).

While vacation visitors have been the key driving force of the income growth in the tourism sector, contribution from business visitors is expected to rise due to the expansion of convention and exhibition activities in Hong Kong and growing business activities with Mainland enterprises following the implementation of CEPA. In terms of per-

Figure 5.24
Per-capita Spending by Purpose of Visit

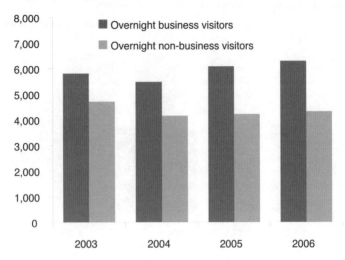

Sources: HKTB and authors' estimates.

Figure 5.25
Spending Pattern of Business Visitors in 2006

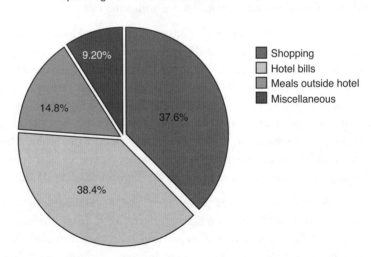

Sources: HKTB and authors' estimates.

Figure 5.26

Number of Events for Conventions and Exhibitions

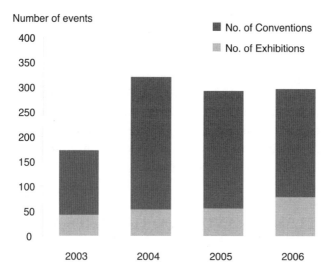

Source: HKTB.

Figure 5.27

Number of Overseas Visitors in Conventions and Exhibitions

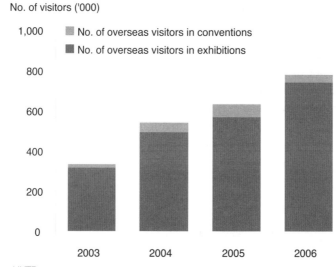

Source: HKTB.

capita spending, business visitors in general create higher value-added to the domestic economy. In 2006, business visitors spent more than HK$6,200 per trip per capita while vacation visitors spent one-third less (Figure 5.24). More than half of business visitor spending goes to hotel and catering services (Figure 5.25).

Reflecting the buoyant convention and exhibition industry in Hong Kong, the number of overseas visitors in these areas increased by 33% per annum between 2003 and 2006, thanks to the renowned and mega-size international exhibitions organised in Hong Kong (Figures 5.26 and 5.27).[9] Spending by exhibitors and exhibition visitors is generally higher than that of other business visitors.

3. CHALLENGES AND OPPORTUNITIES AHEAD

The near-term prospects for service exports will depend on the developments in the external environment, which has become more uncertain given the economic slowdown in the US and tighter macroeconomic measures on the Mainland. While deterioration in cyclical conditions may weigh on the external demand for services produced in Hong Kong, the potential service demand unleashed from liberalisation of the Mainland's service sector would be a strong structural factor supporting service exports in Hong Kong over the medium term.

However, keener competition within and outside Asia and growing pool of talent on the Mainland may erode the role of service intermediary performed by Hong Kong. Service providers have to strengthen their expertise in trade and financial areas by diversifying and expanding the range of services to maintain their competitiveness. The challenges and opportunities faced by service providers in Hong Kong are discussed in the following paragraphs.

---

9. For instance, Hong Kong Trade Development Council (HKTDC) organised nearly 30 world-class international trade fairs in Hong Kong each year—some of which are the largest in Asia.

Figure 5.28
Gross Margin by Types of Trade in 2006

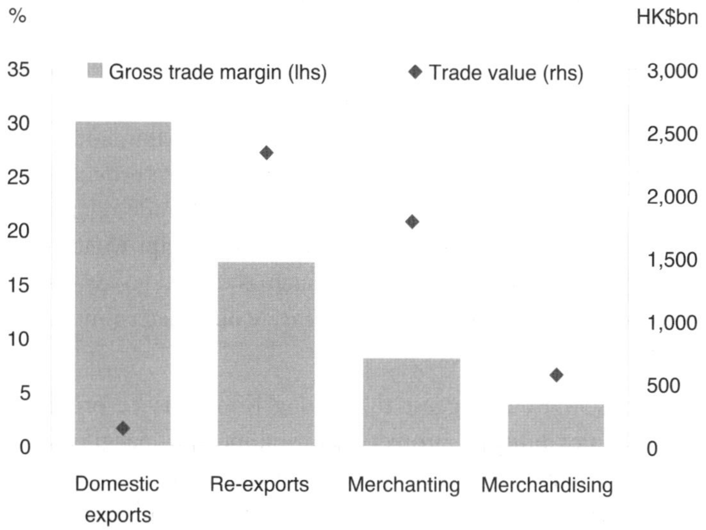

Source: C&SD.

3.1   Offshore trade

As Mainland China is such a large driver of Hong Kong's offshore trade, one natural question that arises from its further development and liberalisation is whether Hong Kong will continue to have a role to play in intermediating China's exports. We note that while there would be less of a role for a middle-man given an increasingly open Chinese economy, there is still an important role for the supply chain specialist to perform sourcing, quality assurance, logistics management, and compliance work, especially as product cycles get increasingly tight.

Offshore trade earnings can grow either through volume or margin expansion. Hong Kong's trade structure has shifted from domestic exports to re-exports, and from re-exports to offshore trade, with gross trade margins declining during the process (Figure 5.28). However, the higher volume that can be handled in re-exports over domestic exports, and subsequently in offshore trade over re-exports, more than offset the decline in margins to enhance overall earnings. For instance, in merchandising, where the commission rate is lower than it is in merchanting, the large merchandiser Li & Fung have expanded their handling volume and bought out the sourcing units of branded goods in ways to boost their earnings. On the other hand, trade margins can be maintained or enhanced if service providers move to provide higher value-added services, such as design and marketing, or develop new or niche markets and product knowledge. Given that Mainland's exporters are moving up the value chain, this would give service providers in Hong Kong opportunities to provide higher value-added trade-related services. Whether and how Hong Kong service providers adapt to accommodate new, higher value-added product types such as capital goods, and expand their supplier markets to increase volume, would determine how Hong Kong's offshore trade would evolve.

Some observations suggest that Hong Kong service providers have adapted with flexibility to protect their volume and margins in the face of increasing competitive pressures. Meanwhile, Hong Kong merchanting service providers are reportedly under mounting challenges in the face of rising cost pressure and the lack of pricing power, with margins being increasingly compressed. In response to this threat, service providers have been broadening their sourcing markets beyond the Mainland to other cost-efficient regional economies. Indeed, in offshore trade of non-Mainland origin, there is a trend towards increasing affiliation between Hong Kong service providers and the suppliers, suggesting strengthening business relationships and a more diversified supplier base. At the same time the range of destination markets has also been broadened beyond traditional markets like the US and Western Europe to such markets as Latin America and Eastern Europe.

The provision of offshore trade services is an extension of Hong Kong's traditional strength in re-exports. Looking further ahead, one might see the potential for Hong Kong service providers to set up affiliates on the Mainland and in other supplier markets to provide more local and immediate trade-related services. CEPA already allows Hong Kong service suppliers to provide logistics, freight forwarding, shipping, and warehousing services in the form of wholly-owned operations on the Mainland, opportunities which Hong Kong service providers can seek to exploit. This may be a significant growth area in the future.

Figure 5.29

Turnover Value of Equities vs Warrants and Equity-linked Instruments

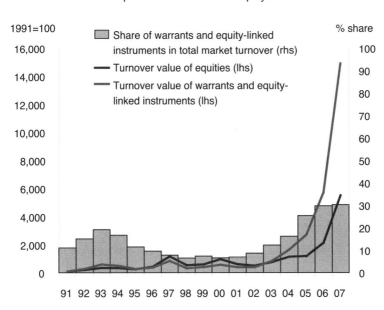

Sources: CEIC and Hong Kong Stock Exchange.

3.2   Financial service exports

Given the strong economic performance and the rapid accumulation of wealth and financial assets, the pace of financial development in Mainland China will be faster and more liberalisation measures will be implemented to meet the growing financing needs of households and firms. A more developed and liberalised financial system on the Mainland will pose challenges to Hong Kong in two aspects. First, the role of Hong Kong as the financial intermediary for Mainland entities could become less prominent. Secondly, growing foreign participation in Mainland's financial service sector may reduce the Mainland's demand for financial services provided by Hong Kong.

Over the medium term, a more developed and open stock exchange in Shanghai or Shenzhen may reduce the number of new listing and turnover of Mainland-related shares in Hong Kong. This could undermine the growth of service income from securities transactions

Figure 5.30
US Financial Service Exports by Service Group

US$bn

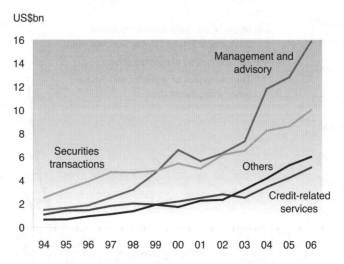

Source: US Bureau of Economic Analysis.

in the form of underwriting and brokerage fee, which has been the key driver of financial service exports in Hong Kong. While the listing and trading of Mainland-related shares in Hong Kong have boosted financial service income from non-residents, disaggregate data show that exchange-traded equity-linked derivatives have gained importance in the stock market turnover recently (Figure 5.29). In fact, it is a global trend for increasing share of derivatives trading in world's leading stock markets like New York and London, as the customised and innovative features of derivatives generate higher service income for financial institutions.

Given the growing global interest in trading and investing in Mainland-related securities, the demand for new derivative instruments for risk management and investment purposes is expected to rise over time. Hong Kong has an edge in creating and promoting new derivative products linked to equities of Mainland enterprises, and there is ample room to further develop the derivatives market following the financial liberalisation on the Mainland.

Although the recent stock market rally in Mainland-related shares has boosted the service income from securities transactions in Hong

Figure 5.31

Hong Kong's Fund Management Business by Source of Investor

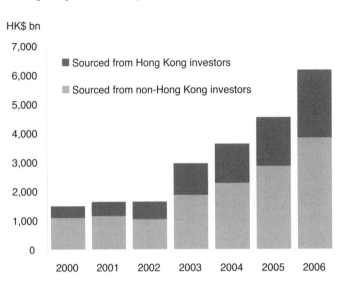

Source: Securities and Futures Commission (SFC).

Kong, this source of income is more volatile in nature and its growth prospects depend much on the pace of financial liberalisation on the Mainland. It is desirable to diversify the sources of financial service income to other areas such as asset management and investment advisory services. In the US, income from providing fund management and investment advisory services to non-residents has registered the fastest pace of expansion among various types of financial services (Figure 5.30). This reflects steady growth in global demand for US dollar assets and the highly developed asset management and investment advisory industry in the US.

Growing interests of Mainland entities to invest overseas provide great opportunities for Hong Kong to develop its fund management industry catering for the demand of private and institutional investors in Mainland China. Depending on the pace and scale of liberalisation of capital account transactions on the Mainland, private assets under management in Hong Kong could increase significantly. This will increase the service income from asset management, investment advisory and securities custody. It is expected that Mainland investors would

Figure 5.32
Average Net Worth of HNWIs in Asia in 2006

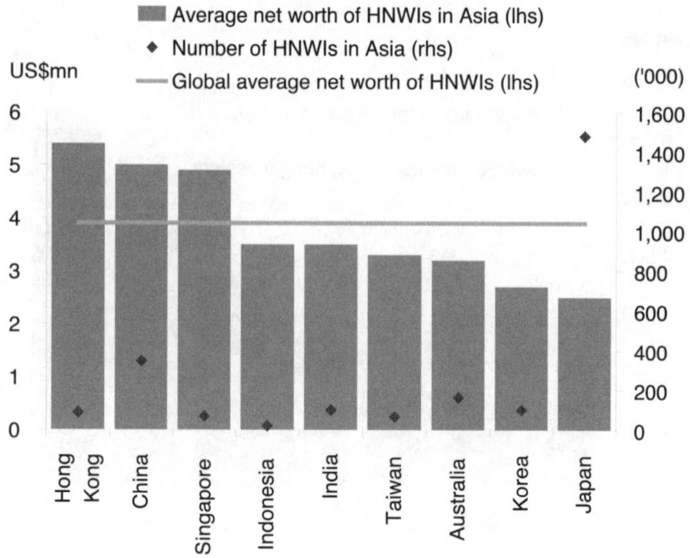

Average net worth of HNWIs in Asia (lhs)
Number of HNWIs in Asia (rhs)
Global average net worth of HNWIs (lhs)
US$mn
('000)
6
5
4
3
2
1
0
1,600
1,400
1,200
1,000
800
600
400
200
0
Hong Kong
China
Singapore
Indonesia
India
Taiwan
Australia
Korea
Japan

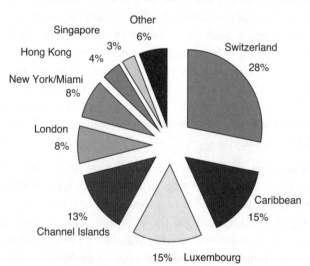

Source: Asia-Pacific Wealth Report 2007.

Figure 5.33
Estimated Destination of Offshore Private Banking Wealth, 2005

Other
6%
Singapore
3%
Hong Kong
4%
Switzerland
28%
New York/Miami
8%
London
8%
Caribbean
15%
13%
Channel Islands
15% Luxembourg

Estimated offshore private assets in 2005: US$5.9 trillion

Source: Wealth Management in Switzerland (2007).

become one of the major client groups for the asset management industry in Hong Kong (Figure 5.31).

Within the asset management industry, private wealth management (or private banking) could be an area with the highest growth potential in the coming years. The rapid pace of wealth accumulation and rising number of high net worth individuals (HNWIs) on the Mainland could boost the private banking business in Hong Kong (Figure 5.32).[10] In comparison to other major players, offshore private assets under management in Hong Kong only accounted for 4% of the world total in 2005, much smaller than the 28% in Switzerland and 8% in London (Figure 5.33). If fund managers in Hong Kong can successfully promote their wealth management and investment advisory services to the HNWIs on the Mainland, this could be another important source of financial service income given the higher value-added nature of private wealth management services.

3.3   Travel service exports

Hong Kong's unique role as an international business hub and global platform for China business will continue to underpin export of travel services. In particular, with China's increasing economic and financial integration with the rest of the world after the accession to the World Trade Organisation, Hong Kong is playing an increasingly important role in helping local and foreign exporters and investors to tap into the Mainland market. Thus, the contribution from business visitors to Hong Kong's travel service exports is expected to increase. In addition, infrastructure projects announced in the 2007 Policy Address will foster cross-boundary transportation between Hong Kong and the Mainland.

Hong Kong should continue to attract more high-yield visitors who spend more and stay longer in general, by hosting more mega international events and exhibitions and promoting the M.I.C.E. (Meetings, Incentives travel, Conventions and Exhibitions) industry, which is one of the fastest growing segments within the tourism industry. Secondly, the Hong Kong Tourism Board should continue to promote

---

10. According to the Asia-Pacific Wealth Report prepared by Capgemini and Merrill Lynch, the number of HNWIs on the Mainland rose from 287,000 in 2003 to 345,000 in 2006.

Hong Kong as an Asian vacation city to long-haul visitors, introduce new scenic spots and promote Hong Kong's traditional festivals.

Over the medium-term, building new exhibition venues is the key to attract business visitors. The second expansion of Hong Kong Convention and Exhibition Centre, which is scheduled for completion in early 2009, will increase the gross exhibition area by 42% to cater for the medium-term demand in the convention and exhibition industry. Hong Kong will strengthen its role as a gateway to the Mainland market and a springboard for Mainland enterprises to venture into the global marketplace, which will attract more convention and exhibition business.

3.4   Possible constraints faced by the service providers

Similar to other highly developed trade and financial service centres, how to maintain and attract talent to work and stay in Hong Kong has been the key priority on the policy agenda of the authorities. Fostering growth and accumulation of human capital is the key to success for a knowledge-based economy like Hong Kong, as information discovery and product innovations have become increasingly important to value creation in a service-oriented economy. Over the past few years, the government has implemented a number of measures to enhance the quality of the labour force and attract more talent from overseas.

On the financial front, a well established legal system and robust financial infrastructure in Hong Kong have built a solid foundation for the future development of the financial industry. While financial liberalisation on the Mainland is a golden opportunity to expand the size and product range in the domestic financial markets, there is room to develop and expand the asset management industry in Hong Kong, particularly in the areas of private wealth management and alternative investment funds. The role of government in providing a favourable legislative environment is important to the growth and success of these specialised segments.

4. POTENTIAL GAINS FROM GROWING INTEGRATION WITH CHINA

Following the implementation of the open-door policy in the late 1970s, the Mainland economy has been growing by nearly 10% per annum from 1980 to 2007, raising per-capita GDP by 40 times to renminbi $19,000. The robust economic expansion and growing personal income have increased the demand for services, boosting the tertiary industry (excluding construction) to GDP ratio from 26% in the 1980s to 39% in 2007. With the Mainland economy moving up the value chain, the tertiary industry is expected to grow faster and ultimately become the largest component in GDP. This shift in the Mainland's economic structure implies spending on services will take up a larger portion in consumption and business investment, which will create enormous business opportunities for service providers in Hong Kong.

To measure the potential gains from the continued expansion of the Mainland economy to the domestic economy, a number of scenarios are used to project the future growth path of service exports in Hong Kong. Our key question is: if the size of the Mainland economy doubles in the next decade (i.e., real GDP grows by 7% a year), how large will be the potential gains to service providers in Hong Kong? Based on some crude assumptions derived from past developments in service trade, we project different future growth paths for offshore trade, financial service exports and inbound tourism over a 10-year horizon.[11]

4.1 Offshore trade

Trade-related service exports are expected to continue to grow at a solid pace in the medium term. Two developments in particular are likely to benefit Hong Kong's trade-related service exports. First, globalisation is likely to continue to drive the trend towards specialised supply chain management. Trade intermediation services are expected to become increasingly customised so that there continues to be a role for trade

---

11. The assumptions used and the rationale behind our projections of service exports of key service groups are set out in the Appendix.

Figure 5.34

Contribution from Mainland China to the Projected Increase of
Offshore Trade Earnings in Hong Kong

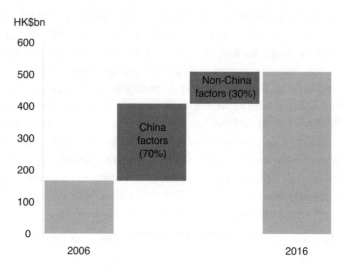

Sources: C&SD and authors' estimates.

service specialists. Secondly, exports of the Mainland are moving up the value chain, which should open up the potential for the provision of higher value-added trade-related services. On the other hand, as Mainland exporters acquire experience in handling marketing and logistics arrangements, there could be a decline in the share of total Chinese exports that Hong Kong service providers help service.

Our projections suggest that, when the size of the Mainland economy doubles from its 2006 level, which we project to take place in 2016, earnings from offshore trade of Mainland origin could reach over 11% of Hong Kong's GDP, up from 8% in 2006. This reflects both the continued importance of exports sourced from the Mainland economy, as well as the upgrading of Chinese exports in the value chain. Our assumptions are for Chinese exports to increase by 12% year on year to 2016, a rate that is slightly faster than the projected 11% growth rate of Chinese nominal GDP, but represents a slowdown from the 18% average annual growth in exports observed in 1996–2006. We also assume that the value of Hong Kong's offshore trade of Mainland origin to gradually

Figure 5.35

Merchanting Trade of Mainland Origin by Types of Goods

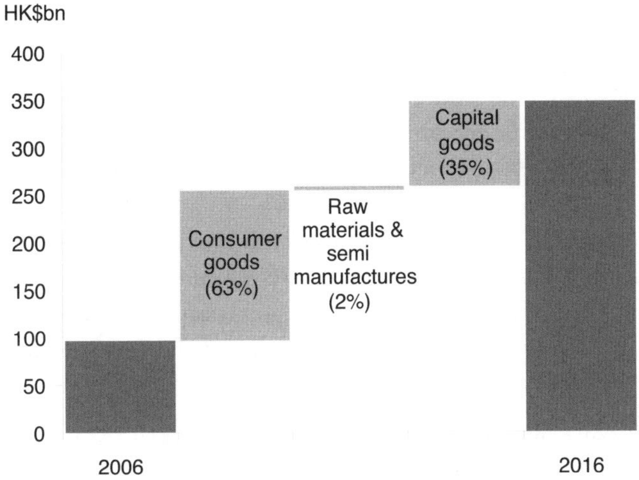

Sources: C&SD and authors' estimates.

decline to represent 12% of the value of the Mainland's total exports by 2016, down from 17% in 2006, as bilateral trade links between the Mainland and its trading partners improve and as Hong Kong service providers who support the lower rungs of the value chain may be displaced. We continue to see a role, however, for Hong Kong service providers in facilitating Chinese exports especially in higher-value-added services and thus expect the decline in the share to taper off at some point. In terms of the trade margin, the assumption is for the weighted merchanting/merchandising margin to remain steady at 8% during our projection period, roughly in line with the 9% observed for 2006, as the upgrading of Chinese exports helps maintain the margin in the face of global and local competitive pressures. Figure 5.34 shows the results of our projections, which suggests that the Mainland factor would account for 70% of the growth in offshore trade earnings between 2006 and 2016.

If we focus on merchanting trade of Mainland origin, our projections suggest a shifting pattern in the underlying product types, reflecting Mainland China's changing export structure and Hong Kong service providers' move to accommodate the change. Indeed recent trends suggest that, within Hong Kong's merchanting trade of Mainland origin, exports of capital goods increased at a faster rate than those of consumer goods, which in turn also grew more quickly than the exports of raw materials and semi-manufactures. In our projections, the assumptions are for consumer goods to increase by 12% per year, raw materials and semi-manufactures by 7%, and capital goods by 20% during our projection period, in line with per annum growth rates of 14%, 8%, and 27% observed in 2003–06 respectively. In terms of trade margins, we assume them to be 11% for consumer goods, 4% for raw materials and semi-manufactures, and 7% for capital goods, in line with trends observed in re-export trade. Figure 5.35 shows the projection results. While consumer goods are expected to remain the largest goods category, capital goods are likely to grow to account for over one-third of the expected increase in merchanting trade earnings between 2006 and 2016.

Meanwhile offshore trade of origin other than the Mainland is also projected to see solid growth, although not at rates as high as those expected of Mainland-originated offshore trade, helped by such trends as the diversification of sourcing markets amid increasing product specialisation, as well as China's rising import demand. We assume that Hong Kong's offshore trade of non-Mainland origin to increase by 12% a year to 2016, slightly faster than the 11% average annual growth rate observed between 2002 and 2006. The weighted merchanting/merchandising trade margin is assumed to remain steady at 4.5%, in line with the 4.4% observed in 2006. Our projections suggest that earnings from Hong Kong's offshore trade of non-Mainland origin would grow to make up almost 5% of Hong Kong GDP by 2016, and to account for 30% of the increase in offshore trade earnings (see Figure 5.34). Together, Hong Kong's total offshore trade could reach 16% of GDP in 2016, up from 12% in 2006, suggesting the continued importance of trade for the Hong Kong economy.

4.2   Financial service exports

Among the key service groups, financial service exports are expected to have the highest growth potential. The growth impetus mainly comes from two sources: growing financial integration between Hong Kong and the Mainland; and financial sector liberalisation on the Mainland.

Over the past few years, a number of initiatives have been introduced to strengthen financial intermediation between Hong Kong and Mainland China, including the conduct of renminbi business in Hong Kong, the listing of H-shares on the Hong Kong Stock Exchange and the implementation of the QDII scheme. These activities have boosted the underwriting fee, brokerage fee and management fee received by financial institutions in Hong Kong. Under the framework of CEPA, an increasing number of financial institutions in Hong Kong have set up their subsidiaries or branches on the Mainland. This also raises the sales of financial services between the parent companies in Hong Kong and their affiliates on the Mainland.

To gauge Mainland's contribution to financial service exports in Hong Kong over the next decade, we project the potential gains in service income from securities transactions, asset management and other financial services. Fee income from securities transactions mainly include underwriting fee for IPO and private placement services, and brokerage fee for trading Mainland-related shares listed in Hong Kong. With the increasing use of equity financing by Mainland enterprises, the ratio of equity funds raised to M2 increased to 1.6% in 2006 on the Mainland. If M2 grows at the same rate as nominal GDP and the ratio of equity funds raised to M2 remains stable, total equity funds raised by Mainland enterprises could increase by nearly two-fold to RMB $1.7 trillion or 2.6% of GDP in 10 years.[12] If about one-third of these funds are raised through the stock market in Hong Kong, total equity funds raised by Mainland enterprises in Hong Kong will double after 10 years. Increased listing of Mainland shares will also boost stock market turnover in Hong Kong. If the turnover of domestic stock market in 2007 doubles in value by 2016, total service income from securities transactions (including underwriting and brokerage fee) attributable to the Mainland factors will increase to 1.5% of GDP in Hong Kong.

Service income from asset management mainly includes fund management fee and advisory fee from M&A activities. Given the bulk

---

12. In 2007, Mainland enterprises raised more than half of their equity funds through the Stock Exchange in Hong Kong. It is expected that a more liberalised stock market on the Mainland will attract more enterprises to raise equity funds in the domestic market in the future. As a result, the projected portion of equity funds raised by Mainland enterprises in Hong Kong may decline over the next decade.

Figure 5.36
Contribution from Mainland China to the Projected
Increase of Financial Service Exports in Hong Kong

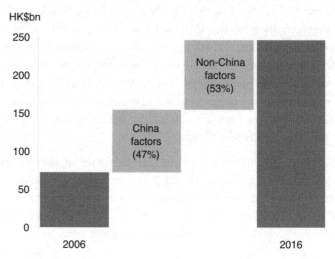

Source: Authors' estimates.

Figure 5.37
Mainland's Contribution to Financial Service Exports by Service Group

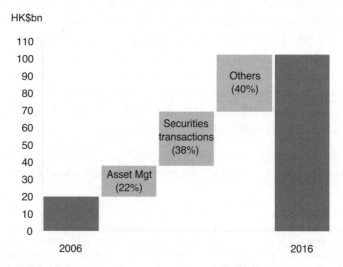

Source: Authors' estimates.

Figure 5.38

Projected Increase in Travel Service Exports by Source of Visitors

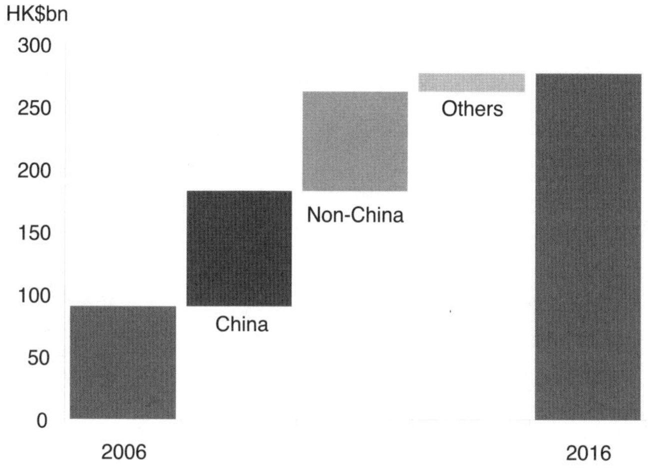

Source: Authors' estimates.

of private savings and limited investment opportunities on the Mainland, the Chinese authorities are expected to further open up its capital account to allow orderly outflow of private capital. Hong Kong will play a pivotal role in channelling these funds to domestic and overseas markets. Our previous studies suggest that if the Mainland economy is mature enough with its capital account as liberalised as in a typical OECD economy, its outward portfolio investment position could increase from the current 9% of GDP to 23% of GDP.[13] Reflecting the rise of Hong Kong's share in world stock market capitalisation as a result of increased listing of Mainland shares, the estimated share of Mainland's outward portfolio investment captured by Hong Kong could increase to around 15%. Based on these estimates and the standard fund management fee of 0.5%, the projected fee income could rise to 0.5% of GDP by 2016. Growing foreign participation in the Mainland's service industry will increase cross-border M&A activities on the Mainland. Suppose its size

13. See "Outward Portfolio Investment from Mainland China: How Much Do We Expect and How Large a Share Can Hong Kong Expect to Capture?" by Lillian Cheung *et. al.*, *Research Memorandum* 13/2006, Hong Kong Monetary Authority, September 2006.

Figure 5.39

Projected Increase in Travel Service Exports by Type of Visitors

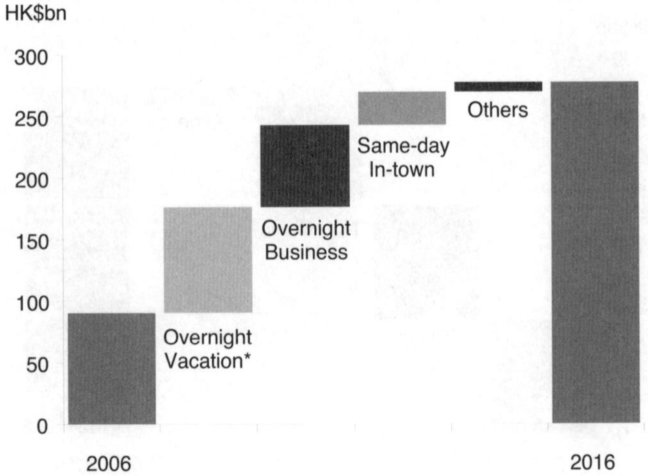

HK$bn

* Include tourists for visiting friends and relatives.

Source: Authors' estimates.

doubles in 10 years and about half of these M&A activities are arranged by financial institutions in Hong Kong, the combined fee income from fund management and M&A advisory services due to the Mainland factors could reach HK$20 billion or 0.6% of GDP.

Combining the projected earnings from the provision of credit facilities, clearing services and other financial services to Mainland entities, the Mainland factors could possibly contribute to 47% of the gain in Hong Kong's financial service exports in 10 years, with the rest of service income generating from places outside China (Figure 5.36). Growing financial integration between Hong Kong and the Mainland suggests that contribution from the Mainland factors to financial service exports in Hong Kong could increase from 28% in 2006 to 42% in 2016. Disaggregate data show that about 38% of Mainland's contribution to the rise in financial service exports is due to securities transactions including underwriting and brokerage fee. The rest is shared by service income from asset management (22%) and other financial services (40%) (Figure 5.37).

If the projected growth path for financial service exports realises over the next 10 years, its share of GDP would increase from 5% in 2006 to 8% in 2016. This will probably raise the share of financial sector output in GDP from the current 14% to 20% in 10 years, comparable to that in London and New York.

4.3   Travel service exports

Based on our assumptions of GDP growth for the Mainland and Hong Kong economies, exports of travel services are expected to increase by 12% per annum to reach 9% of GDP in 2016. Breakdown by source of visitors suggests that more than half of the increase in inbound tourism earnings is due to Mainland visitors, thanks to the stronger renminbi and the expected extension of the IVS (Figure 5.38). We adjust downward the spending growth of overnight vacation visitors from the Mainland, but expect stronger spending growth of overnight business visitors over the next 10 years (Figure 5.39).[14]

4.4   Projected contribution from service exports to GDP

Given the projected growth paths of offshore trade, financial and travel service exports, separate projections on exports of transport services and other business services are made to come up with the estimated growth path for total service exports over a 10-year horizon. Since trade in transport services tracks closely re-export trade and the flow of passengers, the weighted average of the growth rates of passenger and freight/cargo transport is used to project growth in transport services, which is about 9% per annum. Hong Kong's exports of other business services, including insurance, professional and personal services, have

---

14. The expenditures of visitors are simply calculated by number of arrivals and per-capita spending. The growth of vacation visitor arrivals is assumed to moderate, reflecting the lack of sightseeing scene in Hong Kong and the more developed tourism industry on the Mainland, which will divert Mainland visitors from Hong Kong. Business visitor arrivals, however, are expected to grow more notably, because of growing business activities and better prospect of the convention and exhibition industry. Per-capita spending of all visitors is also assumed to grow steadily, in line with the expected inflation rate in Hong Kong and increasing foreign household income. In particular, spending by Mainland visitors would continue to rise on the back of robust economic growth on the Mainland.

Figure 5.40
Projected Service Exports to GDP Ratio by Service Group

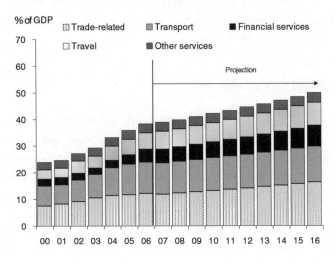

Sources: C&SD and authors' estimates.

Figure 5.41
Projected Contribution from the Mainland Factors to Service Exports

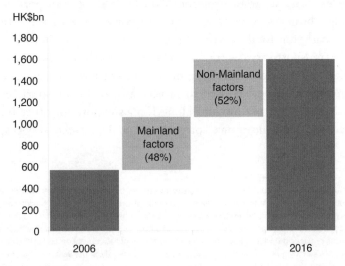

Source: Authors' estimates.

been largely offset by imports during the past two decades, thus the growth paths for exports and imports of other business services are projected to be roughly the same, and similar to the growth rate of nominal GDP.

Based on the projections on exports of the five key service groups (offshore trade, financial, travel, transport and other business services), service exports are projected to grow by 11% per annum in nominal terms over the next 10 years, raising its ratio to GDP from 38% in 2006 to 50% in 2016. Offshore trade is likely to remain the largest component in service exports, while financial service exports would be the fastest growth area thanks to financial sector liberalisation on the Mainland. This will raise the share of financial service exports in total service exports from 13% in 2006 to 15% by 2016 (Figure 5.40).

What does our projection mean to the Hong Kong economy? First, Mainland China is expected to be the major driver of service exports in Hong Kong, as nearly half of the gain projected over 2006–16 could be attributable to the Mainland factors (Figure 5.41). Secondly, the robust expansion in trade in financial services will strengthen the status of Hong Kong as an international financial centre, serving the growing financial needs from Mainland entities. Finally, growing importance of trade in services to the Hong Kong economy could be a catalyst for service providers to move up the value chain in the face of keener global competition.

5. CONCLUSIONS

This Chapter provides an overview of the recent developments in service exports in Hong Kong. It shows how service exports have become an increasingly important contributor to economic growth, and looks at the drivers behind the growth of three key service groups, namely trade-related, financial and travel services.

The Chapter also offers a baseline scenario on the growth of service exports in the medium term. The projection results suggest that service exports would take on an increasingly important role in the Hong Kong economy, accounting for 50% of GDP in 2016, up from about 40% in 2006. While trade-related service exports are expected to remain the largest service group, financial service exports have the highest growth potential. Meanwhile, travel service exports are expected to grow faster than imports to result in a surplus in this service group.

Mainland factors feature prominently in the projected growth path of Hong Kong's service exports. Because of the rapid economic growth and rising service demand in Mainland China, as well as the deepening economic and financial integration between Hong Kong and the Mainland, Mainland factors are expected to contribute to 48% of the growth of service exports between 2006 and 2016.

While our baseline scenario suggests a positive outlook, there are challenges and risks. A central challenge common to all service groups is the need to move up the value chain. This is especially important in the face of increasing domestic and foreign competition on the Mainland and in other regional economies, markets which are likely to be the key drivers of Hong Kong's service exports growth. At the policy level, the need to develop and retain human capital becomes increasingly important for a service-oriented economy like Hong Kong.

Appendix 5

Key Assumptions Used in the Projection of Service Exports

I. General assumptions for the Mainland economy

Assumptions	Remarks
• Real GDP to double from 2006 to 2016	This is equivalent to 7% per-annum growth. Real GDP last doubled in the eight years from 1998 to 2006.
• GDP deflator to grow by 4% per annum	GDP deflator grew by 2.1% a year during 1998-2006. The faster growth rate reflects higher inflation pressures driven by domestic demand in the coming years.
• The renminbi appreciates to 5.0 per US dollar by 2016	This is equivalent to a 5% appreciation of the RMB against the USD per year over the projection period.

II. General assumptions for the Hong Kong economy

Assumptions	Remarks
• Real GDP to grow by 5% a year in 2006-16	Official medium-term forecast.
• GDP deflator to grow by 3% per annum	This is higher than the official medium-term forecast, in part reflecting a faster growth in Mainland's GDP deflator.
• The Hong Kong dollar weakens to 1.6 per renminbi by 2016	This reflects the linked exchange rate between HKD and USD, and the gradual appreciation of renminbi against the USD.

III.   Assumptions used in the projection of trade-related service exports

Assumptions	Remarks
Mainland related assumptions	
• Mainland's exports to grow by 12% a year to 2016	Mainland's exports grew by an annual average of 24.7% in 2001-2006. A slowdown is assumed as the Chinese economy becomes more domestic demand oriented.
• Value of Hong Kong's offshore trade of Mainland origin to equal to 12% of China's exports in 2016	The share observed in 2006 was 17%. The assumption is for a gradual decline in the share as bilateral trade links between the Mainland and its trade partners improve.
• The weighted trade margin of Hong Kong's merchanting and merchandising trade of Mainland origin to average 8% over the projection period	The equivalent was 9% in 2006.
Value of Hong Kong's merchanting trade of Mainland origin by product category	
• Consumer goods to grow by 12% per year	The annual average growth rate was 14% in 2003-06.
• Raw materials and semi-manufactures to grow by 7% per year	The annual average growth rate was 8% in 2003-06.
• Capital goods to grow by 20% per year	The annual average growth rate was 27% in 2003-06.
Trade margin of Hong Kong's merchanting trade of Mainland origin	
• Consumer goods to be 11%	The overall rate averaged 10.6% in 2002 to 2006. Our assumed trade margins for different product categories are made based on trends observed in re-export trade.
• Raw materials and semi-manufactures to be 4%	
• Capital goods to be 7%	
Other assumptions	
• Value of Hong Kong's offshore trade of non-Mainland origin to grow by 12% per year	The annual average growth rate was 11% in 2003-06.
• The weighted merchanting / merchandising margin of Hong Kong's offshore trade of non-Mainland origin to be 4.5%	The rate was 4.4% in 2006.

IV.　Assumptions used in the projection of financial service exports

Assumptions	Remarks
• Equity funds raised by Mainland enterprises in Hong Kong to double by 2016, equivalent to 7% growth per annum	Assume the total equity funds raised by Mainland enterprises (A-shares and H-shares) remain stable at 1.6% of Mainland's M2, and about one-third is raised in Hong Kong.
• Stock market turnover to double by 2016 from its level in 2007	This reflects the rapid expansion in trading of Mainland-related shares and equity-linked derivatives listed on the Hong Kong Stock Exchange. The participation rate of overseas investor is projected to rise to 50% in 2016 from 40% in 2006.
• Cross-border M&A in Hong Kong to double in 10 years	Assume about half of cross-border M&A arranged in Hong Kong is related to Mainland enterprises.
• Assume Hong Kong captures 15% of outward PI from the Mainland by 2016, equivalent to HK$3.4 trillion	Total outward PI from the Mainland is projected to be 23% of its nominal GDP.
• Interest income from providing credit services through the banking sector to double in 10 years	Mainland entities are projected to generate one-third of credit service business for the Hong Kong banking sector, compared to around 20% in 2006.
• Mainland demand would account for about 40% of exports of other financial services	This reflects increases in custody fee and securities lending fee from managing the sizable PI assets held by Mainland entities, and growing contribution from Mainland business to financial service providers in Hong Kong.
Fee structure of financial services	
• Underwriting fee for IPO and private placement services is assumed to be 2.5%	Average underwriting fee for arranging IPO and private placement services for Asian and Mainland companies is around 2.5–3.0%.
• The standard brokerage fee for securities transactions is 0.25% of the trading size	
• Financial advisory fee for M&A services is about 2.0%.	Advisory fee for legal and accounting services for M&A is about 2.0%.
• The standard management fee for fund management is about 0.5% of the asset size	Asset management fee varies for different types of funds, ranging from as little as 0.15% for passive funds to 2.0% or more for actively managed equity funds.

V.   Assumptions used in the projection of travel service exports

Assumptions	Remarks
Number of visitors	
Mainland visitors	
• Overnight visitors: Arrivals to grow by 5% per annum in 2006–16.	The growth rate reflects the effect of extension of the IVS and tourism developments on the Mainland.
• Same-day in-town visitors: Growth of arrivals is assumed to decline starting in 2009, averaging 5% per annum in ten years.	Improvement in the tourism industry on the Mainland will divert Mainland tourists from Hong Kong.
Non-Mainland visitors	
• Overnight visitors: Growth of arrival is expected to ease gradually, averaging 5% per annum in 2006–16.	Due to improvement in the tourism industry and better transportation system on the Mainland.
• Same-day in-town visitors: Growth is assumed to decline starting in 2009, averaging 5% per annum in ten years.	Same as the above.
Vacation visitors	
• Growth of vacation visitor arrivals is expected to decline, from 10% per annum in 2004–06 to an average rate of 6% per annum in ten years.	Reflecting the lack of sightseeing scene in Hong Kong and improvement in the tourism industry on the Mainland.
Business visitors	
• Growth of business visitor arrivals is assumed to increase, from 6% per annum in 2004–06 to an average rate of 7% per annum in ten years.	Growing business activities and boom in the convention and exhibition sector in Hong Kong.

V.   Assumptions used in the projection of travel service exports (Continued)

Assumptions	Remarks
Per-capita spending	
Mainland visitors	
• Overnight visitors: per-capita spending is expected to grow at 5% a year.	Average annual growth rate of 4% in 2004-06. The expected higher growth rate reflects renminbi appreciation and per-capita income growth.
• Same-day in-town visitors: Growth rate is assumed to decline gradually, averaging 9% per annum in ten years.	Average annual growth rate of 21% in 2004-06. The lower growth rate is due to development of tourism industry on the Mainland, which will divert Mainland visitors from Hong Kong.
Non-Mainland visitors	
• Overnight visitors: Growth is expected to increase by 6% per annum in 2006-16.	More high-yield visitors are expected because of more business and long-haul vacation visitors with higher spending power.
• Same-day in-town visitors: Growth rate is assumed to decline until reaching 3%.	
Vacation visitors	
• Per-capita spending by vacation visitor is projected to grow by 5% per annum in ten years.	Due to foreign income growth and expected domestic inflation.
Business visitors	
• Per-capita spending by business visitor is projected to grow in line with past growth in 2004–06, at an average annual growth rate of 7%.	More high-yield business visitors amid a booming convention and exhibition industry are expected.

VI. Assumptions used in the projection of transportation service exports

Assumptions	Remarks
Passenger	
• Total number of visitor arrivals to grow as projected in the travel service section	
• Value of passenger transportation service exports per visitor to grow at 6% a year to 2016	The annual average growth rate was 8% in 2005–06.
Freight	
• Hong Kong's exports to grow by 8% per year to 2016	The annual average growth rate was 9% in 2000–06.
• The ratio of freight service exports to Hong Kong's exports is assumed to stay at 4%.	The ratio was 4% in 2006.
Others (including airport/port operations and ship chartering)	
• Airport/port operations and other transportation service exports to grow at 11% per year to 2016	The annual average growth rate was 10% in 2002–06.

VII. Assumptions used in the projection of other business service exports

Assumptions	Remarks
• Exports of other business services grow by 9% per annum.	Past experience shows that exports of other business services generally grow faster than nominal GDP. We expect this to continue given the growing service demand from the Mainland. Contribution of demand from Mainland entities is projected to increase to one-third of the total by 2016, up from 24% in 2006.

REFERENCES

Annual Report, Airport Authority Hong Kong, various years.

Annual Report, Li&Fung Limited, various years.

Asia-Pacific Wealth Report 2007, Capgemini and Merrill Lynch.

Banga, Rashmi, 2005, "Trade in Services: A Review," *Global Economy Journal*, Volume 5 (2), pp.1–22.

Cash Market Transaction Survey 2006/07, Hong Kong Exchanges and Clearing Limited, January 2008.

Cheung, Lillian, Kevin Chow, Jian Chang and Unias Li, 2006, "Outward Portfolio Investment From Mainland China: How Much Do We Expect and How Large A Share Can Hong Kong Expect to Capture?" *Research Memorandum 13/2006*, Hong Kong Monetary Authority.

Cocca, D. Teodoro, 2005, "The International Private Banking Study," Swiss Banking Institute, University of Zurich.

Economic Impact of the Hong Kong Exhibition Industry Report 2006, Hong Kong Exhibition and Convention Industry Association, 2007.

Fund Management Activities Survey 2006, Securities and Futures Commission, July 2007.

Koncz, Jennifer, Anne Flatness, 2007, "U.S. International Services: Cross-Border Trade in 2006 and Sales Through Affiliates in 2005," *U.S. Bureau of Economic Analysis*, October 2007.

Kwong, Kai Sun, 1997, *Tourism and the Hong Kong Economy*, City University of Hong Kong Press.

Manual on Statistics of International Trade in Services, United Nations, European Commission, International Monetary Fund, Organisation for Economic Co-operation and Development, 2002, United Nations Conference on Trade and Development, World Trade Organisation.

Maude, D., 2006, *Global Private Banking and Wealth Management*, Wiley Finance.

Statistics on Conventions and Exhibitions, Hong Kong Tourism Board, various years.

Statistics on Corporate Events, Hong Kong Tourism Board, various years.

Su Zhixin, 2006, "On Hong Kong's Trade Transformation and its Intermediary Role," Hong Kong Trade Development Council.

Tourism Expenditure Associated to Inbound Tourism, Hong Kong Tourism Board, various years.

Visitor Profile Report, Hong Kong Tourism Board, various years.

Walter, Ingo, 1999, "The Global Asset Management Industry: Competitive Structure and Performance," in *Financial Markets, Institutions and Instruments*, New York University Salomon Centre, November 1999.

Wealth Management in Switzerland: Industry Trends and Strategies, Swiss Bankers Association, January 2007.

Wong, Yue-Chim Richard, 2002, "The Role of Hong Kong in China's Economic Development," *The University of Hong Kong Working Paper Series*, vol. 2002–26.

Chapter 6

How Much of Hong Kong's Import from Mainland China Is Retained for Domestic Use?

Frank LEUNG
Kevin CHOW

1. OVERVIEW

As the renminbi continues to appreciate against the US dollar, question has been raised on how such appreciation will affect the inflation outlook in Hong Kong. The size of the impact depends on how much of Hong Kong's retained imports is sourced from Mainland China (China). Data on retained imports are not directly available and have to be estimated using figures of total imports, re-exports and re-export margins compiled by the Census and Statistics Department (C&SD).[1] It is estimated that retained imports of China origin amounted to HK$25 billion or only 4.3% of total retained imports in Hong Kong for 2005.

The estimated share of retained imports from Mainland China appears to be quite small considering the growing trade and economic linkages between Hong Kong and China. In fact, an analysis of various related statistics suggests that the published re-export margin of 23.5% for China could have been under-stated, probably as a result of the marked increases in round-tripping trade between China and Hong Kong in recent years. As a result, retained imports of China origin tend to be under-estimated.

This note uses alternative methods to obtain estimates of retained imports from Mainland China. Specifically, based on different assumptions on re-export margins, it is estimated that the actual share of retained imports from Mainland China could fall within a range of 9% -17% in 2005, higher than the 4.3% figure derived from the headline re-export margin for China.

Although Hong Kong's retained imports from Mainland China are likely to be materially higher than the headline figure, the impact of renminbi appreciation on consumer price inflation in Hong Kong is still likely to be modest. Specifically, a 10% renminbi appreciation is estimated to increase the Composite CPI inflation rate at most by 0.4 percentage points in Hong Kong, assuming that China's share of Hong Kong's retained imports is 14%, which is the mean of our estimates, and that there is complete exchange rate pass-through to consumer prices.

---

1. The C&SD only publishes data of total imports and do not differentiate between imports for re-exports and imports for domestic use. Retained imports are estimated using re-export margins compiled based on survey data.

2. ESTIMATION OF RETAINED IMPORTS FROM CHINA

Trade statistics in Hong Kong mainly cover total imports, domestic exports and re-exports. No official statistics are available to directly measure the size of imports retained for domestic use, and the figure has to be estimated using re-export margin statistics. Re-export margin measures the price difference between re-exports and imports expressed as a percentage of re-export prices.[2] It captures the value-added to imports for re-export purposes. Given the re-export margin, retained imports can be derived by deducting re-exports measured at import prices from total imports. In other words, retained imports are equal to total imports minus re-exports discounted by the re-export margin, as represented by the following equation.

Retained imports = Total imports – Re-exports*(1 – re-export margin) (1)

Based on survey data, C&SD has compiled the overall re-export margin, re-export margins for goods imported from China and non-China trading partners, and re-export margins by five end-use categories (Figures 6.1 and 6.2).[3] In terms of country of origin, the re-export margin for China has been much higher than that for other trading partners.[4] On the other hand, breakdown by end-use category shows that consumer and capital goods usually command higher re-export margins than fuels and raw materials.

The 2005 figures show that re-export margins for China and the rest of the world are 23.5% and 7.8% respectively, with the overall margin being 17.5%. Using equation (1), retained imports from China are estimated to be HK$25 billion, equivalent to 4.3% of total retained imports in Hong Kong. The share is relatively small compared with other major trading partners such as Japan and the US (Table 6.1).

---

2. I.e., re-export margin = (re-export prices – import prices) / re-export prices.

3. The five main types of goods by end-use category include foodstuffs, raw materials and semi-finished goods, consumer goods, capital goods and fuel.

4. The higher re-export margin for China may reflect the practice of transfer pricing, which is a profit-booking arrangement used by manufacturers for tax reasons.

Figure 6.1
Re-export Margin by Country of Origin

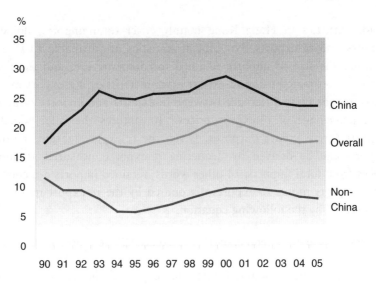

Source: C&SD.

Figure 6.2
Re-export Margin by End-use Category

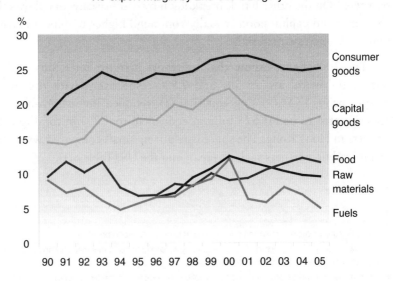

Source: C&SD.

Table 6.1
Retained Imports from Major Trading Partners in 2005

2005 (HK$bn)	Imports by origin	Re-exports by origin	Re-export margin1 (%)	Retained imports	Share of HK's retained imports (%)
Mainland China	1,030	1,313	23.5	25	4.3
US	106	64	7.8	46	7.9
Japan	266	186	7.8	95	16.2
Euro area	135	75	7.8	65	11.2
Taiwan	172	152	7.8	32	5.4
Korea	129	74	7.8	61	10.4
Others	492	249	7.8	261	44.7
Total	2,329	2,114	17.5	585	100.0

Note: The re-export margin for non-China trading partners is estimated to be 7.8% on average for 2005.

Sources: C&SD and authors' estimates.

Figure 6.3
Retained Imports by Country

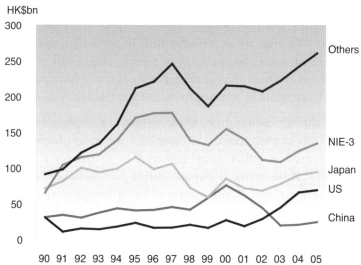

Sources: C&SD and authors' estimates.

169

Figure 6.4
Trade Share by Country

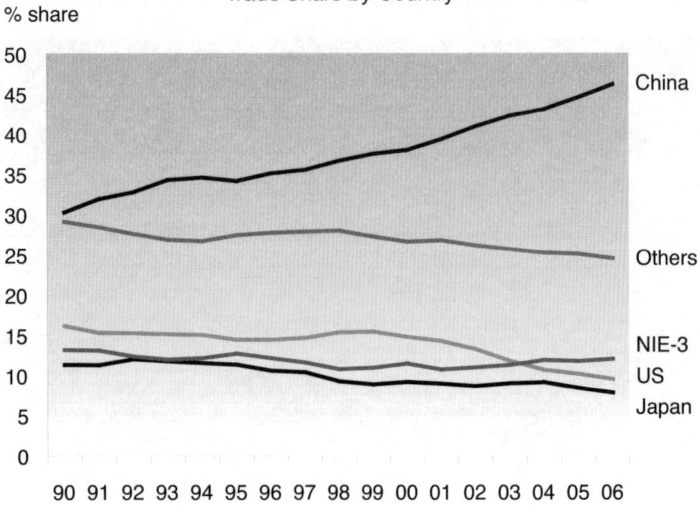

% share

Sources: C&SD and authors' estimates.

One noteworthy development is that while retained imports from most trading partners have been picking up along with rising domestic demand in recent years, retained imports from China have been declining (Figure 6.3). This trend seems to be at odds with the growing importance of China trade in Hong Kong compared with other economies (Figure 6.4), and raises question whether the re-export margins for goods originated from China are under-estimated. In particular, as 60% of re-exports in Hong Kong originates from China, even small sampling or reporting errors in the re-export margin statistics may have considerable impact on the estimate of retained imports from China.

To test the sensitivity of the share of retained imports from China to changes in re-export margin, 5% and 10% deviations from the mean estimate are used to reflect sampling errors in the survey data.[5] Table 6.2 shows that if the actual re-export margin for China is 5% and 10% above the mean estimate, China's share of Hong Kong's retained imports would rise to 6.7% and 9.1% respectively for 2005. However, the share

---

5. Based on the sampling errors from the survey data, a 10% deviation from the mean estimate of re-export margin is equivalent to a 95% confidence interval within which the true re-export margin would fall.

Table 6.2

Sensitivity of Retained Imports from China to Re-export Margins

2005	Re-export margin for China (%)	Retained imports originated from China (HK$bn)	China's share of HK's retained imports (%)
Mean - 10%	21.2	-5.8	-1.0
Mean - 5%	22.3	9.7	1.7
Mean estimate	23.5	25.1	4.3
Mean + 5%	24.7	40.5	6.7
Mean + 10%	25.9	55.9	9.1

Note: We assume that re-export margins for other trading partners will remain unchanged, and total retained imports will change along with different re-export margins used for China.

Sources: C&SD and authors' estimates.

would turn negative if the actual re-export margin is 10% below the mean estimate, which is not a sensible outcome.

The trend of declining retained imports from China suggests that the re-export margin of 23.5% for China appears to be under-stated. It is possible that the actual re-export margin for China is 10% higher than the published figure, yielding a margin of 26% for 2005. Assuming that re-export margins for other trading partners remain unchanged, the share of imports from China for domestic use would rise from 4.3% to 9.1%, while total retained imports in Hong Kong would increase from HK$585 billion to HK$616 billion.

3. THE BREAKEVEN RE-EXPORT MARGIN FOR CHINA

The hypothesis of a higher re-export margin for China could also be justified by past movements in the breakeven re-export margin and shifts in the product composition of re-exports originated from China. The breakeven re-export margin is defined as the margin which will lead to zero retained imports. It can be derived by re-arranging Equation (1) and setting retained imports to zero, that is,

$$\text{Breakeven re-export margin} = 1 - (\text{Imports / Re-exports}) \qquad (2)$$

In other words, the breakeven re-export margin is the difference between re-exports and imports expressed as a percentage of re-exports. Positive retained imports require the actual (or estimated) re-export margin to be higher than the breakeven re-export margin. The larger the difference between the two, the higher will be the retained imports.

Past developments showed that the breakeven margin and headline re-export margin (published by C&SD) for China tended to move together during the period of 1995–2000, with the spread between the two widening gradually from 6 percentage points to 9 percentage points. However, the headline re-export margin has started to decline since 2001, meanwhile the breakeven margin has risen. As a result, the spread declined notably to 2 percentage points in 2005 (Figure 6.5). However, the composition of re-exports from China shows that manufacturers have shifted to produce goods with higher valued-added such as machinery and electronics products, whose combined share increased from 26% in 1995 to 49% in 2005 (Figure 6.6). This suggests that the profit margin for China-originated re-exports should have improved or at least remained stable, which is consistent with the rising breakeven margin but at odds with the falling headline margin (Figure 6.5).

Supposing that the true re-export margin follows the movement of the breakeven margin as shown in Figure 6.5 and the spread between the two remains stable over time, the actual re-export margin for China would be higher than the headline figure of 23.5%. Using the average spread of 7 percentage points during 1995–2000, the derived re-export margin for China would rise to 28.6%, with a range estimate of 27.7%–30.6%. As a result, the share of imports from China for domestic use would increase to an average of 14.1% for 2005 (Table 6.3).

4. ROUND-TRIPPING TRADE AND THE MEASUREMENT OF RE-EXPORT MARGINS

The above analysis suggests that the 23.5% re-export margin for China appears to be small and inconsistent with increased value-added contents in exports from China. While sampling errors have increased the uncertainty and variability in the estimation of re-export margins,

Figure 6.5

Breakeven and Headline Re-export Margins for China

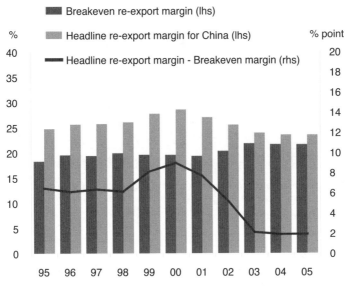

Sources: C&SD and authors' estimates.

Figure 6.6

Re-exports Originated from China by Commodity Group

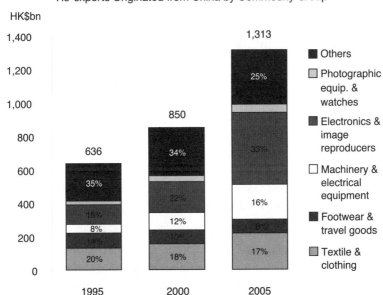

Sources: C&SD and authors' estimates.

Table 6.3

Re-export Margin for China Derived from the Spread

between the Breakeven and Headline Margins

	Spread for the period 1995-2000 (% point)	Derived re-export margin for 2005 (%)	China's share of retained imports in 2005 (%)
Smallest	6.1	27.7	12.5
Largest	9.0	30.6	17.4
Average	7.0	28.6	14.1
Breakeven re-export margin		21.6	

Note: We assume that re-export margins for other trading partners will remain unchanged, and total retained imports will change along with different re-export margins used for China.

Sources: C&SD and authors' estimates.

the recent change in the trade pattern between Hong Kong and China could have distorted the measurement of re-export margins significantly. Specifically, the rise in round-tripping trade between Hong Kong and China, in which goods imported from China are subsequently re-exported back to China, might lead to under-estimation of the re-export margin for China.

In recent years, the share of round-tripping trade in re-exports originated from China has increased markedly, rising from around 10% in 2000 to above 30% in 2006 (Figure 6.7). This has coincided with the fall in the headline re-export margin for China over the same period (Figure 6.5). Although there is limited information about the nature and motive of the round-tripping trade, breakdown by commodity group suggests that the re-export margin for this type of trade has been improving, reflecting the rising share of high value-added goods such as machinery and electronics in the product mix. Their combined share increased from 19% in 1995 to 66% in 2005 (Figure 6.8).

If the re-export margins of the round-tripping trade and re-exports to overseas (both originated from China) are expected to improve over time, in what ways would the growing importance of the round-tripping trade lead to under-estimation of the re-export margin for China? This hinges on whether the profit margin of re-exports back to China is

Figure 6.7
Share of the Round-tripping Trade in Re-exports from China

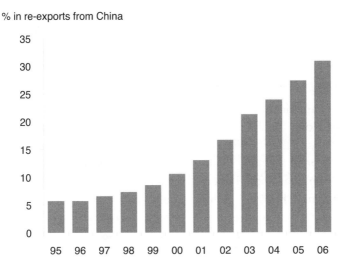

Sources: C&SD and authors' estimates.

Figure 6.8
Product Composition of the Round-tripping Trade with China

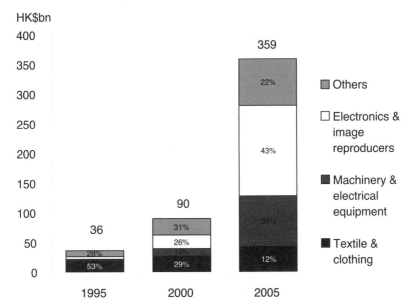

Sources: C&SD and authors' estimates.

lower than that to other places. Since such a breakdown is currently not available, re-export margins by destination have to be estimated based on some broad assumptions.

In general, imports originated from China can be used for three purposes, that is, for re-export to overseas markets (excluding China), for domestic use, and for re-export back to China (round-tripping trade), which can be illustrated by Figure 6.9.

The numerical figures in the Figure 6.9 are trade flows from China to Hong Kong for 2005. Assuming a re-export margin of 26%, which is 10% above the headline margin published by C&SD, imports from China retained for domestic use is estimated to be HK$56 billion (Table 6.2). Given that total imports of China origin is HK$1,030 billion, the remaining HK$974 billion should be for re-export purposes. To disaggregate the balance into re-exports to overseas market and back to China, it is assumed that imports involving outward processing in China, which amount to HK$692 billion, will be subsequently re-exported to overseas markets except China.[6] As a result, the derived re-export margin for this type of trade is 27.5%. The remaining imports, which amount to HK$282 billion, are expected to be re-exported back to China, with a derived re-export margin of 21.4%.

If the re-export margin for goods shipped to overseas markets is generally higher than for those shipped back to China, the rising share of the round-tripping trade may drag down the overall re-export margin for China as the chance of selecting samples with lower re-export margins in the re-export margin survey increases. This possibly explains the steady decline of the headline re-export margin for China since 2001, when the share of round-tripping trade started to pick up (Figure 6.7). Anecdotal evidence also suggests that some of the round-tripping trade involve little further processing and value-added activities in Hong

---

6. The usual outward processing arrangement is to export raw materials or semi-finished goods from or through Hong Kong to China for processing and assembly, with a contractual arrangement for subsequent re-importation of the processed goods into Hong Kong. It is believed that the majority of imports related to outward processing will be re-exported to overseas markets through Hong Kong. Although some of these outward-processing-related imports may be retained for domestic use or re-exported back to China, their proportions are assumed to be small.

Figure 6.9

Decomposition of Imports and Re-exports Originated from China in 2005

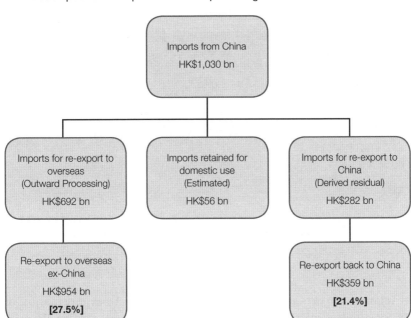

Note: Bold figures in square bracket are derived re-export margins

Sources: C&SD and authors' estimates.

Kong.[7] Nevertheless, the validity of a higher re-export margin for goods shipped to overseas markets relative to China hinges on the estimate of retained imports and the assumption made on imports related to outward processing. Any under- or over-statement of these figures could lead to substantial changes in the estimates of re-export margins.

5. RETAINED IMPORTS AND IMPORTED INFLATION

Based on an assumed range of 26%–31% for the re-export margin, the share of imports from China retained for domestic use could lie between 9% and 17% for 2005 (Table 6.4). The mean estimate of China's share

---

7. Some possible motives for the round-tripping trade could include tax reasons, restrictions of selling exported products in domestic markets, profit booking and logistic arrangements.

Table 6.4
Retained Imports from China under Different Assumptions
on Re-export Margin

2005	Re-export margin for China	China's share of retained imports
Headline (published by C&SD)	23.5%	4.3%
Headline + 10%	25.9%	9.1%
Spread over the breakeven margin	28% - 31%	13% - 17%
Plausible range	26% - 31%	9% - 17%
Mean estimate	28.5%	14%

Note: We assume that re-export margins for other trading partners remain unchanged, and total retained imports change along with different re-export margins used for China.

Sources: C&SD and authors' estimates.

of retained imports in Hong Kong is 14% given a re-export margin of 28.5%, higher than the 4.3% share calculated from the headline re-export margin. The higher 14% share of retained imports from China seems to be in line with the general perception that a growing portion of consumer and capital goods sold in Hong Kong are made in China. It is also comparable to the levels seen in the early 2000s.

A higher portion of imports from China retained for domestic use is expected to increase inflationary pressure in Hong Kong given the continued strengthening of the renminbi. Assuming China's share of retained imports is 14% and there is a one-to-one exchange rate pass-through to consumer prices, a 10% renminbi appreciation could increase the Composite CPI inflation by 0.4 percentage points, as tradable goods only account for 30% of household expenditure in the Composite CPI basket (that is, 10%*0.14*0.3). However, the overall impact of a stronger renminbi on consumer price inflation could be larger or smaller than the above estimate, depending on the degree of exchange rate pass-through, the indirect impact on service prices, and the actual share of retained imports from China.

Although Hong Kong's retained imports sourced from China are likely to be materially higher than the headline figure, the upwardly

Table 6.5

Retained Imports from Major Trading Partners

Based on Revised Re-export Margin for China

2005 (HK$bn)	Imports by origin	Re-exports by origin	Re-export margin (%)	Retained imports	Share of HK's retained imports (%)
Mainland China	1,030	1,313	28.5	91	13.9
US	106	64	7.8	46	7.1
Japan	266	186	7.8	95	14.6
Euro area	135	75	7.8	65	10.0
Taiwan	172	152	7.8	32	4.9
Korea	129	74	7.8	61	9.3
Others	492	249	7.8	263	40.3
Total	2,329	2,114	20.7	652	100.0

Note: We assume that re-export margins for other trading partners will remain unchanged, and total retained imports will change along with different re-export margins used for China.

Sources: C&SD and authors' estimates.

revised share of retained imports from China is not large compared to other major trading partners. This suggests that the impact of renminbi appreciation on consumer price inflation in Hong Kong is still likely to be modest. Moreover, since a significant portion of retained imports originates from countries other than China and the US, inflationary pressures on domestic consumer prices due to the general weakness in the US dollar should be more significant than the effect due to renminbi appreciation.

6. CONCLUSION

To summarise, our analysis suggests that the share of retained imports from China is likely to be within a range of 9%–17%, higher than the 4.3% estimate based on the headline re-export margin of 23.5% for China. In comparison with other major trading partners, the mean estimate of a 14% share for China raises the ranking of China to be one of the top importers of goods for domestic use (Table 6.5).

While a higher re-export margin of 28.5% is plausible for goods of China origin, it at best serves as an alternative estimate to the headline re-export margin published by C&SD, as the validity of the assumptions used to come up with the estimate has yet been subject to test. Inferring the "actual" re-export margin based on historical relationships between the breakeven and headline re-export margins also has its own shortcomings. In view of these caveats, the purpose of this analysis is to identify factors that could have distorted the estimation of the re-export margin and retained imports for China.

In general, there are two major sources of errors which render the estimation of retained imports imprecise. First, since re-export margins are estimated based on survey data, sampling and reporting errors may result in under-estimation of retained imports if the re-export margin is under-reported by the respondents.[8] Secondly, since imports and re-exports from the same origin could not be mapped or traced based on official Customs trade data, measurement errors may result in considerable mismatch between these two sets of statistics, which further complicates the estimation of retained imports by country of origin.[9]

To improve the estimation of re-export margins, one needs to increase the sample size to enhance the precision of the estimates with detailed breakdowns. It would also be useful to research further the nature, motives and characteristics of the round-tripping trade between Hong Kong and China.

---

8. There could be incentive for trading firms to under-state their re-export margins due to tax considerations and other commercial reasons.

9. For example, goods assembled in Hong Kong and re-exported to overseas markets may involve components from more than a single place of origin. However, exporters in Hong Kong may report the place of origin of the key component which contributes most to the formation of the final product, such as China, in the trade declaration form. As a result, the value of re-exports originated from China could be over-stated as the value of imports only covers the key component of the finished product.

Chapter 7

Cross-border Fund Flows
and
Hong Kong Banks' External Transactions
vis-à-vis
Mainland China

Joanna SHI

Andrew TSANG

1. INTRODUCTION

This Chapter explores what information about cross-border fund flows can be extracted from existing statistics on banking transactions, and to study how such fund flows may influence monetary conditions in Hong Kong. Data on external transactions between Hong Kong banks and Mainland China (the Mainland) have been volatile. Following a general trend of decline between 2000 and mid-2003, Hong Kong banks' external claims and liabilities *vis-à-vis* the Mainland have increased notably since mid-2003. During 2004 to 2006, gross claims rose steadily, while gross liabilities registered some fluctuations, but still increased in general. As gross liabilities have exceeded claims since mid-1999, the Mainland has become a net supplier of funds (in terms of both Hong Kong dollar and foreign currency) to the banking system in Hong Kong (Figures 7.1 and 7.2). These developments have raised questions about the stability and importance of such a funding source to our banking system. In particular, sharp fluctuations in Hong Kong dollar positions held by Mainland entities may impact money and foreign exchange markets in Hong Kong.

This Chapter is organised as follows. Section 2 outlines the major channels of fund flows between Hong Kong and the Mainland and their impact on external transaction statistics between Hong Kong and the Mainland. Section 3 examines how Hong Kong's net external transactions can be explained by existing statistics on trade, services and investment, and Section 4 assesses the monetary implications for Hong Kong. The final section concludes.

2. CHANNELS OF FUND FLOWS

Equation (1) represents a balance of payments (BoP) accounting identity, showing that how the change in net foreign assets (NFA) of an economy is determined by trade and services account balances, net factor income, and capital account balance. A change in NFA of an economy reflects all its economic transactions with the rest of the world, as well as capital gains and losses on existing external assets and liabilities over a period of time.

Figure 7.1

Hong Kong Banks' External Transactions *vis-à-vis* Mainland China

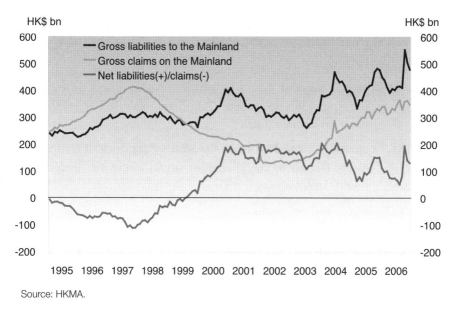

Source: HKMA.

Figure 7.2

Hong Kong Banks' Net External Transactions *vis-à-vis* Mainland China

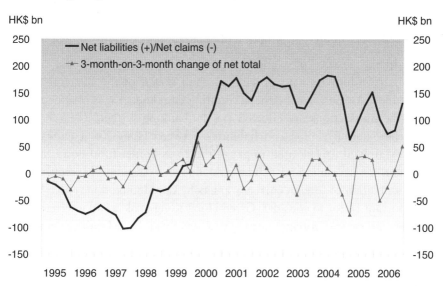

Source: HKMA.

$$\Delta NFA_t = CA_t + KA_t + KG_t + EO_t \qquad (1)$$

where

CA_t = current account balance, which equals the sum of balance on goods, services and current transfers, and investment income balance,

KA_t = capital account balance, which includes direct investment (DI), portfolio investment (PI), financial derivatives (FD) and other investment (OI),

KG_t = capital gains and losses on the outstanding stock of net foreign assets (equals to the change in stocks minus the underlying flows), and

EO_t = errors and omissions.

In principle, this accounting equation also holds on a bilateral basis. However, bilateral BoP statistics are seldom compiled due to difficulties in collecting the data. Thus, one can only get a partial picture of bilateral BoP by making use of statistics such as those on trade of goods and services. In the case of Hong Kong and the Mainland, comprehensive and timely bilateral statistics on merchandise exports and imports are available. In addition, data on trade of services, inward and outward direct investment are also available but with a time lag. However, there are only very limited information on bilateral portfolio investment flows.

In the absence of a complete data set, one may make use of the available information to provide a rough sketch of the bilateral flows of funds. As indicated by the accounting equation, if it is assumed that all the transactions are effected via the banking system,[1] then changes in the external claims and liabilities between Hong Kong banks and the Mainland can be used to gauge the cross-border fund flows related to current account, and capital and financial account. Moreover, the accumulation of foreign currency assets by the Mainland may also be an important factor to consider. Given Hong Kong's role as an international financial centre, foreign currency assets held by Mainland entities,

---

1. Since formal fund flows in most cases are reflected in banks' external liabilities and claims positions, it is justified to assume all the cross-border transactions are effected via the banking system.

Table 7.1

Linkages between Channels of Fund Flows and
Hong Kong's External Claims and Liabilities against the Mainland

	Claims	Liabilities
Increase	Hong Kong's exports of goods and services to China	Hong Kong's imports of goods and services from China
	China's direct investment in Hong Kong	Hong Kong's direct investment in China
	China's portfolio investment in Hong Kong	Hong Kong's portfolio investment in China
	Hong Kong banks' other investment in China	China banks' other investment in Hong Kong
Decrease	Hong Kong's imports of goods and services from China	Hong Kong's exports of goods and services to China
	Hong Kong's direct investment in China	China's direct investment in Hong Kong
	Hong Kong's portfolio investment in China	China's portfolio investment in Hong Kong
	China banks' other investment in Hong Kong	Hong Kong banks' other investment in China

including the People's Bank of China, may be placed in Hong Kong or channelled through Hong Kong's banking system to other countries. These should also be reflected in Hong Kong's statistics of external claims and liabilities.

Table 7.1 provides a matrix on the theoretical linkages between the major channels of fund flows and their relations with external claims and liabilities of Hong Kong banks *vis-à-vis* the Mainland. Specifically, exports of goods and services from Hong Kong to the Mainland, Mainland's direct investment and portfolio investment in Hong Kong, and Hong Kong banks' placements on the Mainland can lead to a rise in claims of Hong Kong banks *vis-à-vis* the Mainland (or a decline in Hong Kong banks' liabilities). Conversely, imports of goods and services from the Mainland, and Hong Kong's direct and portfolio investment on the Mainland result in a rise in our gross liabilities (or a decrease in claims) of Hong Kong banks *vis-à-vis* the Mainland.

To illustrate, suppose Hong Kong runs a current account surplus with the Mainland, and assume that all payments are arranged via the banking system, in accordance with the double-entry principle of the balance of payments account, a credit entry is booked in the current account representing the surplus, while a debit entry is booked in the financial account.[2] On the balance sheets of banks in Hong Kong, the debit entry represents an increase in Hong Kong banks' claims on a Mainland entity. At the same time, there is a matched increase in deposits, assuming the ultimate beneficiary (i.e. the Hong Kong exporter) places the fund with banks in Hong Kong.

Likewise, when there is capital inflow from the Mainland to Hong Kong, on the balance sheet of Hong Kong's banking system, there will be an increase in bank deposits, representing the amount which is owed by banks to the recipient of the funds.[3] This will be matched by an increase in the balances due from Mainland banks on the asset side (i.e. a rise in claims on the Mainland). In short, external claims of Hong Kong's banking sector on the Mainland would rise, should there be an increase in net receipts arising from current account activities or cross-border capital flows.

3. FACTORS BEHIND CHANGES IN NET EXTERNAL TRANSACTIONS VIS-À-VIS MAINLAND CHINA

This section attempts to establish the linkages between the external claims and liabilities between Hong Kong and the Mainland and bilateral fund flows arising from trade and financial activities based on available data. Table 7.2 and Figure 7.3 provide a summary of the stock as well as the change of external claims and liabilities of Hong Kong banks, compared with the data on bilateral current account and capital and financial account activities between Hong Kong and the Mainland during the past few years. The first panel of Table 7.2 shows the stock of net liabilities and the year-on-year change of this stock, with the latter taken as an indicator of net flows of funds between Hong Kong and the Mainland. The second panel shows the estimated bilateral BoP components. Data in Table 7.2 are commonly available on a quarterly basis, providing an ex-post framework to keep track of fund flow between Hong Kong and the Mainland on a quarterly basis.

---

2. Balance of payments statistics are compiled based on the double-entry principle. A surplus in the current account is matched by a deficit in the capital and financial account.

3. The deposits refer to Hong Kong banks' liabilities to the recipient but not the Mainland.

Table 7.2

Possible Factors Explaining Changes in Net External Transactions of
Hong Kong Banks *vis-à-vis* the Mainland

HK$ billion	1998	1999	2000	2001	2002	2003	2004	2005	2006
Net liabilities (+)/ net claims (-)									
Level	-34	17	172	136	162	147	140	151	130
Change	68	51	155	-36	26	-15	-7	11	-21
Possible factors explaining changes in net external transactions of Hong Kong banks vs. the Mainland									
due to goods accounts [1]	-139	-94	-113	-137	-147	-196	-245	-267	-323
due to services accounts [2]	-3	-4	-9	-17	-34	-44	-51	-57	-61
due to investment income [3]	-3	-1	-4	-8	-14	-26	-27	-21	-37
due to direct investment [4]	123	88	10	92	108	100	86	67	48
due to portfolio investment [5]	4	4	52	7	18	48	60	159	306
residuals	*87*	*57*	*219*	*27*	*95*	*103*	*170*	*130*	*45*

(1)   Exports and imports were adjusted to exclude outward processing trade.

(2)   Data on trade in services between Hong Kong and the Mainland are from Report on Hong Kong Trade in Services Statistics.

(3)   From survey data.

(4)   HK's foreign direct investment (FDI) to the Mainland based on data from the Mainland, while the Mainland's FDI in Hong Kong are from Balance of Payments Statistics.

(5)   Data refer to funds raised by Mainland companies in the Hong Kong Stock Exchange, while data on Mainland's portfolio investment in Hong Kong are not available.

Sources: HKMA, various Government publications and authors' estimates.

Table 7.2 and Figure 7.3 show that banks in Hong Kong have been registering net liabilities against the Mainland since 1999. Meanwhile, Hong Kong registered current account surpluses with the Mainland, thus reducing the net liabilities to the Mainland (under the assumption that all transactions are effected through the banking system). Moreover, Hong Kong has been a net investor in the Mainland, increasing banks' external liabilities with the Mainland. The difference between changes in the banks' net external transactions and the observable data on current account and capital and financial account is taken as a residual, which reflects those fund flows that are not covered by existing surveys. Such a residual contributed to increases in the banks' liability with the Mainland during the past few years. It should be noted that this calculation has some caveats. For example, the above sketch of cross-border fund flows may be inaccurate if the shipment of goods and

Figure 7.3

Possible Factors Explaining the Change in Net External Transactions of
Hong Kong Banks *vis-à-vis* the Mainland

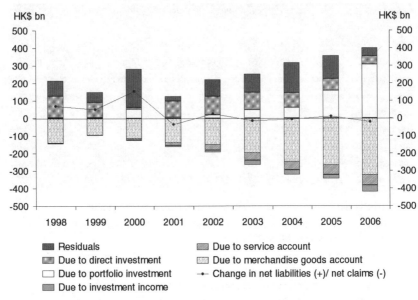

Residuals | Due to service account
Due to direct investment | Due to merchandise goods account
Due to portfolio investment | Change in net liabilities (+)/ net claims (-)
Due to investment income

Sources: HKMA, various Government publications and authors' estimates.

payments for merchandise are not entirely synchronised, or if the custom value of shipment is not the same as the actual payment.

Major developments in the goods account, service account, factor income account, and capital and financial account are reviewed as follows.

3.1   Goods Account

Hong Kong has been running a current account surplus with the Mainland, contributing to banks' claims on the Mainland if all the payments are effected through the banking system.[4] Specifically, such

---

4.   A current account balance is the sum of the balance of goods and service account and net income of assets.

Figure 7.4

Trade between Hong Kong and the Mainland and Net Liabilities

A. Exports and imports

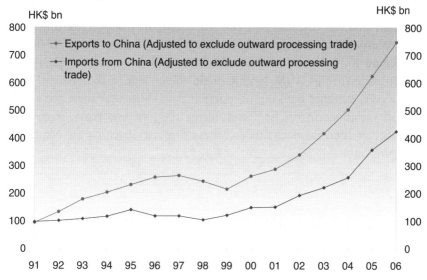

B. Trade balance and external banking transactions

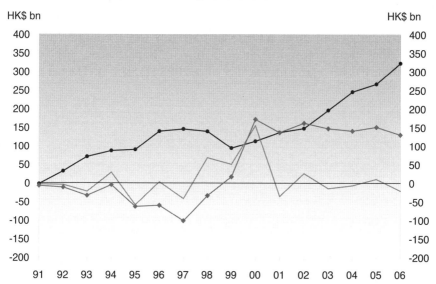

Sources: C&SD, HKMA and authors' estimates.

surplus is attributable mainly to merchandise trade with the Mainland (after adjusting to exclude outward processing trade).[5] The bilateral trade surplus amounted to HK$267 billion and HK$323 billion in 2005 and 2006 respectively, or up by 21% year on year (Figure 7.4a). As discussed earlier, a trade surplus with the Mainland, in principle, will lead to a corresponding increase in net claims or a decline in net liabilities of Hong Kong banks *vis-à-vis* the Mainland. In terms of magnitude, such trade surplus is the largest single component in the bilateral BoP. However, external banking transaction data show that there were only small variations in net liabilities during the past few years, suggesting that other fund flows channelled these surpluses back to the Mainland (Figure 7.4b).

3.2   Service Account

Within the current account, Hong Kong also recorded bilateral surpluses in the trade of services with the Mainland in recent years. The service account surplus increased from less than HK$10 billion in 2000 to HK$61 billion in 2006. Analysed by categories, the surplus from merchanting and other trade-related services was the largest, followed by that from transportation and travel.[6] In particular, net tourism income has been growing steadily since 2003 (Table 7.3). The net gain in

---

5.   Outward processing trade refers to arrangements made between Hong Kong companies and manufacturing entities in the Mainland under which the companies concerned sub-contract the whole or part of the production of their products to the Mainland entities. Raw materials and semi-manufactures are normally exported to the Mainland for such processing. Both exports and imports are adjusted to exclude outward processing activity, as such activities only involve payments of processing fees rather than the value of products or materials involved. As a result, only processing fee payments will be included in external claims and liabilities statistics.

6.   There are six major categories of service trade, namely, transportation, travel, insurance services, financial services, merchanting and other trade-related services, and other services.

Table 7.3

Tourism Income

HK$ bn	Spending by Mainland tourists in Hong Kong	Spending by HK tourists in Mainland China	Net spending in Hong Kong
1999	15	42	-27
2000	15	36	-21
2001	18	35	-16
2002	29	33	-3
2003	35	27	7
2004	40	32	9
2005	44	32	12
2006	50	34	17

Source: Report on Hong Kong Trade in Services Statistics.

favour of Hong Kong was mainly attributable to the relaxation of travel restrictions from the Mainland as well as the amount of the foreign exchange that may be carried abroad by Mainland residents.[7&8]

3.3   Factor Income Account

The factor income account contains cross-border receipts and payments of income arising from factors of production (such as compensation of employees and investment income). Hong Kong maintains a net inflow of factor income from the Mainland, and such inflow has increased markedly in recent years. While a breakdown of the nature of factor income is not available, such income is likely generated mainly from earnings of Hong Kong's direct investment in the Mainland. According

7. The Individual Visit Scheme, the liberalisation of travelling restrictions on individual travellers, was first introduced in four Guangdong cities (Dongguan, Zhongshan, Jiangmen, Foshan) on 28 July 2003. The coverage of the Scheme has expanded since implementation. The scheme was further extended to 49 cities in January 2007.

8. Mainland individuals travelling overseas are allowed to purchase up to US$3000 for trips less than six months and US$5000 for those above six months from 1 October 2003. Since 1 February 2007, the cap was lifted to US$50,000 per person each year, regardless the length of trips.

Table 7.4

FDI Flows

HK$ bn	Hong Kong's FDI in Mainland China	Mainland China's FDI in Hong Kong	Net FDI in the Mainland
1995	155	NA	NA
1996	160	NA	NA
1997	160	NA	NA
1998	143	20	123
1999	127	39	88
2000	121	111	10
2001	130	39	92
2002	139	32	108
2003	138	38	100
2004	148	62	86
2005	140	73	67
2006	157	109	48

Notes: Hong Kong's foreign direct investment (FDI) in the Mainland are from Mainland data source.
Mainland China's FDI in Hong Kong are based on Hong Kong sources.

Sources: CEIC and authors' estimates.

to statistics on Hong Kong's inward and outward investment, the position of Hong Kong's direct investment on the Mainland amounted to HK$2,117 billion at end-2006 (the latest data available), equivalent to about 143% of GDP in Hong Kong.

3.4   Capital and Financial Account

Hong Kong has been a net investor on the Mainland in terms of foreign direct investment (FDI). Table 7.4 shows that Hong Kong's FDI on the Mainland increased steadily from HK$121 billion to HK$157 billion during 2000–06. Meanwhile, Mainland's FDI in Hong Kong was less than Hong Kong's direct investment on the Mainland and was quite volatile. On balance, net FDI contributed to an increase in Hong Kong banks' liabilities to the Mainland, though its contribution varied a lot during the recent years.

Figure 7.5

Funds Raised by Mainland Companies in Hong Kong

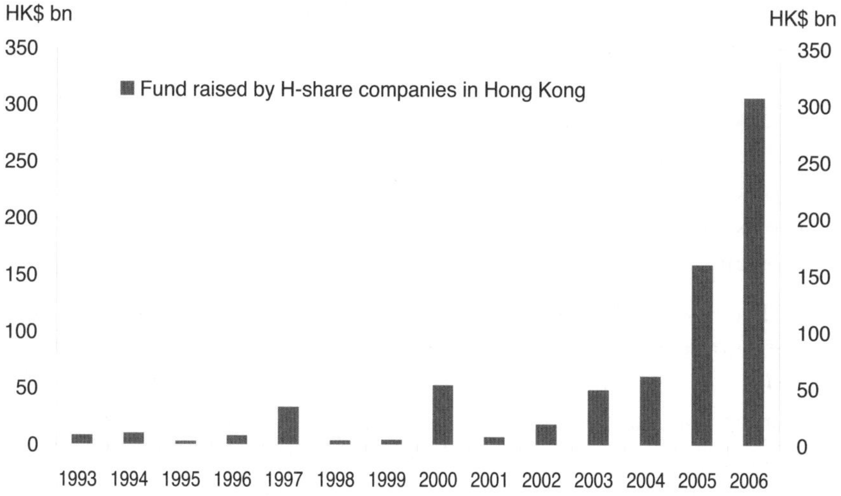

Source: Hong Kong Exchanges and Clearing Limited website.

In terms of portfolio investment, fund-raising activity of Mainland enterprises, mainly through equity listings and bond flotations, is another conduit of funds flowing to the Mainland. Mainland enterprises can acquire foreign funds through equity markets in Hong Kong or Shanghai and Shenzhen B-shares markets. However, fund-raising activity in the two B-share markets has not been active in the past few years. At the same time, fund-raising activity by Mainland firms in Hong Kong increased markedly. Mainland companies raised HK$159 billion and HK$306 billion in 2005 and 2006 respectively from the Hong Kong stock market (Figure 7.5).[9] Past experience suggests that some of the proceeds have been placed with our banking sector, thereby increasing our external liabilities *vis-à-vis* the Mainland.[10] However, it should be noted that the funds placed by these Mainland firms with banks in Hong Kong are usually temporary in nature.

---

9. Mainland enterprises refer to H-share companies listed in Hong Kong stock market.

10. Funds deposited by a Mainland company with banks in Hong Kong are treated as Hong Kong's liabilities to the Mainland, as external positions are reported based on the status of the counterparty and his address.

3.5   Residual Fund Flows

As discussed above, the residual term in Table 7.2 represents fund flows between Hong Kong and the Mainland that are not explained and/or captured by existing surveys. Such residual contributed to increases in net liabilities of Hong Kong banks *vis-à-vis* the Mainland during the past few years. This may be associated with the build-up of foreign currency reserves by the Mainland authorities and the re-cycling of surplus foreign currency liquidity by the non-government sector on the Mainland.

Placements of funds abroad by the Mainland can be a possible explanation for the residual term in net liabilities of Hong Kong banks *vis-à-vis* the Mainland.[11] Indeed, the Mainland has rapidly built up foreign exchange reserves since 2000. In particular, foreign exchange reserves increased markedly by US$207 billion (11% of GDP), US$209 billion (9% of GDP) and US$247 billion (9% of GDP) in 2004, 2005 and 2006 respectively.[12] A BIS study suggests that the rise in total foreign exchange reserves across Asia since 2002 has coincided with an equally sharp increase in the stock of external liabilities *vis-à-vis* banks in the region. The growth in deposits placed with BIS reporting banks seemed to be associated with the accumulation of reserves by the monetary authorities in the region.[13] In particular, it is estimated that, globally, some 15% of US dollar-denominated reserve assets are held as deposits with banks.

---

11. The residual fund flows also capture valuation changes due to factors like revaluation of the renminbi. That said, the impact of renminbi revaluation was immaterial in 2005 and 2006. On the other hand, this residual term may over-estimate the actual amount of placements of funds abroad by the Mainland, as data on Mainland's portfolio investment in Hong Kong are not included in the calculation. Anecdotal evidence suggests that portfolio investment in Hong Kong by Mainland citizens is increasingly popular following the introduction of Individual Visit Scheme.

12. It is noted that the visible trade surplus and FDI inflows only accounted for about half of the increase in Mainland's foreign exchange reserves in 2004, suggesting that capital inflows from other channels played a significant role.

13. "Choosing Instruments in Managing Dollar Foreign Exchange Reserves," *BIS Quarterly Review*, March 2003, pages 39–46. This study estimates that, globally, 3% of total US dollar denominated reserve assets are held as deposits in banks in the United States, and an additional 12% in banks offshore.

Table 7.5

Change in Reserves and Liabilities

US$ billion	2002 vs. 2001	2003 vs. 2002	2004 vs. 2003	2005 vs. 2004	2006 vs. 2005	Dec 06 vs. the trough in Jul 03 [1]
Change in forex reserves of the Mainland	74.2	116.8	206.7	208.9	247.5	709.9
Assuming 15% of the change in forex reserves placed with banks abroad (based on BIS studies)[2]	11.1	17.5	31.0	31.3	37.1	106.5

Notes:

1. The trough position referred to the recent low of Hong Kong banks' gross liabilities with the Mainland.

2. The assumption of 15% of reserve assets being placed as deposits with banks abroad is from the March 2003 issue of BIS Quarterly Review.

Sources: BIS, HKMA and authors' estimates.

While data on Mainland's placements of official reserves abroad are not available, if the above ratio is applied to the Mainland's data, then the rises in foreign exchange reserves could imply that US$31 billion and US$36 billion might be placed by the Mainland authorities with banks abroad (including those in Hong Kong) in 2005 and 2006 respectively (Table 7.5). BIS reporting banks' liabilities *vis-à-vis* the Mainland increased by around US$22 billion and US$14 billion in 2005 and 2006 respectively. In particular, Hong Kong banks' gross liabilities to the Mainland accounted for 34% (US$9.4 billion or HK$73 billion) of the total in 2004 and 45% (US$10 billion or HK$76 billion) of the total in 2005, despite some declines in the share of Hong Kong banks' gross liabilities in 2006. Therefore, it is likely that part of the residual net liabilities of Hong Kong banks against the Mainland was due to the placement of funds made by the Mainland authorities.[14]

---

14. Renminbi (RMB) deposits in Hong Kong are treated as Hong Kong banks' external claims on the Mainland. The stock of RMB deposits with banks in Hong Kong amounted to RMB22.6 billion (equivalent to HK$21.7 billion) at end-2005, and the amount changed slightly to RMB23.4 billion (equivalent to HK$23.3 billion) at end-2006.

4. IMPLICATIONS

The impacts of net inflow of Hong Kong dollars and foreign currencies from the Mainland can be different. Inflow of foreign currencies only has limited impact on Hong Kong's financial markets and economic activities, as it mostly reflects Hong Kong's role in re-exporting the foreign currency liquidity to other parts of the global banking system.

Meanwhile, the stock of net Hong Kong dollar liabilities of banks with the Mainland only accounted for about 4% of the total Hong Kong dollar funding of our banking system (end-2006 figure). However, changes in net Hong Kong dollar liabilities of banks with the Mainland were sizable as compared to changes in overall Hong Kong dollar funding sources since 2000 (Table 7.6). In other words, monetary conditions in Hong Kong can potentially be influenced by the Mainland's placement of Hong Kong dollar funds into the local banking system.[15]

Table 7.6

Sources of HKD Funds

HKD billion	At the end of the period							Change during the year						
	2000	2001	2002	2003	2004	2005	2006	2000	2001	2002	2003	2004	2005	2006
Total HKD funds of the banking sector *	2,324	2,336	2,323	2,369	2,505	2,650	3,034	124	12	-13	46	135	145	384
Of which														
Net HKD funds from Mainland China	136	94	70	89	64	94	112	72	-43	-24	19	-24	29	19
as % of total source of HKD funds	5.9	4.0	3.0	3.7	2.6	3.5	3.7							

Note: Total HKD funds include deposits, net balances due to banks abroad, and capital, reserves and other liabilities.

Source: HKMA.

---

15. For example, during the China Construction Bank IPO subscription period in October 2005, there was 25% increase in Hong Kong dollar liabilities to banks outside Hong Kong (particularly banks on the Mainland) in that month. Meanwhile, increased demand for Hong Kong dollar tightened monetary condition in Hong Kong during the IPO subscription period.

In 2004, overall HKD funds of the banking sector increased substantially, leading to a significant discount of HIBORs over LIBORs. However, data in Table 7.6 suggest that the inflow of funds was not from the Mainland. In fact, the Mainland contributed to withdrawals of Hong Kong dollar funds from the banking system during the year, likely due to the low Hong Kong dollar interest rates. In 2005, as Hong Kong dollar interest rates caught up with the US dollar counterparts, there appeared to be Mainland funds flowing back to Hong Kong dollar deposits. In 2006, overall HKD funds of the banking sector increased markedly, and the discount of HIBORs over LIBORs enlarged again. Similar to 2004, the inflow of funds was not from the Mainland. This suggests that, in the recent periods, the fund flows associated with Mainland entities reacted to changes in Hong Kong dollar interest rates and were not an "autonomous" force influencing monetary conditions in Hong Kong.

5. CONCLUSION

This Chapter provides a sketch of the bilateral BoP between Hong Kong and the Mainland, and also provides a framework for analysing how these bilateral flows of funds may influence monetary conditions in Hong Kong. This can be used as a preliminary framework for understanding the impact of increasing integration between the Mainland and Hong Kong economies on the financial and monetary fronts.

Hong Kong ran a current account surplus with the Mainland in the past few years, contributing to a rise in claims of Hong Kong banks on the Mainland (or a decline in liabilities). At the same time, Hong Kong was a net investor in the Mainland in terms of direct investment and portfolio investment, implying an increase in liability of Hong Kong banks *vis-à-vis* the Mainland. Taking the difference between Hong Kong banks' net changes in liabilities with the Mainland and the fund flows related to current account, direct and portfolio investment, Hong Kong banks had a net "residual" liability with the Mainland. Placement of foreign currency reserve assets by the Mainland was likely to be a factor behind this residual liability.

Although net Hong Kong dollar liabilities of Hong Kong banks *vis-à-vis* the Mainland remain a small fraction of total Hong Kong dollar funding of our banking system in recent years, they tend to be volatile and can potentially be an important influence on monetary conditions in Hong Kong. Nonetheless, in the recent episodes, these Mainland funds appeared to react to changes in Hong Kong dollar interest rates and were not an autonomous force driving local monetary conditions.

Chapter 8

How Do Macroeconomic Developments in Mainland China Affect Hong Kong's Short-term Interest Rates?

Dong HE

Frank LEUNG

Philip NG

1. INTRODUCTION

Economic integration between Hong Kong and Mainland China has gathered pace in recent years and economic links through bilateral trade, foreign direct investment, and tourism have increased substantially. With over 130 H-share and red-chip companies listed on the Hong Kong Stock Exchange accounting for about half of the total market capitalisation, Mainland companies have become more influential in affecting market sentiments and fund flows in Hong Kong. Hong Kong's monetary conditions seem to be significantly affected by Mainland's macroeconomic developments in recent years. For example, the persistently negative spreads of the Hong Kong Interbank Offered Rate (HIBOR) against the corresponding US dollar London Interbank Offered Rate (LIBOR) in 2003–05 appeared to have been the result of large fund flows into the Hong Kong dollar market, driven by market expectation that the Hong Kong dollar might appreciate along with the renminbi. Mainland-related shocks therefore seem to be more readily transmitted to Hong Kong through the financial channel.

But under the Linked Exchange Rate system (LERS), Hong Kong's exchange rate is fixed against the US dollar within a narrow range, and Hong Kong dollar interest rates should be broadly aligned with US dollar interest rates. So the US factors in theory should have a dominant effect on Hong Kong's monetary conditions.

Against this backdrop, this Chapter analyses how Hong Kong's interest rates have been affected by Mainland macroeconomic developments and compares the relative importance of US and Mainland shocks. The Chapter is organised as follows. Section 2 recapitulates some historical episodes of large interest rate movements in Hong Kong, analyses the statistical properties of the spreads between HIBOR and LIBOR, and discusses their implications for model selection. Section 3 presents econometric evidences obtained from a seven-variable vector auto-regression (VAR) model. The final section concludes.

2. NARRATIVE DESCRIPTION OF HISTORICAL DATA

Short-term interbank interest rates in Hong Kong have broadly tracked their corresponding US dollar rates since the establishment of the LERS (Figure 8.1). Although the differential between the three-month HIBOR and the three-month LIBOR has been fluctuating around zero most of the time, temporary or somewhat persistent deviations did occur due to various shocks (Figure 8.2).

Table 8.1 shows periods of large interest rate spreads and the major causes of the deviations. Movements in the US dollar exchange rate were a major driver of the interest rate spread in the early periods of operation of the LERS. Shortly after the return of Hong Kong to Chinese sovereignty in 1997 came the Asian financial turmoil, during which Hong Kong witnessed the largest positive interest rate spread in history. Recently, Mainland-related factors seemed to have been the main explanation behind large movements in the interest rate spread. In particular, the negative interest rate spread from September 2003 to May

Figure 8.1

Movements between Hong Kong and US Interest Rates

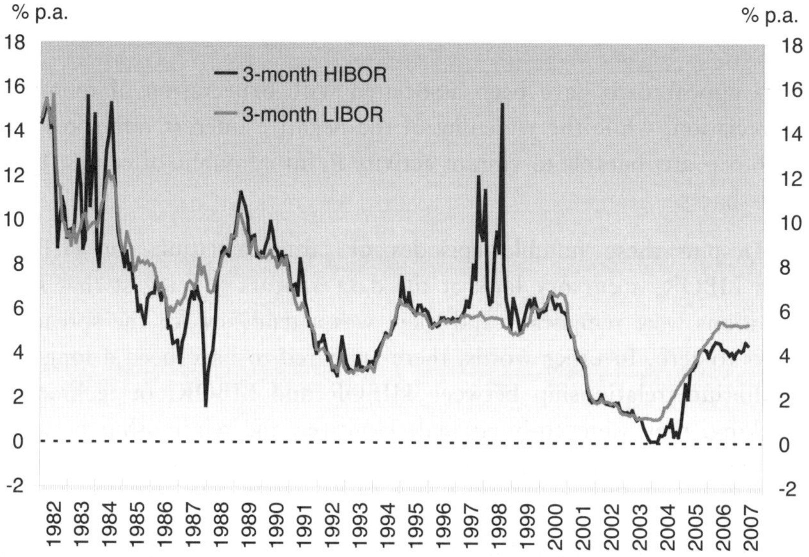

Note: Month-end data.

Source: HKMA.

201

Figure 8.2

Historical Movements of Interest Rate Spread

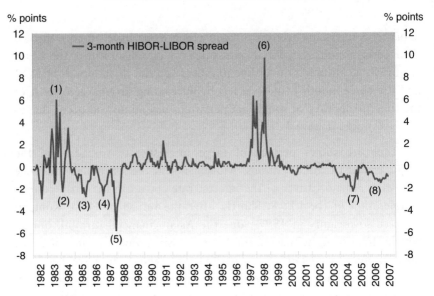

Notes: Month-end data. The numbers in the bracket refer to the episodes of extreme interest rate spreads discussed in Table 8.1.

Source: HKMA.

2005 appeared to have been associated with expectation of renminbi appreciation, while the widening of the negative interest rate spread in 2006 was attributable to vibrant activity in initial public offerings (IPO) of H-shares.

Despite these notable episodes of large deviations of HIBOR from LIBOR, a cursory look at the data appears to suggest that such deviations were temporary and there was a tendency for the spread to revert to zero. In other words, there appeared to have been a long-run equilibrium relationship between HIBOR and LIBOR, or technically speaking, they were co-integrated. However, the relationship between the two has been more complicated than long-run co-integration given the institutional features of the LERS.

Prior to the introduction of a weak-side Convertibility Undertaking in September 1998, the fixed exchange rate of HK$7.8 per US dollar

Table 8.1

Historical Episodes of Interest Rate Spreads

	Period	Maximum/ minimum 3-month HIBOR-LIBOR spread	Reported cause of spreads
1	Sep 1983 – Oct 1983	+600 bps	The depreciation of the Hong Kong dollar, under the then free floating regime, was made worse by speculative attacks and by the escalating crisis of confidence over the future of Hong Kong.
2	Feb 1984 – Mar 1984	-225 bps	Market considered that the official rate under-valued the Hong Kong dollar.
3	May 1985 – Feb 1986	-269 bps	US dollar declined rapidly.
4	Jan 1987 – Feb 1987	-263 bps	US said it could not accept the large trade deficits with the newly industrialised countries.
5	Nov 1987 – Feb 1988	-575 bps	US and European governments criticised Hong Kong's LERS.
6	Oct 1997 – Sep 1998	+969 bps	Hong Kong was struck by the Asian financial crisis and short term interest rates shot up due to currency speculation.
7	Sep 2003 – May 2005	-227 bps	Market speculations about Hong Kong dollar appreciation alongside the renminbi after the G7 Communiqué to urge greater exchange rate flexibility in Asian countries. Prolonged weakness in the US dollar.
8	Jan 2006 – Dec 2006	-149 bps	Ample interbank liquidity made the interbank rate persistently low. This partly reflected capital inflows associated with vibrant H-share IPO activities.

Notes: Interest rate spread figures are based on month-end data. See also Figure 8.2.

Sources: HKMA; Jao and King (1990).

applied only to cash notes, and in principle, there was nothing in the institutional design of the system that would prevent a large and persistent deviation of Hong Kong dollar money market interest rates from the US dollar counterparts. The Government had to intervene frequently in the foreign exchange and the money markets to ensure that the spread was contained (Latter, 2007).

The weak-side Convertibility Undertaking introduced an automatic mechanism to ensure that the Hong Kong dollar spot exchange rate would not depreciate beyond HK$7.8 per US dollar. If this commitment was credible, then the Hong Kong dollar exchange rate would be bounded on the weak side, implying that the HIBOR-LIBOR differential, a proxy for the risk premium required to compensate for the possibility of currency devaluation, would be bounded on the upside. But it does not necessarily imply that the spread would have a tendency to converge to zero (or more generally to a constant value). In fact, it may persistently stay away from zero without compromising the credibility of the exchange rate regime.

The introduction of a strong-side Convertibility Undertaking in May 2005, together with the weak-side Convertibility Undertaking, implies that the Hong Kong dollar spot exchange rate would be bounded on both the strong and the weak sides, implying that the interest rate spreads would be bounded on both the downside and the upside (Genberg, He and Leung, 2007; Hui and Fong, 2007). Again, such a bounded process does not necessarily mean that the interest rate spread will have a tendency to revert to zero or a constant mean, and HIBOR and LIBOR may not have a fixed long-run equilibrium relationship.

Empirical tests indicate that the null hypothesis that there is no co-integration between HIBOR and LIBOR, and that the interest rate spread is not a stationary process, cannot be rejected (Appendix 8A). This conclusion has important implications for the selection of the right empirical model to study the relationship between HIBOR and LIBOR. If the two series were co-integrated, then a vector error-correction model (VECM) would be a suitable choice since it would capture both the long-run equilibrium relationship and short-run dynamics. A simple VAR model is subject to specification error because it fails to capture the long-run dynamic convergence of the two variables. However, given the lack of co-integration relationship between HIBOR and LIBOR, the VAR specification is an appropriate model to summarise the data patterns.

3. STATISTICAL DESCRIPTION OF DATA USING A VAR MODEL

Mainland-related shocks can influence Hong Kong dollar interest rates through both the real-sector channel and the financial-market channel, as well as investor and consumer sentiment. The demand and supply of Hong Kong dollars in the money market will react to changes in the expectation of relative returns on assets induced by various Mainland shocks. Equity-related fund flows are particularly sensitive to Mainland-related shocks, as Mainland-related (H-share and red-chip) companies listed on the Hong Kong stock exchange have become a dominant force in recent years.

The response of HIBOR to a particular shock relating to the Mainland, however, is theoretically ambiguous, depending on the prevailing macroeconomic and market conditions, as well as investor sentiment. For example, a positive output shock could be indicative of improved earnings of Mainland companies. This may induce increased investments in their stocks on the Hong Kong market and the resultant higher demand for Hong Kong dollars relative to supply could raise the short-term HIBOR. On the other hand, a positive output shock on the Mainland could signal a build-up of overheating pressure and affect market sentiment negatively. This could lead to reduced investments in Mainland-related stocks on the Hong Kong market and a lower demand for Hong Kong dollars relative to supply, prompting a decrease in the short-term HIBOR.

We construct a seven-variable VAR model to understand dynamic responses of the three-month HIBOR to Mainland shocks. Among the seven variables in the VAR, three of them are US variables, another three are Mainland variables, and the remaining one is the three-month HIBOR. Table 8.2 lists the VAR variables and summarises the theoretical impacts they may exert on the three-month HIBOR. The sample period is between September 1998 and December 2006. Through the estimated VAR, plausible shocks can be identified from the estimated statistical residuals. Following Genberg, Liu and Jin (2006), identification of shocks is achieved by exploiting a small-economy assumption: because of the size of the US economy, the US shocks will affect both Hong Kong and the Mainland, but not vice versa; and because of the relative sizes

Table 8.2

Variables in the VAR Model

Variable	Economic Relationship	Theoretical Effect of a Positive Shock on Three-month HIBOR
US non-farm payroll (seasonally adjusted)	• An unexpected stronger employment growth typically signals heightened inflation pressure in the future, which in turn is likely to lead to increases in the US Federal funds target rate and LIBOR, and eventually HIBOR.	Positive
Three-month LIBOR	• Under the LERS, HIBOR tends to rise or fall with the US dollar counterparts because of arbitrage trades. • The short-term trends of HIBOR and LIBOR, however, could diverge, but in theory their spreads should be constrained by the width of the Convertibility Zone under a credible target zone regime.	Positive
US nominal effective exchange rate index (trade weighted)	• A weak US dollar tends to reduce the demand for Hong Kong dollars relative to supply because of expectations of higher inflation in Hong Kong, or to increase the supply of Hong Kong dollars relative to demand because of the expectation that the Hong Kong dollar exchange rate will be revalued, thus putting downward pressure on HIBOR.	Positive
Mainland industrial production, i.e value added of industry (seasonally adjusted)	• A positive output shock on the Mainland could signal a build-up of overheating pressure and affect market sentiment negatively, reducing the demand for Hong Kong dollars relative to supply and prompting a reduction in the short-term HIBOR (negative effect). • On the other hand, a positive output shock could be indicative of improved earnings of Mainland companies. This may induce increased investments in their stocks and the resultant higher demand for Hong Kong dollars relative to supply will raise the short-term HIBOR (positive effect).	Positive or negative
Mainland policy interest rate (a weighted average of one-year nominal lending and deposit interest rates, and the weight is equal to loans/(deposits+loans) for the lending rate and is similarly defined for the deposit rate.)	• A positive interest rate shock could signal tightened liquidity or reduced future earning growth, negatively affecting market sentiment and reducing HIBOR through lower demand for Hong Kong dollars relative to supply (negative effect). • Alternatively, a positive interest rate shock could indicate that the central bank has taken control of an otherwise unfavourable situation, thereby boosting investor confidence, increasing the demand for Hong Kong dollars relative to supply and raising HIBOR (positive effect).	Positive or negative
Mainland monetary aggregate M2 (seasonally adjusted)	• Money aggregate M2 is one of the intermediate targets of Mainland's monetary policy. It is widely observed by the market practitioners to gauge the future actions of the central bank as an above-target growth may signal a tightening of monetary policy, reducing the demand for Hong Kong dollars and lowering HIBOR (negative effect). • Alternatively, a positive money supply shock could point to a recovery from a depressed business environment on the Mainland, thereby boosting investor confidence, increasing the demand for Hong Kong dollars and raising HIBOR (positive effect).	Positive or negative
Three-month HIBOR		Positive by definition

of Hong Kong and the Mainland, Mainland shocks are transmitted to Hong Kong but not the other way round. More technical details of the VAR model are provided in Appendix 8B.

3.1 Dynamic effects of US and Mainland shocks on the three-month HIBOR

We use the impulse response function analysis to trace out the model's reaction to a current shock in one of the VAR variables, assuming no further shocks occur for all other variables and in subsequent periods. It establishes the dynamic effects of various shocks on the three-month HIBOR. (Appendix 8B discusses how the shocks are identified using a Choleski decomposition scheme.)

US shocks

The responses of three-month HIBOR to a positive shock in each US variable are in line with the theoretical prediction, but with richer dynamics (Figure 8.3):

- Non-farm payroll. Faster-than-expected growth in US non-farm payroll leads to a positive and hump-shaped response of the three-month HIBOR, with maximal impact after 17 months. However, the impulse response function (solid line) is not significantly different from zero, as evidenced by the wide standard error band (dashed lines), which covers the zero-line.

- Three-month LIBOR. The response of the three-month HIBOR to a three-month LIBOR shock is instantaneous, positive and somewhat persistent in the short and medium run (one to 17 months). Moreover, the impacts are significantly different from zero in this period. The positive effect then gradually decreases to zero.

- Nominal effective exchange rate index. A greater-than-expected strengthening of the US dollar has a positive impact on the three-month HIBOR. The positive impacts are short-lived, with statistically significant response only in the first two months. Five months after the initial shocks, the impulse response function declines near to zero.

Figure 8.3

Impulse Response Functions of Three-month HIBOR to US Shocks

Shock: growth rate of non-farm payroll (sa) increases by 0.1 percentage point

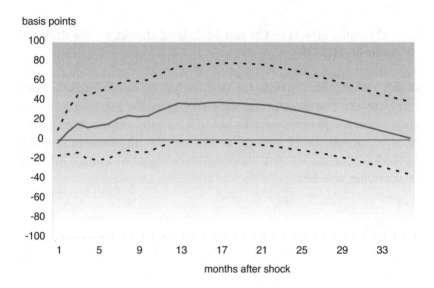

Shock: 3-month LIBOR increases by 193 basis points

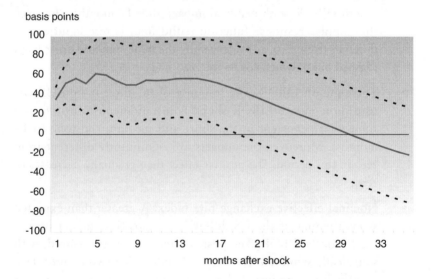

Shock: growth rate of nominal effective exchange rate index increases by 1 percentage point

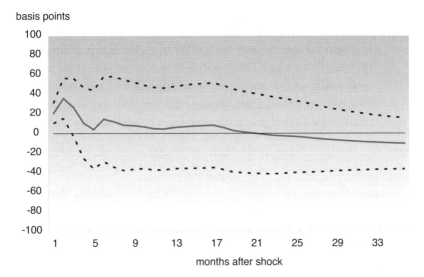

basis points

Notes: The impulse response functions (solid lines) and the standard error bands (dashed lines) are measured in basis points. Each shock value corresponds to one standard deviation of the specific VAR variable. The sample period is between September 1998 and December 2006.

Mainland shocks

The responses of the three-month HIBOR to a positive shock in the Mainland variables (Figure 8.4) appear sensible and are described as follows:

• Industrial production. Stronger-than-expected growth in Mainland industrial production induces a slightly positive response in the three-month HIBOR in the first five months, and the response function thereafter becomes close to zero. This result is possibly due to offsetting economic forces at work. Moreover, the impacts are not significantly different from zero over the specified 36-month period.

• Policy interest rate. The dynamic effect of a policy interest rate shock on the three-month HIBOR is negative in the short run (one to nine months), with statistically significant impacts in the first three months. The impacts are positive after nine months but are not significantly different from zero.

- Monetary aggregate M2. Faster-than-expected growth in monetary aggregate M2 leads to a positive and hump-shaped response of the three-month HIBOR, with maximal impact in the fourth month. The positive impacts are short-lived, with statistically significant response within the first two months. Ten months after the initial shocks, the impulse response function turns negative and gradually converges to zero in the long run.

Figure 8.4

Impulse Response Functions of Three-month HIBOR to Mainland Shocks

Shock: growth rate of industrial production (sa) increases by 1 percentage point

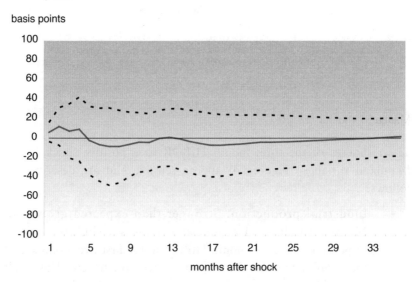

Shock: policy interest rate increases by 52 basis points

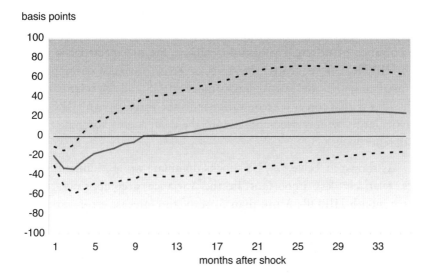

Shock: growth rate of monetary aggregate M2 (sa) increases by 0.4 percentage points

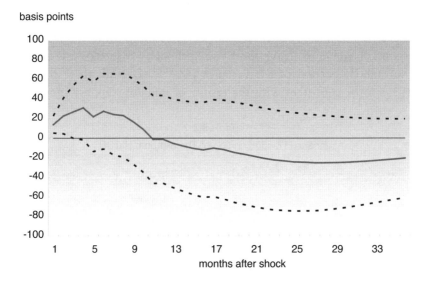

Notes: The impulse response functions (solid lines) and the standard error bands (dashed lines) are measured in basis point. Each shock value corresponds to one standard deviation of the specific VAR variable. The sample period is between September 1998 and December 2006.

3.2 Relative Importance of US and Mainland Shocks

While the impulse response function estimates the dynamic effects of shocks on the three-month HIBOR, the method is silent on the relative importance of different shocks in causing the unexpected changes in the HIBOR. Consequently, the (forecast error) variance decomposition is used to gauge the relative importance of US and Mainland shocks. The idea is that forecast error variance of the three-month HIBOR at a particular horizon is decomposed into the components accounted for by different shocks.

As shown in Table 8.3, US shocks dominate while Mainland shocks are relatively less important in the variance decomposition of the three-month HIBOR. More than 50% of the forecast error variance is accounted for by the US shocks (combining non-farm payroll, LIBOR and nominal effective exchange rate index shocks) at the three reported horizons: 3 months (short run), 18 months (medium run) and 36 months (long run). The Mainland shocks (comprising industrial production, interest rate and monetary aggregate shocks), on the other hand, account for less than a quarter of the variance.

Across different horizons, the contribution of US shocks is the largest over the medium (82.7%) and long (72.8%) run. Mainland shocks (24.5%) and HIBOR shocks (17.1%), however, have their largest contributions in the short run, although US shocks still explain a substantial portion of the variance (58.4%). Overall, these patterns appear to be consistent with the results of impulse response functions,

Table 8.3
Variance Decomposition of Three-month HIBOR

Forecast Horizon (Months)	Forecast Error Variance Decomposition (Percentage Points)		
	US	Mainland	HK (HIBOR)
3	58.4	24.5	17.1
18	82.7	12.6	4.7
36	72.8	22.9	4.3

Note: The sample period is between September 1998 and December 2006.
Source: Authors' estimates.

which indicate that the impacts of Mainland shocks are statistically significant only in the short run.

3.3 Has the Influence of Mainland Shocks Become More Important in Recent Years?

One potential problem with the above analysis is that the relationship between the variables has changed in recent years as financial integration between Hong Kong and the Mainland has gathered pace. The significance of Mainland shocks in causing unexpected changes in HIBOR is likely to have become more prominent in the recent past, since the market capitalisation of the H-shares and red chips has increased substantially since 2001 (Figure 8.5), reaching $7.6 trillion at the end of June 2007 to account for 48% of the total market capitalisation on the main board. In addition, funds raised by H-share companies surged to almost $300 billion in 2006 (Figure 8.6).

Figure 8.5

Market Capitalisation of China-related Stocks (Main Board)

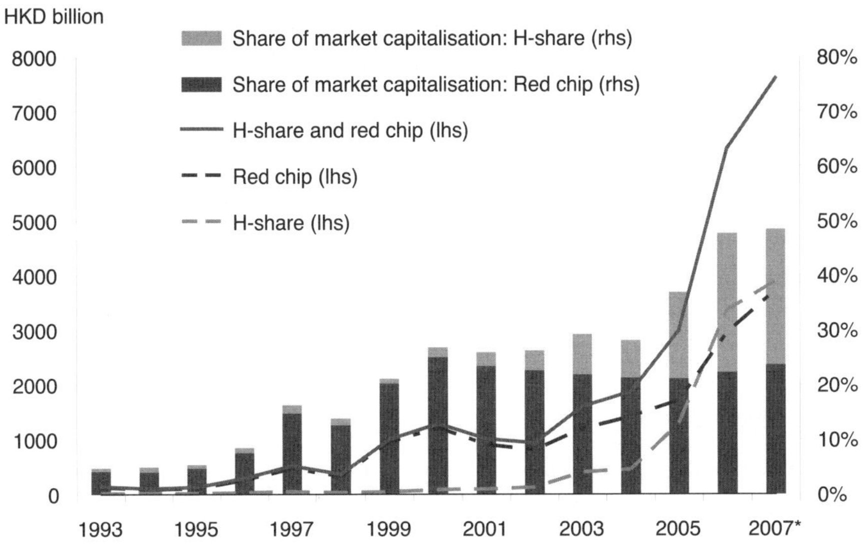

* as at the end of June 2007

Source: Hong Kong Exchanges and Clearing Limited website.

213

Figure 8.6

Equity Funds Raised by China-related Companies (Main Board)

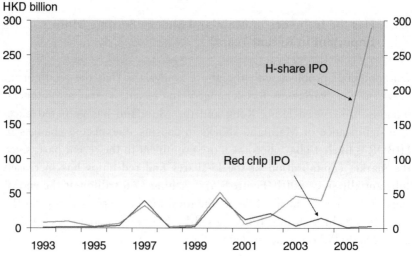

Source: Hong Kong Exchanges and Clearing Limited website.

To take this recent development into account, we re-estimate the VAR model by using a sub-sample that covers January 2001 to December 2006. The starting year roughly coincides with the takeoff of the H-share market and should be able to isolate more recent effects of Mainland shocks. In this more recent sub-sample period, the response of HIBOR to Mainland shocks appeared to be stronger than in the whole sample (Panel A, Figure 8.7).[1] In particular, the initial (one month) positive impact of industrial production now becomes significantly different from zero, and the positive impact of M2 is much larger and more long-lasting (up to six months) than in the whole sample. On the other hand, the impact of policy interest rate has become less pronounced in the short run but more significant in the nine-to-twelve-month period.

With more pronounced dynamic impacts, the contribution of Mainland shocks to the forecast error variance of the three-month

---

1. Regarding the responses to US shocks, the qualitative results obtained using the recent sub-sample are not substantially different from those using the whole sample.

Figure 8.7

Impulse Response Functions of Three-month HIBOR to Mainland Shocks

Shock: growth rate of industrial production (sa) increases by 1 percentage point

Panel A: sample period between January 2001 and December 2006

basis points

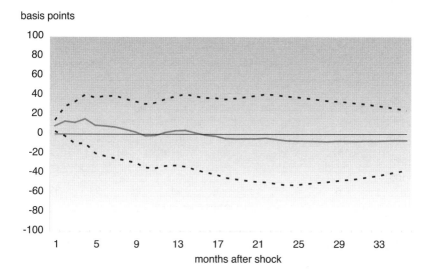

months after shock

Panel B: sample period between September 1998 and December 2006

basis points

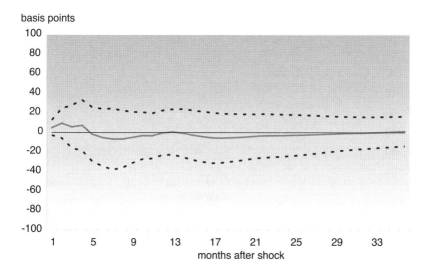

months after shock

215

Shock: policy interest rate increases by 18 basis points

Panel A: sample period between January 2001 and December 2006

basis points

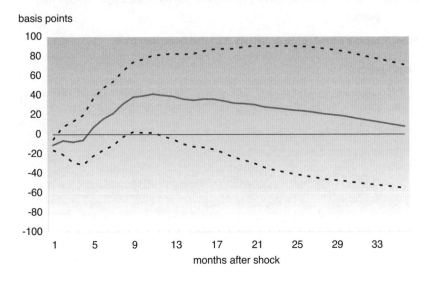

months after shock

Panel B: sample period between September 1998 and December 2006

basis points

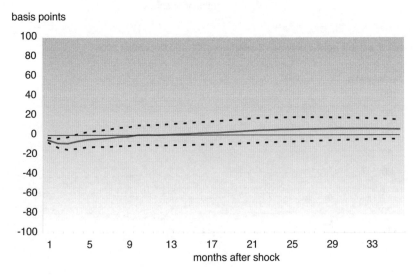

months after shock

Shock: growth rate of monetary aggregate M2 (sa) increases by 0.4 percentage points

Panel A: sample period between January 2001 and December 2006

basis points

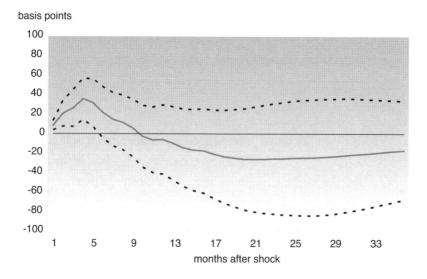

months after shock

Panel B: sample period between September 1998 and December 2006

basis points

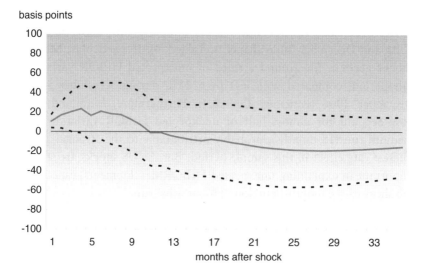

months after shock

Notes: The impulse response functions (solid lines) and the standard error bands (dashed lines) are measured in basis point. Each shock value corresponds to one standard deviation of the specific VAR variable. For ease of comparison, Panel B generates the impulse response functions using the full sample.

Table 8.4

Variance Decomposition of Three-month HIBOR

Forecast Horizon (Months)	Forecast Error Variance Decomposition (Percentage Points)		
	US	Mainland	HK (HIBOR)
Panel A. Sample period: 1998:09-2006:12			
3	58.4	24.5	17.1
18	82.7	12.6	4.7
36	72.8	22.9	4.3
Panel B. Sample period: 2001:01-2006:12			
3	34.8	33.9	31.3
18	39.4	49.0	11.6
36	44.9	39.0	16.1

Notes: The sample period in panel A (the full sample) corresponds to the time when explicit
convertibility undertaking was introduced in the LERS. The sample period in panel B sees
the growing importance of Mainland-related (predominantly H-share) stocks in Hong Kong.

Source: Authors' estimates.

HIBOR increases considerably for the sample period between January 2001 and December 2006 (Panel B, Table 8.4). In particular, Mainland shocks account for around a third of unexpected HIBOR variation in this period, compared with less than 25% during September 1998 to December 2006 (Panel A, Table 8.4). Furthermore, Mainland shocks now account for almost half of unexpected HIBOR variation in the medium run (18 months), probably attributable to the stronger positive interest rate effect in this sample period. But the US shocks are still very important in explaining unexpected HIBOR developments, especially in the short (three months) and long (36 months) run.

3.4   Historical decomposition of HIBOR

We conducted a further statistical exercise to decompose the in-sample actual value of HIBOR into a part that is forecast on the basis of the estimated dynamics of the VAR system and a part that depends on

Figure 8.8

Historical Decomposition of 3-month HIBOR

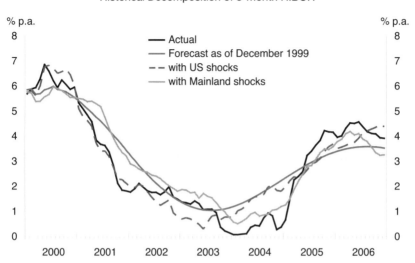

Note: The forecast is based on data until December 1999.

shocks that have occurred during a particular period of time.[2] Figures
8.8 and 8.9 are designed to shed light on the relative importance of US
and Mainland shocks in determining the historical evolution of 3-month
HIBOR. The solid black line in Figure 8.8 represents the actual value
of HIBOR, and the solid dark grey line represents the forecast based on
data until December 1999, which effectively means that it is based on the
assumption that there will be no shocks from then onwards. The dashed
line represents the forecast path plus the effects of the actual shocks
to US variables from January 2000 onwards, and the solid light grey
line represents the forecast path plus the effects of the actual shocks to
Mainland variables from January 2000 onwards. Figure 8.9 shows the
respective contributions of US shocks, Mainland shocks and Hong Kong
domestic shocks to the forecast errors.

The decomposition shows that, between 2000 and 2002, virtually
all of the unexpected variations in the 3-month HIBOR could be
explained by US shocks. Thus the dashed line tracked closely the solid

---

2. Genberg (2003) contains a good explanation of the historical decomposition methodology in a
   VAR system.

Figure 8.9

Decomposition of Forecast Errors of 3-month HIBOR

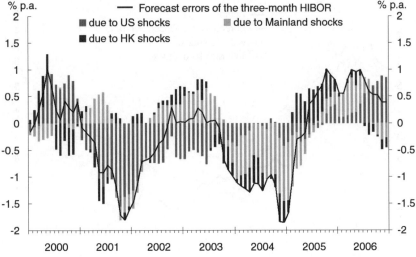

Note: The forecast is based on data until December 1999.

black line during that period. On the other hand, Mainland shocks accounted for most of the unexpected HIBOR movements during 2003–05, with the solid light grey line tracking more closely the solid black line. This is consistent with the impression that the easing of short-term HIBOR in this period was the result of large speculative fund flows into the Hong Kong dollar market, driven by market expectation that the Hong Kong dollar might appreciate along with the renminbi. In 2006, unexpected HIBOR movements were again mainly due to Mainland factors, reflecting buoyant IPO activities of Mainland firms.

4. CONCLUDING REMARKS

This Chapter has attempted to answer the question of how macroeconomic developments in Mainland China affect Hong Kong's short-term interest rates, after controlling for the US factors. Preliminary results from a simple VAR model show that an unexpected rise in Mainland policy interest rate, or higher-than-expected growth in

Mainland output or money supply, in general produces a positive and hump-shaped effect on the three-month HIBOR. The effect of these Mainland shocks has become more prominent in recent years, in part attributable to the fast-growing China-related stocks listed on the Hong Kong stock market.

Despite the increasing importance of Mainland-related stocks, variance decomposition shows that US shocks still dominate, especially in the medium and long run, in explaining unexpected HIBOR developments. However, the influence of Mainland shocks has been rising, as evidenced by the growing contribution of these shocks to the unexpected variation in HIBOR over the more recent time.

With the introduction of the three-refinements in May 2005, the determination of the interest rate spread may have undergone a structural change. Under the refined LERS, HIBOR should follow a bounded process. In other words, HIBOR should move within a band defined by the LIBOR and a spread, which reflects the width of the Convertibility Zone.[3] This Chapter implies that movement of HIBOR within the band could be increasingly influenced by Mainland-related shocks.

This Chapter should be seen as a preliminary step towards a better understanding of the forces that determine short-term interest rate movements in Hong Kong. Further work is needed to understand the channels of transmission of Mainland-related shocks that affect the demand and supply of funds in the Hong Kong dollar interbank market. The analysis would require a structural model, which is an area of further research by the Research Department of the HKMA.

---

3. Genberg, He and Leung (2007) argue that the spread should be no larger than 127 basis points, if transaction cost is assumed to be zero, given the 1000-pip width of the Convertibility Zone.

Appendix 8A

Test for Co-integrating Relationship between Three-month HIBOR and LIBOR

Introduction

If LIBOR and HIBOR are co-integrated, the use of VAR instead of VECM could introduce specification errors. This section attempts to test for the presence of co-integrating relationship between the three-month HIBOR and LIBOR.

Formal test results

Econometric evidence does not support a co-integrating relationship between the three-month HIBOR and LIBOR. First, the standard tests of stationarity and unit root give mixed results regarding HIBOR, LIBOR and their spread (Table 8A1 summarises the results). Secondly, a widely used test for cointegration suggests no cointegrating relationship between the two interest rates.

With the sample period spanning from September 1998 to December 2006, the Augmented Dickey-Fuller test indicates that both the three-month HIBOR and LIBOR are integrated processes at the 1% significance level. However, the KPSS stationarity test shows the reverse: HIBOR and LIBOR are stationary processes. This demonstrates the low power of these unit root tests and the difficulty of empirically confirming whether interest rates are stationary or unit-rooted. Using the Johansen method, both trace test and maximum eigenvalue test indicate no co-integrating relation between HIBOR and LIBOR at the 5% level. Moreover, the HIBOR-LIBOR spread is not stationary and the data do not reject the null hypothesis that the spread is a unit root process.

Table 8A1

Tests of Unit Root and Stationarity

	3-month HIBOR	3- month LIBOR	Their Spread
ADF unit root test (1% level)	unit root	unit root	unit root
KPSS stationarity test (1% level)	stationary	stationary	non-stationary

Source: Authors' estimates.

Appendix 8B

Details on the Seven-variable VAR Model

Vector auto-regression (VAR)

The estimated VAR contains seven variables: US non-farm payroll, three-month LIBOR, US nominal effective exchange rate index, Mainland industrial production, Mainland policy interest rate, Mainland monetary aggregate M2, and the three-month HIBOR.[4] The sample is composed of monthly data from September 1998 to December 2006. The number of lag is six.[5] Figure 8B1 plots the data. The time series (except the interest rates) are transformed into log-difference to ensure stationarity before estimation.

Impulse response function (IRF)

A Choleski decomposition is imposed based on the following ordering: US non-farm payroll, three-month LIBOR, US nominal effective exchange rate index, Mainland industrial production, Mainland monetary policy interest rate, Mainland monetary aggregate M2, and the three-month HIBOR. Implicit in this ordering, it is assumed that, because of the size of the US economy, the US shocks will affect both Hong Kong and the Mainland, but not vice versa. And because of the relative sizes of Hong Kong and the Mainland, Mainland shocks are transmitted to Hong Kong but not the other way round. The variables are ordered in the VAR in such a way that some variables respond contemporaneously to shocks and others do not. For example, it is assumed that the US interest rate responds contemporaneously to US output shocks but not vice versa.[6]

---

4. The number and the choice of variables in the model involve a trade-off. Preferably, all variables that have significant impacts on the three-month HIBOR should be included. This is why indicators of real activities, monetary conditions and policy actions of both the Mainland and the US are incorporated in the model. However, these variables should not be excessive to prevent the model from being over-fitted and the estimation hampered by inadequate observations.

5. In fact, mixed results are obtained using information criteria to determine the number of lags. Some researchers recommend including lags covering more than one year to capture seasonal effects. A seven-variable VAR model and a sample size of around 100, however, exclude such a choice. A longer lag structure, though capturing the dynamic interactions more satisfactorily, might risk overfitting the model. As a compromise, lags covering half a year are adopted. Partly as a result of this, the time series are seasonally adjusted where appropriate.

6. Whether these assumptions are reasonable or not can be roughly checked by computing the correlation coefficients between the derived shock series. If the underlying assumption is true, the empirical correlation coefficients between different shock series should be low or equal to zero. Empirical results show that this is indeed the case.

Figure 8B1
Data Plots of the VAR Variables

US non-farm payroll (sa)

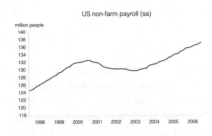

Three-month LIBOR

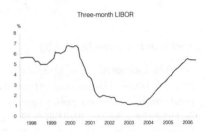

US nominal effective exchange rate

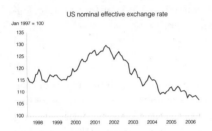

Mainland industrial production (sa)

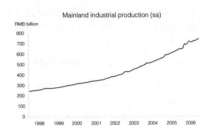

Mainland weighted sum of one-year deposit and lending rates

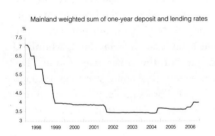

Mainland M2 (sa)

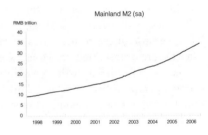

Three-month HIBOR

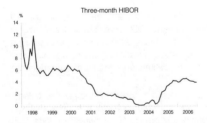

Sources: CEIC and authors' estimates.

REFERENCES

Genberg, Hans, 2003, "Foreign versus Domestic Factors as Sources of Macroeconomic Fluctuations in Hong Kong," *HKIMR Working Paper No. 17/2003*, Hong Kong Institute for Monetary Research.

Genberg, Hans, Li-gang Liu, and Xiangrong Jin, 2006, "Hong Kong's Economic Integration and Business Cycle Synchronisation with Mainland China and the US," *HKMA Research Memorandum (11/2006)*, Hong Kong Monetary Authority.

Genberg, Hans, Dong He, and Frank Leung, 2007, "The "Three Refinements" of the Hong Kong Dollar Linked Exchange Rate System Two Years On," *Quarterly Bulletin* June 2007, Hong Kong Monetary Authority.

Ha, Jiming, and Kelvin Fan, 2003, "The Monetary Transmission Mechanism in the Mainland," *HKMA Research Memorandum (11/2003)*, Hong Kong Monetary Authority.

He, Dong, Chang Shu, Raymond Yip, and Wendy Cheng, 2006, "The Macroeconomic Impact on Hong Kong of Hypothetical Mainland Shocks," *HKMA Research Memorandum (12/2005)*, Hong Kong Monetary Authority.

Hui, Cho-hoi and Tom Fong, 2007, "Is the Hong Kong Dollar Exchange Rate "Bounded" in the Convertibility Zone?" *HKMA Working paper 13/07, September 2007*, Hong Kong Monetary Authority.

Jao, Y. C., and Frank King, 1990, "Money in Hong Kong," Centre of Asian Studies, University of Hong Kong.

Latter, Tony, 2007, "Rules versus Discretion in Managing the Hong Kong Dollar, 1983–2006," *HKIMR Working Paper No. 2/2007*, Hong Kong Institute for Monetary Research.

Laurens, Bernard J., and Rodolfo Maino, 2007, "China: Strengthening Monetary Policy Implementation," *IMF Working Paper (WP/07/14)*, International Monetary Fund.

Peng, Wensheng, and Frank Leung, 2005, "A Monetary Conditions Index for Mainland China," *HKMA Research Memorandum (01/2005)*, Hong Kong Monetary Authority.

Shi, Joanna, and Andrew Tsang, 2005, "Cross-Border Fund Flows and Hong Kong Banks' External Transactions vis-à-vis Mainland China," *HKMA Research Memorandum (07/2006)*, Hong Kong Monetary Authority.

Chapter 9

Outward Portfolio Investment from Mainland China: How Much Do We Expect and How Large A Share Can Hong Kong Expect to Capture?

Lillian CHEUNG

Kevin CHOW

Jian CHANG

Unias LI

1. INTRODUCTION

Since the introduction of the reform and opening-up policy, China has made eye-catching progress in developing its economy. China's economic growth has averaged almost 10% per year over the past two decades, with per capita income doubling every 8 years since the late 1980s. China's growth represents one of the most sustained and rapid economic transformations ever seen in the world economy. Great advancements have been made in transforming its foreign exchange control regime into an increasingly market-oriented arrangement. Although foreign exchange controls have been maintained, including restrictions on cross-border capital flows as well as quantitative and regulatory controls on exchange between the renminbi and foreign currencies, a limited and selective capital account liberalisation has been introduced, and the country has recently encouraged outward foreign portfolio investment through the Qualified Domestic Institutional Investors (QDII) scheme.

Nevertheless, while China's gross foreign direct investment (FDI) as a percentage of GDP had caught up to the world average by the early 1990s, foreign portfolio investment flows have continued to lag behind. This might be explained by past liberalisation policies that have strongly favoured FDI over foreign portfolio investment, reflecting the fact that most of the concerns relating to rising capital account convertibility are related to foreign portfolio investment, which together with bank loans, are far more vulnerable than direct investment to serving speculative ends and more subject to abrupt reversal.

As such, foreign portfolio investment flows are likely to have the greatest scope to respond to further capital account liberalisation in the future. While in general, capital account liberalisation helps create an attractive environment for capital inflows, it will also result in capital flowing from countries with high savings to countries that offer more profitable investment opportunities and a greater diversity of financial products. While much literature has been focusing on international capital flows from developed to developing countries, the high savings rate in China is likely to represent enormous potential to the developed economies. Given China's high savings rate of around 50% of GDP, together with the limited channels of investment domestically and the relatively low interest rates offered to domestic investors, an opening up of the capital account could lead to considerable outflows of capital from China to the developed economies where their portfolios could be better diversified, given their more sophisticated financial markets. This is likely to have important implications for the rest of the world.

This Chapter aims to provide an analytical framework for an educated guess of the potential volume of outward portfolio investment from Mainland China, should its capital account be as open as any other developed economies. Given the close link with the Mainland, question arises as to how large a share Hong Kong could capture from such investment. The next section provides a brief overview of China's capital account liberalisation process. Section 3 compares where China stands in terms of foreign portfolio investment holdings based on some stylised facts, including international portfolio investment position, Japan's experience in capital account liberalisation and the allocation pattern of international bilateral portfolio investment. The first part of our empirical analysis is provided in Section 5, where we attempt to quantify the potential volume of China's outward portfolio investment based on experience in the OECD countries, should China's capital account be as open as in any of these economies. Section 6 provides the second part of our empirical analysis by investigating factors that determine the pattern of international cross-border portfolio transactions, and then estimating the potential portfolio investment from the Mainland that would be captured by Hong Kong. The last section concludes by discussing the policy implications and caveats of the analysis.

2.   CAPITAL ACCOUNT LIBERALISATION IN CHINA

The Mainland government has adopted a gradual and pragmatic approach to the convertibility of the renminbi and capital account liberalisation. Several patterns regarding the liberalisation sequence are observed: controls on inflows were deregulated before outflows; the current account was opened before the capital account; and within the capital account, long-term direct investment flows were liberalised before short-term portfolio investment flows.[1]

Specifically, during the early stage of reform (from the late 1980s

---

1.   The major milestones of the evolution of capital controls in China are given in Appendix 9B.

to early 1990s), only FDI—which is believed to facilitate transfer of technology and management know-how from abroad—was encouraged. Since then, restrictions on non-FDI capital inflows have been relaxed. In fact, the government announced in the mid-1990s its intention to implement capital account convertibility by 2000, although the vulnerability of the neighbouring countries to international capital flows during the Asian crisis caused a rethinking among the Mainland policymakers.

With the economy continuing to expand at a rapid pace and financial markets becoming increasingly integrated with the international financial system, especially following the WTO accession in 2001, the government has reiterated publicly that capital account convertibility is a medium-term objective. While the exact time table for full capital account convertibility will depend on the economic conditions, some decisive steps in liberalising capital flows in both directions (inflows and outflows) have recently taken place. In an effort to further open up and attract foreign portfolio investment to the domestic capital market, the government launched the Qualified Foreign Institutional Investors (QFIIs) scheme in late 2002, allowing overseas financial institutions to invest in the renminbi-denominated domestic stock and bond markets. By June 2006, the total investment quota approved for purchase by QFIIs has reached US$7 billion.

Restrictions on capital outflows have also been eased recently. While the official guidelines used to be "encouraging inflows and restricting outflows" and "holding the foreign currencies by the country", policies have shifted to emphasise "promoting capital outflows" and "allowing the people to hold foreign exchanges", especially against the backdrop of the recent rapid build-up of international reserves. In fact, eligible commercial banks have long been allowed to use their own foreign currency holdings to invest in fixed-income products overseas. But it is not until April 2006 that the government approved the Qualified Domestic Institutional Investors (QDII) scheme, which allows certain qualified banks, insurers and fund management companies to purchase foreign currencies for offshore portfolio investment.[2] Moreover, since July 2006, the government has removed restrictions on the amount of

---

2. Specifically, commercial banks are now allowed to invest overseas on behalf of their clients.

foreign currency allowed to be purchased by domestic investors for qualified foreign direct investment.

3. WHERE CHINA STANDS: AN INTERNATIONAL COMPARISON

Until the early 1990s, China's capital inflows had been negligible. Following gradual deregulation and increasing integration with the global economy through trade, gross capital inflows, predominantly in the form of FDI, rose dramatically in the mid-1990s and reached US$145 billion in 2005 (Figure 9.1). Excluding other investment, gross capital outflows remained minuscule until 2004, reflecting outward capital controls which were eased only recently.

That said, foreign portfolio flows appear to be growing. In addition, errors and omissions in China's balance of payments have suggested relatively large outflows until recently, further indicating considerable cross-border activity. Up until 2001, there had been large, negative errors and omissions in China's balance of payment, averaging around US$12

Figure 9.1

Capital Flows in China

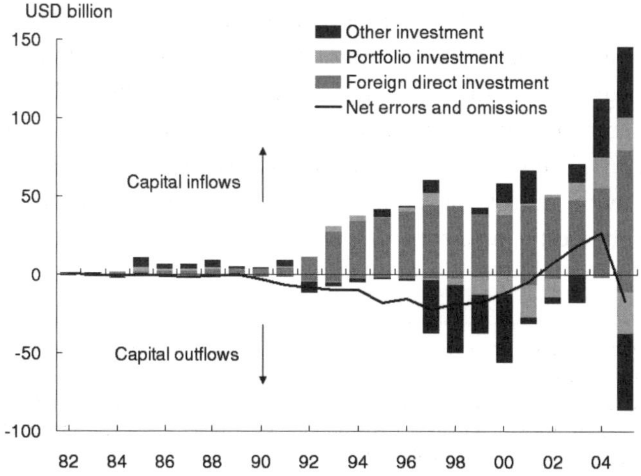

Source: CEIC.

231

billion per year between 1990 and 2001. These "errors and omissions" item may reflect capital flows that were not captured by official statistics, particularly non-FDI flows including portfolio and other investment.[3] The negative errors and omissions imply that there could possibly be large amounts of capital outflows not officially recorded during this period. Although the errors and omissions have switched sign since 2001 reflecting expectations of renminbi appreciation, the cumulative errors and omissions since 1982 still stood at around minus US$114 billion by 2005.[4]

3.1   An international comparison of foreign investment position

In terms of gross international investment position, FDI as a percentage of GDP in China averaged approximately 30%, which is close to that for East Asia of 36%, though less than the OECD average of 54% (Table 9.1).[5] However, there is a significant difference between China and other economies in their gross portfolio investment positions. While the figure as a share of GDP was over 100% for the OECD countries and as high as 34% for East Asia, China's gross portfolio investment position was only 8% of its GDP, with outward portfolio investment position at 5% of GDP. Although China's outward portfolio investment position rose significantly from US$92 billion in 2004 to US$117 billion in 2005, it has continued to lag far behind most other economies.

The small size of portfolio investment in China reflects the government's restrictions on flows of non-FDI capital in either direction. As such, further capital account liberalisation in China is likely to lead to both larger portfolio investment inflows and outflows. In particular, the latter is likely to be driven by China's huge amount of savings together with a lack of domestic investment opportunities and the desire of domestic investors to diversify their portfolios. First, China

---

3.   Given that changes in foreign reserves, the current account balance and net FDI are deemed more easily accounted for than non-FDI flows.

4.   It is not clear how much of these cumulative errors and omissions are attributed to the discrepancy between the market value and the government's valuation of its international reserves, and how much to actual unofficial outflows.

5.   The data for the OECD and East Asia is averaged over 2001–05. For China, the position data is only available for 2004 and 2005, we therefore take the average over these two years.

Table 9.1

International Comparison of Investment Position, Average over 2001–05

(% of GDP)	PI Asset	PI Liability	PI Total	FDI Asset	FDI Liability	FDI Total
OECD	46	57	103	30	24	54
US	24	46	71	24	22	46
UK	95	102	197	61	36	97
Germany	55	67	123	61	36	97
Japan	38	19	57	8	2	10
China[1]	5	3	8	3	28	30
E. Asia[2]	12	22	34	14	22	36
Indonesia	1	8	10	-0.4	10	9
Korea	3	26	28	4	12	16
Malaysia	2	13	15	11	24	35
Philippines	4	24	28	1	16	17
Singapore	84	61	145	102	157	258
Taiwan[3]	32	27	58	27	12	38
Thailand	1	17	19	2	31	34

Note:

1. Simple average of 2004 to 2005.

2. East Asia includes NIE-3 and ASEAN-4.

3. Accumulated sum of capital flows from March 1981 to December 2005.

Source: CEIC.

has a high savings rate compared with most major economies. This partly reflects precautionary savings due to the lack of a full coverage of the social safety net. At the same time, these savings have limited investment opportunities with unattractive returns. This reflects in part a small and underdeveloped domestic capital market, with total stock market capitalisation of only around US$0.4 trillion and the speculative nature of the stock markets limiting its role as an attractive alternative channel of investment for the general public. As such bank deposits play a predominant role as a channel for investment. By 2005, the corporate and households' total deposits in the banking system have reached approximately US$3.5 trillion.[6] However, these savings earn very low returns, with the three-month time deposits currently earning a nominal

---

6. This includes demand, saving, time and foreign currency deposits as reported in the monetary survey published by the People's Bank of China.

return of around 1.8% per annum and one-year time deposits 2.5% per annum. The sheer size of savings and limited investment opportunities in China suggests that the potential amount of funds to be invested overseas could be huge.

3.2 Implications of Japan's capital account liberalisation experience for China

A study on the experience of Japan in overseas investment after the opening of the capital account may shed some light on the future path of China's outward portfolio investment. From a historical perspective, there are a number of similarities shared by Japan and China in capital account liberalisation. Governments in both countries have adopted a gradualist approach in opening up their current and capital accounts, and private savings rates are high in both economies.

The high private savings rates relative to investment rates in the two countries is attributable to two main factors. First, both economies have experienced rapid income growth following the liberalisation of current account transactions and foreign direct investment, as increased export earnings and investment by foreign enterprises raised household income significantly. Growth in real per capita income rose to an annualised rate of 3.2% in Japan in the 1980s and 9.4% in China in the 1990s. Given the high propensity to save in both countries, domestic savings also picked up notably during these periods.

At the same time, both countries have earned sizable current account surplus over the past few decades. Low labour and rental costs at the early stage of development in Japan and China increased their export competitiveness in international markets, while the promotion of trade-oriented policy by the government also helped to boost domestic exports. Both Japan and China have recorded sizable current account surplus starting from the 1980s and 1990s respectively, mainly reflecting increased surplus in the trade account (Figures 9.2 and 9.3).

Limited investment opportunity in domestic capital markets also contributed to high excess savings in China and Japan before the capital account was liberalised. With high savings rates and rising current account surplus, savings are accumulated at a much faster pace than

Figure 9.2
Japan's Current Account

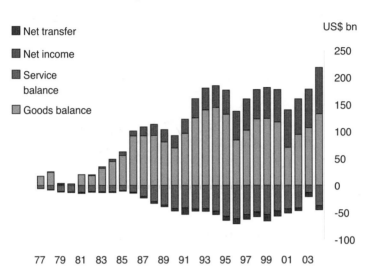

Source: IMF.

Figure 9.3
China's Current Account

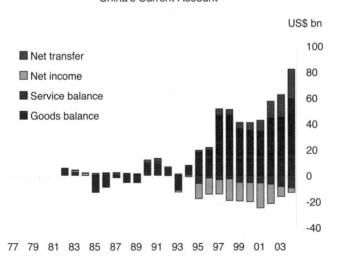

Source: IMF.

Figure 9.4
Saving-investment Gap in Japan and China

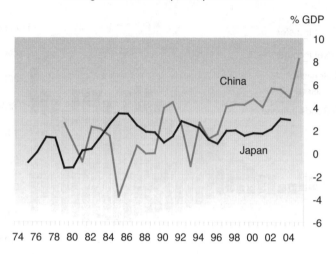

% GDP

China

Japan

Source: IMF.

domestic investment (Figure 9.4). Similar to Japan, where the saving-investment gap increased rapidly during the period before the capital account was liberalised in the mid-1980s, the gap in China has increased significantly over the past decade, and is even higher than the level experienced in Japan.

The positive saving-investment gap in Japan has been the major driver of outward portfolio investment in the country. Past developments in Japan show that there has been a strong co-movement between the saving-investment gap in the private sector and gross portfolio investment outflows, with the former appearing to be driving the latter (Figure 9.5). The sheer size of private sector savings accumulated during the period of rapid income growth and relatively low returns on bank deposits have increased the attractiveness of overseas investment when the capital account was fully liberalised in Japan in the 1980s. During the early stage of liberalisation, the size of outward portfolio investment flows was relatively small as only a limited number of qualified financial institutions were allowed to invest in securities overseas, but such flows have increased along with the liberalisation process. After years of financial sector reforms and deregulations, Japan's gross outward

Figure 9.5

Saving-investment Gap and Gross Portfolio Investment Outflows in Japan

US$ bn

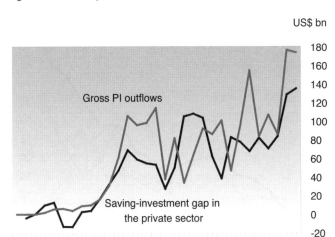

74 76 78 80 82 84 86 88 90 92 94 96 98 00 02 04

Source: IMF.

portfolio flows have increased from US$4 billion (0.3% of GDP) in 1980 to US$196 billion (4.3% of GDP) in 2005.

In terms of the share of GDP, outward portfolio investment position in Japan was around 5% before the opening of the capital account in 1984, similar to the current level in China (Figure 9.6). After the opening, outward portfolio investment position increased to 18% in 10 years' time and further to the current level of over 40% in another 10 years. As a result, Japan has become one of the largest holders of foreign assets in the world, with its net international investment position (excluding foreign reserve assets) rising from US$2.3 billion (0.2% of GDP) in 1982 to US$738 billion (16% of GDP) in 2005.

Given the similarities between the two countries and the experience in Japan, would China follow Japan to become a key investor in the global financial markets? While in China, the domestic financial markets are less-developed and heavily regulated, experience in Japan suggests that given the high savings rates and limited domestic investment opportunities, the potential of portfolio investment overseas could be comparable to that in Japan following the capital account liberalisation in China.

Figure 9.6
Portfolio Investment Position as a Percentage of GDP in Japan

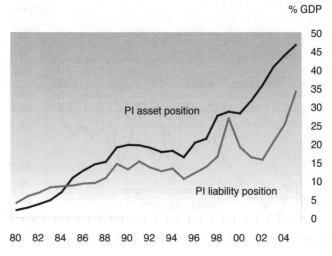

% GDP

Source: IMF.

3.3 Allocation patterns of international portfolio investment

Given the huge potential outward portfolio investment from China, how will it be allocated across different financial markets? An overview of the allocation pattern of international bilateral portfolio investment may provide some insights on the potential overseas portfolio investment behaviour of China should its capital account be as open as in a typical OECD country (Table 9.2). Global portfolio investment has expanded rapidly in recent years, with cross-border portfolio investment asset positions growing at an annual rate of 22% between 2001 and 2004. The increase is across countries, and is mainly attributable to marked increases in overseas securities investment by the US and the EU area, particularly in France. The rapid accumulation of global portfolio investment asset positions suggests that home bias in securities investment might have been diminishing in recent years.[7]

---

7. According to the international Capital Asset Pricing Model (CAPM), an investor should hold domestic assets in his/her portfolio in proportion to their country's share of world capitalisation. In this context, home bias refers to the deviation from the international CAPM allocation, where investors hold portfolios that are overweighted in domestic securities.

Table 9.2

Bilateral Portfolio Investment Asset Position, 2004

(% of total) Source Country	Recipient country									
	US	Euro area	UK	Switzerland	Japan	HK	Singapore	China	OFCs	Sum Total
US	–	25	20	4	10	1	1	0.3	10	70
Euro area	14	58	9	1	3	0.3	0.1	0.1	3	89
UK	25	39	–	2	6	1	1	0.3	4	79
Switzerland	13	52	6	–	2	0.1	0.1	0.0	4	77
Japan	35	30	6	1	–	0.5	0.2	0.2	14	86
NIEs	17	14	16	0.4	3	1	1	5	18	77
ASEAN-4	38	19	12	1	1	3	6	0.2	3	82
OFCs	65	10	5	0.4	2	0.1	0.0	0.0	6	90

Note: OFCs refers to offshore financial centres.

Source: IMF, CPIS.

The US and Europe are the largest destination of cross-border portfolio investment. In 2004, over 70% of global portfolio investment was invested in the US and the European markets. The dominant role of the US and Europe in the global financial markets reflects their highly developed and sophisticated markets, with a huge market size offering a great diversity of financial products. The combined size of their equity markets constitutes to around 70% of the world equity market capitalisation.

Apart from financial market size, bilateral portfolio investment data show that geographical location may also affect the distribution of global securities investment. Information asymmetry due to differences in geographical locations among key financial markets may affect investor preference toward domestic and foreign securities. For example, time zone differences may cause delay in the dissemination of timely information, thus increasing investment risks and trading costs. Table 9.2 shows that the euro area is the major destination of portfolio investment assets from the European community including the UK and Switzerland. The significant share of intra-regional portfolio investment within the euro area partly reflects lower trading cost and exchange rate risk due to the use of a common currency. At the same time, the strong economic ties and proximity of financial markets among European countries are also important in attracting securities investment within the region.

In Asia, while most of the outward portfolio investment assets are invested in the US and Europe, geographical location also plays a role. For example, the NIE economies (Hong Kong, Korea and Singapore) have a larger share of outward portfolio investment in China, while the ASEAN economies (Indonesia, Malaysia, the Philippines and Thailand) have a larger share of outward portfolio investment in Singapore relative to other Asian neighbours.

4. ESTIMATING PORTFOLIO INVESTMENT FROM MAINLAND CHINA

International experiences do not only provide insights on the potential portfolio investment behaviour in Mainland China through the above stylised facts, but are also used as a basis for our empirical analysis. The first part of our empirical analysis aims at estimating how much foreign portfolio investment China would hold should the capital account be as liberalised as any other developed economies. We first build a model to explain the international portfolio investment position based on the experience in countries with open capital account (excluding off-shore financial centres), and then draw inferences for China based on some reasonable projections about the explanatory variables.

4.1   The model

While our interest is to explain a country's outward investment position, most of the related research has focused on studying the determinants of international investment position (a total of the inward and outward positions) or international diversification. Based on data for 19 OECD countries, Lane (2000) attempted to explain the general trend in a country's gross international investment position as well as its portfolio, equity and debt components individually. He found that countries with a high degree of trade openness and larger domestic financial markets tend to hold more foreign assets and liabilities. In a similar study, Lane and Milesi-Ferretti (2003) employed a panel data set for 18 OECD countries and identified trade openness, GDP per capita, and stock market capitalisation as important in explaining international financial integration.[8] In explaining patterns in international portfolio diversification, Amadi (2004) explored factors that determined equity home bias using panel data.[9] In addition to variables such as return differentials and the share of foreign firm listed in the domestic stock markets, he also incorporated information variables including internet penetration and mutual fund capitalisation, and found that they had a significant impact on the dependent variable.[10]

With reference to the above literature, we construct the following model to estimate the share of outward portfolio investment in GDP:

$$PI_{it} / GDP_{it} = \alpha_i + \alpha_1 SWCAP_{it} + \alpha_2 RTNDIFF_{it} + \alpha_3 PFFL_{it} + \alpha_4 Openness_{it} \quad (1)$$
$$+ \alpha_5 Internet_{it} + \alpha_6 \ln GDPC_{it} + \varepsilon_{it}$$

where

PI/GDP = Gross portfolio investment assets as a percentage of GDP

$SWCAP$ = Domestic stock market capitalisation as a percentage of world capitalisation (-)

$RTNDIFF$ = Difference between domestic and world stock market return (-)

$PFFL$ = Number of foreign firms over total firms listed in the domestic stock market (+)

$Opennes$ = percentage share of imports and exports in GDP (+)

$Internet$ = percentage share of internet users in total population (+)

$GDPC$ = per capita GDP (+)

---

8. International financial integration was measured as total international investment position over GDP.

9. Recent studies on the home bias puzzle include Baele, Pungulescu and Horst (2006), Kho, Stulz and Warnock (2006), and Sorensen *et al* (2006). However, these studies have a different context from our study here.

10. Bohn and Tesar (1996) found that "return-chasing" behaviour plays an important role in determining US equity investment in foreign markets, and Ahearne, Griever, and Warnock (2004) found that the share of foreign firms listed in the domestic stock markets was significant in explaining foreign diversification in the US.

Parentheses after the variables give their expected signs in the regression. The rationale of incorporating these variables is explained as follows.[11] First, sophistication of the domestic financial markets matters. A large and well-developed domestic stock market provides domestic residents with alternative investment opportunity and could thus reduce their incentives to invest abroad given their relative unfamiliarity with the foreign markets and the exchange rate risks involved. Financial theory also suggests that investors should diversify their portfolio according to their country's share of world capitalisation. That is, if a country's share of world capitalisation is high, domestic residents would hold less foreign assets.

The difference between local and world market return could also be an important factor in determining the flow of capital. It is generally believed that investors would increase their foreign portfolio holdings when domestic market underperforms the rest of the world. This is sometimes called investors' "return-chasing" behaviour.

The number of foreign firms over total firms listed in the domestic market is included. The listing of foreign firms in the local stock market would allow domestic residents to gain foreign exposure at a relatively lower cost, leading to an increase in foreign portfolio holdings. It should be noted that investment in locally-listed foreign firms is considered as outward portfolio investment in the balance of payment data.

Besides affecting a country's total trade and hence financial flows directly, a country's openness to the rest of the world could also influence its residents' familiarity with the foreign markets and their general willingness to invest abroad.

Following the recent "home bias" literature that emphasises the importance of information variables on cross-border portfolio flow, we also include the percentage internet users in total population as a proxy measure for the ease of each country to access foreign information.

GDP per capita is also considered. In addition to the general belief that countries with higher GDP per capita tends to hold more external

---

11. We have also attempted to include the size of mutual funds capitalisation as the mutual funds industry has been gaining more foreign scope. This variable, however, is not significant in our sample.

assets (and liabilities), Lane and Milesi-Ferretti (2003) found that income per capita appears to influence the propensity to engage in international asset trade to the extent that higher income is associated with lower risk aversion.

4.2   Estimation results

Subject to data availability, 19 OECD countries are chosen as our sample as these countries have opened their capital account for a reasonably long and stable period of time.[12] As outward portfolio investment behaviour is determined more by cross-country differences relatively to variation over time, estimation using a cross-sectional regression might be more appropriate. Nevertheless, the use of cross-sectional data alone gives too few data points, and the model is estimated here using a panel data regression based on the sample countries for the period 2000– 04 to increase the number of observations.[13] The estimation is carried out using country fixed effects and White diagonal standard errors and covariance to correct for heteroscedasticity and serial correlation.[14] Table 9.3 summaries the results for different specifications. In each case, an additional explanatory variable is added, and the parameter estimates are robust to different specifications when a new variable is added to the model. Column (6) represents the full model.

The model appears to be able to explain portfolio investment position in the OECD countries reasonably well. In all specifications the model has a very high explanatory power of over 90%. This is in part due to the inclusion of country dummies under the presence of country

---

12. Based on the information published by the IMF, we first selected 43 countries using a rough criterion that countries which have no restrictions on more than half of the 13 types of capital account transactions are considered to have open capital accounts. Due to data limitation, the number of sample countries is reduced to 19. It should be noted that based on this selection criterion, Australia is not considered as having an open capital account. However, most of the country's measures imposed on the capital account do not represent major barriers to cross-border capital flows, and we have therefore also added this country to our sample.

13. Our sample includes Australia, Austria, Canada, Denmark, Finland, France, Germany, Greece, Israel, Italy, Japan, Netherlands, New Zealand, Portugal, Spain, Sweden, Switzerland, UK and the US with annual data from 2000-2004.

14. Diagnostic testing including Hausman tests and Chow test are conducted, and the results suggest that time-invariant country specific effects are present in our sample. Accordingly, the fixed effects estimation procedure is used to estimate the model.

Table 9.3
Fixed Effects Panel Regression Results

Dependent variable: Plit / GDP it						
Independent variable:	(1)	(2)	(3)	(4)	(5)	(6)
$RTNDIEF_{it}$	-0.144 (-3.57)***	-0.068 (-2.32)**	-0.078 (-3.08)***	-0.096 (-3.53)***	-0.072 (-2.35)**	-0.072 (-2.35)**
$Ln(GDPC_{it})$	–	0.340 (8.02)***	0.360 (9.08)***	0.360 (10.04)***	0.318 (7.37)***	0.318 (7.38)***
$PFFL_{it}$	–	–	1.774 (4.68)***	1.272 (3.667)***	1.328 (3.76)***	1.327 (3.76)***
$Openness_{it}$	–	–	–	0.906 (3.56)***	0.935 (3.56)***	0.936 (3.56)***
$Internet_{it}$	–	–	–	–	0.229 (1.68)*	0.230 (1.69)*
$SWCAP_{it}$	–	–	–	–	–	-0.029 (-0.12)
Adjusted R^2	0.964	0.982	0.986	0.988	0.988	0.988
No. of observations	95	95	92	92	92	92

Note: Figures in parentheses are t-statistics. Standard errors are corrected for heteroskedasticity and serial correlation.

***   denotes significance at 1% level
**   denotes significance at 5% level
*   denotes significance at 10% level

fixed effects, for which the estimated coefficients are not shown in the table. Nevertheless, regression using the explanatory variables only still gives an R-square of over 80%.

All variables have the expected signs and are highly significant, except for the domestic share of stock market capitalisation. Although the domestic share of stock market capitalisation turns out to be insignificant, the sign is correctly negative. Its insignificance might suggest that investors, on average do not follow financial theory as closely as one would expect. The results suggest that recent developments including free trade and the advancement in information technology such as the internet, might have made it more cost-effective to invest overseas for a better risk-return trade-off.

Based on the proportion of variation in the dependent variable explained by the variation in each explanatory variable, the most important determinant of outward portfolio investment is Openness, followed by the share of foreign firms listed in the local stock market (PFFL) and per capita GDP (GDPC). An increase in the trade-to-GDP ratio by 1% is found to raise outward portfolio investment as a percentage of GDP by 0.9 percentage points. Similarly, both an increase in the share of foreign firms listed in the domestic stock market and a rise in per capita income will increase outward portfolio investment. For the rest of the variables, while higher internet penetration will increase portfolio investment overseas, domestic residents will tend to hold less foreign portfolio investment assets when domestic stock market return is higher than the rest of the world.

4.3 Potential outward portfolio investment from China

Given these results and assuming the same relationship identified in the estimated Equation (1) to hold for China by the time its capital account is as liberalised as in a typical OECD country, we apply the model estimates to predict the volume of outward portfolio investment for China, based on some projections about the explanatory variables for the country. In order to provide reasonable assumptions, it would be useful to look at where China stands internationally in terms of the determinants of outward portfolio investment. For most of the determinants, China is at a far lower level than the average of the OECD countries, including the domestic share of world stock market capitalisation, the share of foreign listed firms, internet penetration and per capita GDP (Figure 9.7). It is only in terms of the share of total trade in GDP, where China is higher than its OECD counterparts. However, it is expected that the dependence of China on trade would decline when the country continues to develop.

4.4 Assumptions

Against this backdrop, we try to make some reasonable assumptions about the future values of the explanatory variables for China by the time its capital account is as liberalised as in a typical OECD country.

Figure 9.7
How China Compares to OECD Countries in the
Determinants of Outward Portfolio Investment

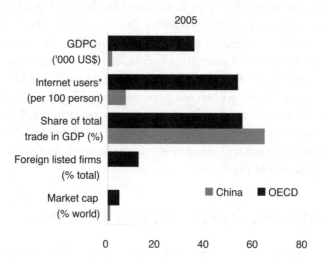

Note: OECD countries include Australia, Austria, Canada, Denmark, Finland, France, Germany, Greece, Israel, Italy, Japan, Netherlands, New Zealand, Norway, Portugal, Spain, Sweden, Switzerland, UK and U.S.

* 2004 figures for internet users.

Sources: World Development Indicators, Balance of Payment Statistics and World Economic Outlook.

We consider three scenarios. The first is a counterfactual exercise, assuming that China has a liberalised capital account today and that the parameter estimates and relationship identified in Equation (1) are applicable, that is, what would be the outward portfolio investment for 2005 given the actual value for the explanatory variables during the year?

However, it should be noted that this counterfactual scenario only serves as a reference based on existing economic and financial conditions in China and provide an easy-to-understand scenario. Given the current development stage of the Mainland economy and the degree of openness of its capital account, it would not be appropriate to assume that Equation (1), which is estimated based on experience in the OECD countries with a reasonably long and stable period of open capital account experience, would hold for China at present. In fact, the aim of this study is to provide an educated guess on what would be the outward portfolio investment holdings by the time the Mainland economy is mature enough to liberalise its capital account to an extent similar to an average OECD country. It should also be noted that we focus on the steady state value in this study, instead of the foreign investment immediately after the full liberalisation.

Therefore, for Equation (1) to be truly applicable, we project ahead in the other two scenarios the values for the explanatory variables by the time China's capital account is as open as in a typical OECD country. Scenario 1 provides a less bullish projection, which could be viewed as a more conservative baseline scenario. First, per capita income (GDPC) is assumed to reach the average level of coastal provinces in China at US$2,983 in 2005, increasing from the current national level of around US$1,700.[15] We do not employ the OECD average as it would be too high to be a realistic assumption—it would take as long as close to 30 years for China to reach that level based on the current pace of growth. INTERNET penetration is assumed to reach the current level in Greece, which was the lowest among OECD countries at 20%, but still much higher than the current level in China of 8.5%. Openness is assumed to be slightly lower at 60%, compared with 64% in 2005. The share of foreign firms listed in the domestic stock market (PFFL) is assumed to reach the level in Japan of around 0.85%, which is the lowest among OECD countries. Assumption based on the OECD average of 10% appears to be too high, given that so far no foreign firm is allowed to be listed in the domestic stock market in China. Finally, the return differential between the domestic and world stock market (RTNDIFF) is assumed to equal to 0, that is, the stock return in China equals the world average. We made this assumption because this factor differs greatly from one year to another, and there is no particular rationale behind what its value would be when the capital account is as liberalised as in a typical OECD country. It would be reasonable to set it to 0 so that the projected portfolio investment would not be affected by these short-term effects.

---

15. It would take approximately 6 years for China's per capita GDP to reach the average level of coastal provinces based on the current pace of growth.

On the other hand, Scenario 2 is based on more bullish assumptions. GDPC is assumed to reach the current level in Shanghai at US$6,277, increasing from the current national level of around US$1,700.[16] INTERNET penetration is assumed to reach the average level in OECD countries of 53% in 2004 which is the latest data available from the World Bank's World Development Indicators. The rest of the assumptions remain the same as in Scenario 1.

4.5 Projections

Table 9.4 summarised the projections under different scenarios. Based on our model estimates, the counterfactual scenario for 2005 suggests that outward portfolio investment relative to GDP will be around 15% in China, which is three times as large as the actual figure of 5%, and equivalent to US$340 billion. Under Scenario 1, the projected volume of outward portfolio investment will reach 23% of GDP by the time the capital account is as liberalised as in a typical OECD country. Under the more bullish Scenario 2, we obtain a figure of 54%. Accordingly, the projected volume of total outward portfolio investment from China

Table 9.4
Potential Outward Portfolio Investment (PI) from China

	2005	Scenario 1	Scenario 2
Actual outward PI position			
(% of GDP)	5.3%	–	–
Projected outward PI position			
(% of GDP)	15%	23%	54%
(USD, billion)	340	904	4,468

Source: Authors' estimates.

---

16. It would take approximately 14 years for China's per capita GDP to reach the level in Shanghai based on the current pace of growth.

would reach US$904 billion and US$4,468 billion for Scenarios 1 and 2 respectively.[17]

These estimates appear to lie within a reasonable range when compared with the average outward portfolio investment-to-GDP ratio of major countries over the past 5 years, with the US being 24%, Japan 38% and the average for OECD countries 46%. They also appear reasonable when compared with the experience in Japan, where as mentioned previously, its outward portfolio investment as a percentage of GDP increased to 18% after 10 years of opening and further to the current 46% after another 10 years (Figure 9.6).

5. HOW LARGE A SHARE CAN HONG KONG EXPECT TO CAPTURE?

The model above suggests that China's outward portfolio investment position could reach US$340 billion should the capital account be as liberalised as in a typical OECD country in 2005. The amount could reach as high as US$900 billion to US$4,500 billion under scenarios based on assumptions projected for the future. Given the strong economic and financial ties, Hong Kong is expected to benefit from the liberalisation of capital account transactions in Mainland China. So how much can Hong Kong capture from this outward portfolio investment from the Mainland? In the second part of the study, we use a gravity model, again based on experience in the OECD countries, to estimate the share of Mainland's portfolio investment that can be captured by Hong Kong.

5.1 The gravity model

Gravity model is widely used in studies of bilateral merchandise trade relationship across countries. The model postulates that trade flows

17. The projected volume of outward portfolio investment from China in terms of US dollar in Scenarios 1 and 2 is derived by multiplying the projected share of GDP with the estimated GDP based on the corresponding per capita GDP used in the projection and assuming population to stay constant at its 2005 level.

between two countries are positively related to the size of the economy (the mass variable) and negatively related to their geographical distance (the distance variable). Previous studies show that the model has a strong explanatory power in analysing international trade relationship. In recent years, financial liberalisation and globalisation have increased research interest in the allocation pattern of international investment position and cross-border capital flows. In earlier studies, Frankel (1997) used a gravity model to analyse the impact of preferential trade arrangements on foreign direct investment (FDI). Stein and Duade (2001) used it to analyse FDI flows from the OECD economies to the host countries, focusing on how institutional characteristics affect the volume of bilateral flows. Loungani *et al* (2003) found that both gravity and information variables played an important role in directing investment flows across countries.

In the context of bilateral portfolio investment flows and holdings, empirical findings generally support the relationship postulated in the gravity model in bilateral investment flows. For example, Lane and Milesi-Ferretti (2004) analysed bilateral equity holdings across countries using a gravity model, and found that they are positively related to trade and negatively related to geographical distance. Moreover, countries with higher per capita income and more developed stock markets tend to have larger cross-border equity asset and liability positions. Portes and Rey (2004) used a gravity model to explain bilateral gross equity investment flows across countries, and found that they are positively related to stock market capitalisation and negatively related to the geographical distance between the source and the recipient country. Their results also suggest that information asymmetry and differences in transaction technology are key determinants of bilateral equity investment flows across countries. Another study by Faruqee, Li and Yan (2004) also found that gravity variables, transaction cost and information asymmetry were significant determinants of international portfolio holdings. In sum, these studies suggest that gravity model has a strong explanatory power for cross-border capital flows and investment positions.

To assess the share of potential outward portfolio investment from the Mainland that could be captured by Hong Kong, we construct a gravity model to identify the key determinants driving bilateral portfolio investment asset holdings across countries with liberalised capital accounts. Specifically, we estimate the model with the following specifications. Parentheses after the variables denote their expected signs in the regression.

$$PI_{ij} / \sum_i PI_i = \alpha_0 + \alpha_1 MKTCAP_i + \alpha_2 MKTCAP_j + \alpha_3 \ln(DISTANCE_{ij}) \qquad (2)$$
$$+ \alpha_4 \ln(Internet_i * Internet_j) + \alpha_5 LANG_{ij} + \alpha_6 RTNDIFFRW_{ij} + \alpha_7 FXVOL_{ij} + e_{ij}$$

where

<u>Dependent variable:</u>

$PI_{ij} / \Sigma PI_i$ = Share of the recipient country in total outward portfolio investment position of the source country

<u>Mass variable:</u>

$MKTCAPi$ = Share of world stock market capitalisation in the source country (+)

$MKTCAPj$ = Share of world stock market capitalisation in the recipient country (+)

<u>Distance variable:</u>

$DISTANCE$ = Geographical distance between the capital cities of the source and the recipient countries, a proxy for information asymmetry (-)

<u>Information variables:</u>

$Internet$ = Cross product of the number of internet users per 1,000 people in the source and the recipient countries, a proxy for information costs (+)

$LANG$ = Dummy variable capturing the similarity of language used in the source and the recipient countries, a proxy for cultural affinity and familiarity with the recipient country (+)

<u>Return-chasing motive variables:</u>

RTNDIFFRW = Difference in stock market return between the source and the recipient countries relative to the global stock market return (-)

FXVOL = Exchange rate volatility of the recipient country's currency against the source country's currency, a measure of exchange rate risk (-)

Since a typical gravity model usually includes the mass and distance variables, we use the share of stock market capitalisation in the source and the recipient countries relative to the world total (MKTCAP) to capture the size effect, and the geographical distance between the capital cities of the two countries (DISTANCE) to capture the distance effect. In the context of a gravity model on cross-border investment, the distance variable is usually regarded as a proxy measure of information flows between the source and the recipient countries.

Apart from the size and distance variables, we identify two information variables and two return-chasing variables to explain the allocation pattern of portfolio investment asset holdings across countries. In general, the lower is the cost of searching information in the source and the recipient countries, the larger will be the size of their bilateral portfolio investment asset holdings. We use the number of internet users per 1,000 people (Internet) as a proxy measure of information costs, as higher internet usage suggests lower costs of searching information. At the same time, we also use a dummy variable (LANG) to capture the cultural ties and market familiarity between the source and the recipient countries, with a value of 1 if they share a common language and zero otherwise. Since using the same language will facilitate residents in the source country to digest the latest market information and developments in the recipient country more easily, this tends to increase the bilateral portfolio investment asset position.

Among the two variables for capturing the effect of return-chasing motives on cross-border securities investment, one is the stock index return differential (RTNDIFFRW) between the source and the recipient countries relative to the global stock market return. If the equity return in the recipient country relative to the world return is higher than that in

Table 9.5
Cross-sectional Regression Results of the Gravity Model

Independent variable:	Dependent variable: $(PI_{ij}/\Sigma PI_i)$				
	(1)	(2)	(3)	(4)	(5)
MKTCAP_i	0.05 (2.69)***	0.04 (2.18)**	0.03 (1.92)*	0.03 (1.42)	0.02 (1.16)
MKTCAP_j	0.55 (6.41)***	0.54 (6.66)***	0.53 (6.53)***	0.54 (6.74)***	0.57 (6.84)***
Ln(DISTANCE_ij)	-0.01 (-7.47)***	-0.01 (-7.05)***	-0.01 (-7.03)***	-0.01 (-7.26)***	-0.01 (-3.96)***
LANG_ij	–	0.02 (2.83)***	0.02 (2.53)**	0.02 (2.56)**	0.02 (2.59)***
Ln(Internet_i*Internet_j)	–	–	0.01 (1.84)*	0.01 (1.79)*	0.01 (2.78)***
RTNDIEFRW_ij	–	–	–	-0.01 (-4.04)***	-0.005 (-4.11)***
FXVOL_ij	–	–	–	–	-0.63 (-3.20)***
Adjusted R²	0.519	0.535	0.537	0.555	0.566
No. of observations	412	412	412	412	412

Note: Figures in parentheses are t-statistics. Standard errors are corrected for heteroskedasticity and serial correlation.

*** denotes significance at 1% level
** denotes significance at 5% level
* denotes significance at 10% level

the source country, the share of outward portfolio investment position in the recipient country would rise. Nevertheless, the higher investment return from overseas may also reflect in part the compensation for higher exchange rate risk. This is captured by exchange rate volatility (FXVOL) in the model, where less portfolio investment is expected to be allocated to countries with large exchange rate movements. A detailed description of the sources and definitions of variables used in the gravity model is provided in Appendix.

5.2   Estimation results

Based on the period averages of annual data from 2001 and 2004 for the sample of OECD countries used in the model in the last section, we estimate the gravity model using a cross-sectional regression.[18] The estimation results show that the parameter estimates have the correct signs and are statistically significant, except for the share of world stock market capitalisation (MKTCAPi) of the source country (Table 9.5). The parameters of the size and distance variables are also robust to different specifications when a new explanatory variable is added to the model. Column (5) represents the full model.

Based on the proportion of variation in the dependent variable explained by the variation in each explanatory variable, the most important determinant of the share of bilateral portfolio investment is the share of world stock market capitalisation of the recipient country (MKTCAPj), followed by DISTANCE and exchange rate volatility (FXVOL). If the share of world stock market capitalisation of the recipient country increases by 1 percentage point, the share of outward portfolio investment position in the recipient country will rise by 0.6 percentage points on average. The distance variable shows that if the source and the recipient countries are far apart, there will be less bilateral portfolio investment asset holdings between the two. The exchange rate volatility variable indicates that less portfolio investment will be allocated to countries with large exchange rate movements.

The relationship of the rest of the explanatory variables with the share of bilateral portfolio investment also conforms to a priori expectations. The language dummy suggests that if the recipient country shares a common language used in the source country, the share of bilateral portfolio investment asset holdings will increase by 2 percentage points. The parameter estimate for the internet variable reflects that more popular use of the internet in the source and the recipient countries will increase bilateral portfolio investment. The regression results also show that if the equity return in the recipient country is greater than the

---

18. The estimation results obtained from cross-sectional regression are robust compared with those obtained from panel regression using pooled cross sectional and time series data. There are little changes in the parameter estimates, and the explanatory variables are significant with the correct signs.

Figure 9.8
How Hong Kong Compares to OECD Countries in its Attractiveness
to Outward Portfolio Investment from China

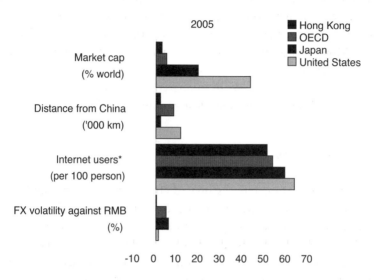

Note: Foreign exchange volatility is the standard deviation of the currency of the source country
       per unit of RMB, standardised by its mean.

* 2004 figures for internet users.

Sources: World Development Indicators, Balance of Payment Statistics and World Economic
          Outlook.

source country by 1 percentage point relative to the global stock market
return, this will increase the share of portfolio investment in the recipient
country by 0.5 percentage points.

5.3   Share of Mainland China's outward portfolio investment captured by Hong Kong

By applying the results from the gravity model, we estimate the share of
Mainland China's outward portfolio investment captured by Hong Kong
if the capital account is as liberalised as in a typical OECD economy. To
enable us in making some reasonable assumptions for the projection, it
is useful to look at how Hong Kong compares with the OECD countries
in terms of its attractiveness to portfolio investment from the Mainland.
These figures suggest that compared with other OECD countries, Hong

Kong could benefit mainly from its close proximity and cultural ties with the Mainland and the relatively low exchange rate volatility against the renminbi (Figure 9.8). In terms of other variables, while internet penetration in Hong Kong is not too far from the OECD average, it does not have an edge over major economies such as the US, UK and Japan. More importantly, compared with major economies, Hong Kong lags behind in terms of the domestic share of world stock market capitalisation. It remains small compared with major markets such as Japan which also has a relatively close proximity to the Mainland.

5.4 Assumptions

Based on the parameters estimated from the gravity model, we project six scenarios using different sets of assumptions. The first is a counterfactual exercise. Using the 2005 data in Mainland China and Hong Kong, we apply the parameters estimated from the gravity model. The other five scenarios are based on different sets of assumptions by the time China's capital account is as liberalised as in a typical OECD country. The assumptions underlying the first 2 scenarios are consistent with those used in our model in the first part of the study.[19] Given the relatively mature financial market developments, MKTCAP and Internet for Hong Kong are assumed to stay at its level in 2005, while exchange rate volatility (FXVOL) is assumed to stay at its average level in 2000-2005.[20]

In Scenario 3, we assume foreign FXVOL to increase to the level between the Japanese yen and the US dollar, while other variables are assumed to be the same as in Scenario 1. The aim of this scenario is to see what would happen when the Mainland increases the flexibility of its exchange rate regime so that the exchange rate volatility of the renminbi against the US dollar and hence the Hong Kong dollar increases to say, a level similar to that of the Japanese yen against the US dollar.

---

19. Internet penetration and return differential between domestic and world stock markets are assumed to be the same as in Scenarios 1 and 2 in the first part of the analysis.
20. Given that exchange rate volatility differs quite significantly from one year to another, the average level over the past years is used, instead of values in one particular year.

In Scenario 4, Hong Kong's share of world stock market capitalisation is assumed to increase along with the projected number of Mainland-related shares listed in the local stock market in the next ten years, while other variables are assumed to be the same as in Scenario 1. This scenario aims to estimate how much more Hong Kong could capture through an increase in its stock market size, as a consequence of the growing importance of its financial market as an avenue to invest in Mainland stocks. We assume the market capitalisation of the locally listed Mainland-related shares to increase at its average pace of growth in recent years.[21] In fact, the recent growth of Hong Kong's stock market capitalisation has been driven by the listing of H-shares. Over the past six years, the market capitalisation of red chips and H-shares has been growing by an average annual rate of around 20%, compared with the average growth rate for the total market of around 9%. For non-Mainland-related stocks, Hong Kong's share of world market capitalisation is assumed to stay constant.

Table 9.6

Projected Share of Mainland China's Outward Portfolio Investment (PI) Captured by Hong Kong

(USD, billion)	2005 Counterfactual	Scenario 1	Scenario 2	Scenario 3	Scenario 4	Scenario 5
Projected China's total outward PI position	340	904	4468	904	904	904
Projected % share of HK in China's total outward PI position	9.4%	10.8%	12.1%	8.6%	13.6%	20.1%
Projected inward PI position from China	32	98	539	78	123	182

Source: Authors' estimates.

---

21. Over the next ten years, the world stock market capitalisation is assumed to grow at 3% based on its average annual growth rate in the past six years. Based on these assumptions, the total market capitalisation of Hong Kong will grow by 12% per annum in the next ten years.

In Scenario 5, we further assume Hong Kong's share of world stock market capitalisation to increase to that of Japan, again with other variables assuming to be the same as in Scenario 1. This scenario tries to estimate how much more Hong Kong could capture if the size of its stock market increases to that in Japan.

5.5   Projections

Based on the 2005 data in Mainland China and Hong Kong, Hong Kong is expected to capture around 9% of the Mainland's outward portfolio investment position (Table 9.6). Based on the counterfactual scenario from the model in the first part which suggests that the Mainland's total outward portfolio investment position would be around US$340 billion in 2005, if 9% of these funds are invested in Hong Kong, this would be equivalent to approximately US$32 billion.

Under Scenario 1, the share captured by Hong Kong is estimated to be around 11%, whereas under Scenario 2, the share is 12%. There are little differences between the projected shares of portfolio investment captured by Hong Kong in the first two scenarios, as there are only slight differences in their assumptions. However, there are significant differences when applying these figures to our previous projections for the Mainland's total outward portfolio investment position. The resulting projected portfolio investment from the Mainland to Hong Kong would be equivalent to US$98 billion and US$539 billion respectively.

The projection in Scenario 3 shows that if exchange rate volatility increases to the level between the Japanese yen and US dollar, Hong Kong will capture 8.6% of the Mainland's outward portfolio investment, which is around 2 percentage points less than its share under the baseline Scenario 1. On the other hand, the projection in Scenario 4 shows that an increase in Hong Kong's share of world stock market capitalisation, as a result of the growing importance of Mainland-related shares in the locally listed stock market, could raise Hong Kong's share of portfolio investment from the Mainland by around 3 percentage points to 14%. The projection in Scenario 5 further suggests that if Hong Kong manages to increase its stock market size to that of Japan, it could almost double its share in the Mainland's outward portfolio investment to 20%.

Table 9.7

Hong Kong's Inward Portfolio Investment Position by Country

2005 (Counterfactual)		
Source Country	USD, billion	% of total
United States	41	24.2
United Kingdom	32	18.9
China	32	18.8
Japan	11	6.3
Luxembourg	10	6.2
Singapore	9	5.4
France	5	2.9
Canada	5	2.7
Netherlands	4	2.5
Ireland	4	2.5

Source: Authors' estimates.

Figure 9.9

Allocation of China's Outward Portfolio Investment across Major Financial Markets
(Based on Counterfactual Scenario for 2005)

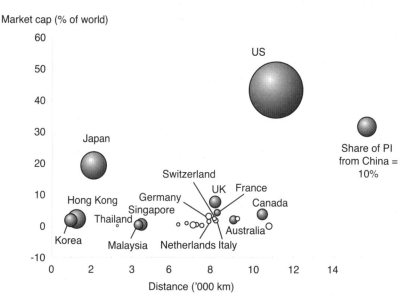

Source: Authors' estimates.

In terms of inward portfolio investment position in Hong Kong, the counterfactual scenario suggests that if 9% of the Mainland's outward portfolio investment is invested in Hong Kong, this is equivalent to about 19% of Hong Kong's total inward portfolio investment position in 2005 (Table 9.7). This will make Mainland China the third largest portfolio investment creditor in Hong Kong after the US and the UK.

It would also be interesting to look at how Hong Kong is competing with other countries in attracting portfolio investment from the Mainland. Figure 9.9 shows the allocation of the Mainland's outward portfolio investment across major financial markets with respect to stock market capitalisation and distance from the country, which are the core determinants of bilateral portfolio investment in the gravity model. The size of the bubble represents the share of portfolio investment from the Mainland captured by each market in 2005. A darker colour denotes higher ranking in terms of the share of portfolio investment captured.

Based on the counterfactual scenario for 2005 from our model estimates, it is expected that while Hong Kong captures a significant share of the Mainland's portfolio investment, a major portion would be invested in the US, Japan and the UK, which have a combined share of around 75% of the global stock market capitalisation. The rest is expected to be invested in Asian economies with developed financial markets given their relatively close proximity and economic linkage with Mainland China, such as Singapore and Korea.

It would be useful to check on the reasonableness of our estimates, based on the existing allocation pattern of China's portfolio investment position across different financial markets. However, there is limited information in this respect and no official data on inward portfolio investment from the Mainland is available in Hong Kong. Nevertheless, according to data reported from Japan, it received US$13 billion of inward portfolio investment from China in 2004, which was equivalent to 14% of China's outward portfolio investment position.[22] This is close to our projections of around 13% for Japan.

---

22. Sources: State Administration of Foreign Exchange, People's Republic of China and Coordinated Portfolio Investment Survey (CPIS), IMF.

6. CONCLUSION AND POLICY IMPLICATIONS

To summarise, based on the existing stage of economic and financial developments, total outward portfolio investment from China can be expected to increase from the current 5% of GDP to 15%, should its capital account be as liberalised as in a typical OECD economy. Assumptions based on our projections for the future suggest that total outward portfolio investment from Mainland China could reach 23% to 54% of GDP by the time the Mainland is mature enough to open its capital account more fully. As a result, Hong Kong could capture around 10% of the outward portfolio investment from the Mainland. This is equivalent to US$32 billion under our counterfactual scenario for 2005, and around US$100 billion to US$540 billion should the Mainland's capital account be as open as in a typical OECD country.

6.1 Policy implications

Naturally, three questions arise from our empirical findings. First, what is Hong Kong's comparative advantage? Secondly, how can Hong Kong increase its competitiveness in attracting portfolio investment from the Mainland? Lastly, what will be the implications for the Hong Kong economy?

With regard to the first question, while the model results show that Hong Kong's proximity and cultural affinity with the Mainland are important determinants, market capitalisation is the most important factor in determining the allocation of cross-border investment, although distance also plays a significant role. Therefore, size matters. It is thus important for Hong Kong to increase its stock market size through maintaining the soundness and sophistication of its capital markets and status as an international financial centre. As discussed earlier, our projections show that an increase in Hong Kong's stock market size as a result of the growing importance of Mainland-related shares listed in the local stock market could increase Hong Kong's share in Mainland's portfolio investment by 3 percentage points, while a further increase in its share in world stock market capitalisation to that of Japan could almost double the share captured by Hong Kong.

However, it should be noted that the former estimates only capture the impact of the growing importance of Mainland-related shares listed in the local stock market through its effect on the total market size, and do not reflect the effect due plainly to the desire of Mainland investors to invest in assets of domestic enterprises.[23] In fact, the attraction of Hong Kong to Mainland investors is more than factors due to proximity of the market, but also its role as a platform to invest in shares of domestic enterprises that are not listed on the Mainland, or that have higher liquidity in Hong Kong's stock market compared to the Mainland's. The former is particularly true as some of the world's largest initial public offerings (IPOs) by major Mainland corporations which are not listed domestically, have taken place in Hong Kong in recent years.

Figure 9.10
Inward Portfolio Investment Position and
Financial Sector Income and Value Added

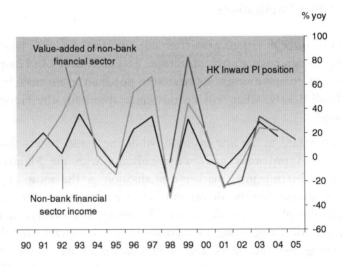

Source: CEIC.

---

23. In order to estimate separately the effect on Mainland's portfolio investment to Hong Kong due to the desire of Mainland investors to invest in assets of domestic enterprises, the share of stocks from the source country listed in the recipient country has to be included in the model. However, due to data limitations, this explanatory variable is not incorporated into our final model.

Nevertheless, such effect could be offset in part by the possibility that the need for cross-border listing in Hong Kong might decline by the time the Mainland has become more developed with a more sophisticated financial market. This would reduce the pace of growth of Mainland-related shares listed in the Hong Kong stock market. It is therefore important for Hong Kong to maintain the sophistication and competitiveness of its financial markets over time not only to increase its stock market size, but also to maintain its role as a major avenue to invest in assets of Mainland enterprises by both Mainland investors and other overseas investors.

In terms of the implications for the Hong Kong economy, increased portfolio investment from the Mainland is expected to benefit the financial services industry in Hong Kong, and increase contributions from this sector to GDP. Past development shows that there has been a strong co-movement between Hong Kong's inward portfolio investment position and non-bank financial sector income (Figure 9.10). The potential sizable portfolio investment from the Mainland would not only boost equity and debt market activities in Hong Kong, but also foster the fund management and custodian services industry.

A rough estimate of past relationship suggests that if growth in Hong Kong's inward portfolio investment position increases by 1 percentage point, growth in the value added of the non-bank financial sector would rise by 0.7 percentage points on average.[24] Based on our counterfactual scenario, liberalisation in the Mainland's capital account would boost Hong Kong's inward portfolio investment position by US$32 billion which is equivalent to a 18%-increase from the actual level in 2005.[25] This would increase GDP growth by 0.3 percentage points and raise the contribution from non-bank financial services to GDP to 3.1% from the current 2.8%.

---

24. Estimates derived by regressing the growth of value-added of the non-bank financial sector on the growth of inward portfolio investment position in Hong Kong.

25. While actual data for inward portfolio investment from Mainland China to Hong Kong is not available, the amount is expected to be very small. As such, the percentage increase in Hong Kong's inward portfolio investment is computed by assuming that the actual amount received in 2005 is minimal, so that the increase is approximately equal to the total projected amount of US$32 billion.

6.2   Caveats

However, it is important to note that these projections are subject to a number of caveats. First, counterfactual scenarios are based on current economic and financial conditions which would have further evolved by the time the capital market is as open as in a typical OECD country, whereas projections in different scenarios are based on assumptions on the future steady state which are subject to a number of uncertainties. These projections are also subject to country-specific factors not captured by the model, including the differences in policy effects across countries, so that the estimated relationship based on experience for the OECD countries may not necessarily be fully applicable to the case of China, and can therefore, only serve as ballpark estimates.

Another caveat is that the size of the debt market, which is an important determinant of bilateral portfolio investment, has not been taken into account in the model estimation due to data limitation. Among the global portfolio investment assets invested in the US and European markets, a large portion of funds is used to purchase debt securities such as government bonds. Therefore, in addition to the equity market, Hong Kong might also need to strengthen its efforts in developing the debt market to attract more portfolio investment.

At the same time, apart from portfolio investment flows directly to Hong Kong's domestic capital markets, Hong Kong could also play the role in providing wealth-management services through which funds from the Mainland could be invested in other overseas markets. It should be noted that portfolio investment data do not capture investment in funds for which Hong Kong is not the custodian, even though investment and wealth management services might be provided in Hong Kong. Investors from the Mainland might invest in overseas funds using Hong Kong's wealth management services without having capital physically flowing into Hong Kong. While such flows would not be reflected in Hong Kong's portfolio investment data, this could nevertheless still benefit Hong Kong's financial sector through the income generated from the services they provide. Therefore, Hong Kong may benefit more than what the estimated inward portfolio investment from the Mainland to Hong Kong would suggest. This also implies that it is important for Hong Kong to strengthen its fund management and custodian services in order to benefit more fully from the liberalisation of the Mainland's capital account.

Appendix 9A

Data Definition and Sources

Panel Data for Equation (1)

Variables	Definition	Sources
PI_{it}/GDP_{it}	Gross portfolio investment asset as a percentage of GDP.	International Financial Statistics, IMF.
$SWCAP_{it}$	Domestic stock market capitalisation as a percentage of world capitalisation.	World Development Indicators.
$RTNDIEE_{it}$	Difference between domestic and world stock market return.	Bloomberg.
$PFFL_{it}$	Number of foreign firms over total firms listed in the domestic stock market.	Websites of various stock exchanges.
$Openness_{it}$	Percentage share of trade flows (exports plus imports) in GDP.	Balance of Payment Statistics, IMF.
$Internet_{it}$	Percentage share of internet users in the total population.	World Development Indicators.
$GDPC_{it}$	Gross domestic product per capita	World Economic Outlook, IMF.

Bilateral cross-sectional data for Equation (2)

Variables	Definition	Sources
$PI_{ij}/\Sigma PI_{ij}$	Outward portfolio investment position of country i to country j as a share of total outward portfolio investment position of country i.	Portfolio investment: CPIS Data, IMF.
$MKTCAP_i$	Domestic stock market capitalisation of country i as a share of world capitalisation.	World Development Indicators.
$MKTCAP_j$	Domestic stock market capitalisation of country j as a share of world capitalisation.	World Development Indicators.
$DISTANCE_{ij}$	Geographical distance between the capital cities of country i and country j.	Forum for Research on Empirical International Trade Website.
$(Internet_i{}^*Internet_j)$	Cross product of internet users per 1000 people of country i and country j.	World Development Indicators.
$LANG_{ij}$	A dummy variable where countries share a common language equal to 1 and 0 otherwise.	CIA, The World Fact Book, 2006. (http://www.cia.gov/cia/publications/factbook/)
$RTNDIFFRW_{ij}$	Stock market return differential between country i and country j relative to the world stock market return.	Bloomberg.
$FXVOL_{ij}$	Exchange rate volatility: standard deviation of country j currency per unit of country i currency, normalised by its mean.	International Financial Statistics, IMF.

Note: Country i denotes the source country and country j denotes the recipient country.

Appendix 9B

Major Milestones of the Capital Account Liberalisation Process in China

1980	China starts borrowing abroad and invest in overseas markets.
	Four cities are first chosen to be Special Economic Zones which aims to promote trade and attract foreign investment in the manufacturing industries.
1982	The first foreign-owned bank opened branch in China to facilitate foreign currency transaction.
1984	Fourteen more selected coastal cities are opened to foreign direct investment.
1989	Domestic enterprises are allowed to invest abroad with their own foreign exchange earnings.
1991	The official exchange rate regime is changed to managed floating from periodical adjustment.
	Domestic residents are allowed to purchase foreign exchange for overseas study, tourism etc. up to a certain limit.
1992	Domestic enterprises can issue foreign currency-denominated shares, which can only be purchased by non-residents.
1993	The first Mainland firm, Qingdao Beer, is listed in the Hong Kong Stock Exchange.
1994	Substantial reforms take place in restructuring the foreign exchange control system: establishing the system of "purchasing and surrendering foreign exchange through designated banks", and unifying dual exchange rates and the managed floating exchange rate regime.
1996	Renminbi becomes convertible under the current account.
	Financial institutions are allowed to issue bonds in the international markets.
2001	World Trade Organization (WTO) accession.
2002	Qualified foreign financial institutions are allowed to invest in the renminbi-denominated domestic stock and bond markets—the so called Qualified Foreign Institutional Investors (QFII) scheme.
2004	Qualified insurance companies are allowed to invest their foreign exchange assets in overseas bond and money markets.
2006	Banks, fund managers, securities houses and insurance companies are allowed to make foreign portfolio investments—the so called Qualified Domestic Institutional Investors (QDII) scheme.
	Upper limits on the foreign exchange holdings are raised to US$500,000 from US$200,000 for domestic firms and to US$20,000 from US$8,000 for individuals.
	Restrictions on the amount of foreign currency allowed to be purchased by domestic investors for qualified foreign direct investment are removed.
	By the end of the year, the financial sector will be opened to full foreign competition, according to the WTO commitment.

Sources: Zhao (2006), Prasad and Wei (2005), and State Administration of Foreign Exchange, People's Republic of China.

REFERENCES

Amadi, Amir Andrew (2004), "Equity Home Bias: A Disappearing Phenomenon?," *Working Paper, University of California at Davis.*

Ahearne, Alan G., Griever, William L., and Francis E. Warnock, 2004, "Information Costs and Home Bias: an Analysis of US Holdings of Foreign Equities," *Journal of International Economics* 62: 313–336.

Baele, Lieven, Crina Pungulescu and Jenke Ter Horst, 2006, "Model Uncertainty, Financial Markets Integration and the Home Bias Puzzle," Paper presented at the ECB Joint Conference: Financial Globalisation and Integration, 17-18 July.

Bohn., Henning and Linda Tesar, 1996, "U.S. Equity Investment in Foreign Markets: Portfolio Rebalancing or Return Chasing?" *American Economic Review Papers and Proceedings* 86(2): 77–81.

Central Intelligence Agency (CIA), *The World Fact Book*, 2006.

Frankel, Jeffrey A., 1997, "Regional Trading Blocs in the World Economic System," *Washington, D.C. : Institute of International Economics.*

IMF, Portfolio Investment: *Coordinated Portfolio Investment Survey (CPIS) Data.*

IMF, World Economic Outlook, April 2006.

Jon Haveman's International Trade Data.
(http://www.macalester.edu/research/economics/PAGE/HAVEMAN/Trade. Resources/TradeData.html)

Kho, Bong-Chan, Rene M. Stulz and France E. Warnock, 2006, "Financial Globalization, Governance, and the Evolution of the Home Bias," Paper presented at the ECB Joint Conference: Financial Globalisation and Integration, 17–18 July.

Lane, R. Philip, 2000, "International Investment Positions: A Cross-sectional Analysis," *Journal of International Money and Finance*, Vol. 19, 513–5.

Lane, R. Philip and Gian Maria Milesi-Ferretti, 2003, "International Financial Integration," *IMF Staff Papers*, Vol. 50 Special Issue, pp. 82–113 (Washington: International Monetary Fund).

Laurenceson, James and Kam Ki Tang, 2005, "China's Capital Account Convertibility and Financial Stability," *No. 5, EAERG Discussion Paper Series*, University of Queensland, School of Economics.

Laurenceson, James and Kam Ki Tang, 2005, "Estimating China's De-facto Capital Account Convertibility', *No 2, EAERG Discussion Paper Series*, University of Queensland, School of Economics.

Loungani, Prakash, Ashoka Mody, Assaf Razin and Efraim Sadka, 2003, "The Role of Information in Driving FDI: Theory and Evidence?" *Scottish Journal of Political Economy*, Vol. 49, pp. 526–543.

Portes, Richard and Hélène Rey, 2004, "The Determinants of Cross-border Equity Flows," *Journal of International Economics*, Vol. 65, 269–296.

Prasad, Eswar and Wei Shang-Jin, 2005, "The Chinese Approach to Capital Inflows: Patterns and Possible Explanations," *IMF Working Papers WP/05/79*, Washington: International Monetary Fund.

Sorensen, Bent E., Yi-Tsung Wu, Oved Yosha and Yu Zhu, 2006, "Home Bias and International Risk Sharing: Twin Puzzles Separated at Birth," Paper presented at the ECB Joint Conference: Financial Globalisation and Integration, 17–18 July.

Stein, Ernesto and Christain Duade, 2001, "Institutions, Integration and the Location of Foreign Direct Investment," in New Horizons for Foreign Direct Investment, *OECD Global Forum on Foreign Direct Investment*, Paris: OECD, pp. 101–128.

World Bank, World Development Indicators, 2004 and 2005.

Zhao, Min, 2006, "External Liberalization and the Evolution of China Exchange System: An Empirical Approach," *No. 4, The World Bank China Office Research Paper*.

Chapter 10

Share Price Disparity
in Chinese Stock Markets[1]

Tom FONG

Alfred WONG

Ivy YONG

1. Authors wish to thank Hans Genberg, Cho-Hoi Hui and Wensheng Peng for valuable comments, and Maggie Mok and Georgina Lok for excellent research background work.

1. INTRODUCTION

The presence of persistent price disparity between A- and H- shares suggests that the two markets are segmented and thus allocation of capital is inefficient. In this paper, we attempt to answer probably the most fundamental question on the phenomenon, identifying the factors contributing to the price disparity, with a view to helping policymakers find solutions to the problem. This paper complements the analysis of the changes in the price disparity by Peng *et al* (2007).[2]

Internationally, when price disparity exists between two shares of the same stock, the one accessible by foreign investors usually commands a premium over the one restricted only to domestic ownership. However, almost all H-shares, which are accessible by foreign investors, are traded at a discount to their counterparts in the A-share market on the Mainland. Nonetheless, this should not be seen as an inconsistency because in most other emerging markets shares accessible by foreign investors are also open to domestic investors—which leaves no opportunity for any discount to exist—while in the Chinese case foreign and domestic investors do not have access to each other's market.[3]

Whether one tries to explain a premium (in the case of other emerging markets) or a discount (in the case of the Chinese markets) should not have any implication for the approaches adopted in empirical studies. Previous studies on price disparity in segmented stock markets are fairly diverse in terms of model specification, due to different hypotheses or explanations. However, despite the diversity, the hypotheses or explanations focus mainly on five factors, namely, market liquidity, shares supply, market risk, information asymmetry and

---

2. While identifying the factors affecting the price disparity can also shed light on the changes in the price disparity, the latter paper differs in that it studies the changes or dynamics by examining the statistical properties of the disparity itself.

3. Foreign investors have in recent years been able to access the A-share market via the qualified foreign institutional investors scheme but the access has remained very limited. During the period under study, the qualified domestic institutional investors scheme was limited to fixed income products and there was no formal channel for Mainland investors to access the H-share market. However, it was recently announced that this rule will be relaxed, allowing Mainland investors to invest in overseas equities.

Table 10.1

Literature Review on Chinese Stock Markets

Author(s)	Markets	No. of Firms	Period	Factors
Ng and Wu (2007)	A-shares	32% of total mkt turnover trade on SH	2001–2002	Risk, market conditions
Guo and Tang (2006)	A- vs H-shares	29 A/H shares	1993–2003	Cost of capital, liquidity
Chan and Kwok (2005)	A- vs H-shares and A- vs B-shares	13 A/H shares 41 A/B shares	1991–2000	Liquidity, supply, risk, information asymmetry
Wang and Li (2003)	A- vs H-shares	16 A/H shares	1995–2001	Liquidity, risk, market conditions, exchange rate
Fung et al. (2000)	A- vs B-shares	20 A/B shares	1993–1997	Dividend yield, exchange rates, bond yield
Sun and Tong (2000)	A- vs B-shares A- vs H-shares	45 A/B shares 10 A/H shares	1994–1998	Risk, bond issued, no.of listed firms, information asymmetry, foreign reserves, inflation, liquidity
Su and Fleisher (1999)	A- vs B-shares	24 A/B shares	1993–1997	Risk, no.of investors, information asymmetry
Chakravarty et al. (1998)	A- vs B-shares	39 A/B shares	1994–1996	Risk, information asymmetry, supply
Ma (1996)	A- vs B-shares	38 A/B shares	1992–1994	Market conditions, Chinese deposit rates, CPIs of China and US
Chen et al. (2001)	A- vs B-shares	36 (SHSE) and 32 (SZSE) A/B shares	1992–1997	Risk, information asymmetry, liquidity
Bailey (1994)	A- vs B-shares	14 A/B shares	1992–1993	Market conditions

Note : The above summary focuses on the modelling of the cross-sectional data in panel data analysis. In the literature, the liquidity factor is represented by the trading volume (or the ratio to market capitalisation or the ratio to total trading volume) and bid-ask spread. The risk factor is represented by the volatility of prices and variance-covariance ratios. The supply factor is represented by the total outstanding shares and tradable market shares. The information asymmetry factor is reflected by total market capitalisation. The factor of market conditions is proxied by the market returns.

general market conditions—in particular in those studies on the Chinese markets (see Table 10.1). All of these are plausible factors contributing to the stock price disparity from a micro perspective. No empirical work has, according to our knowledge, considered the channels through which recent macroeconomic imbalance of China's economy has played an increasingly important role.

The macroeconomic imbalance has arguably impacted the prices of the A- and H-share markets, and hence their disparity, in at least three ways. First, an undervalued currency and thus expectations of future revaluation or appreciation have provided strong motivation for foreign investors to acquire H-shares as a proxy for "renminbi" assets, though H-shares, which are denominated in Hong Kong dollars, are not renminbi assets *per se*. Second, the external imbalance resulting from an undervalued renminbi has been manifested into rising internal imbalance as evidenced by rapidly growing bank deposits. With limited choice of financial products available domestically, stock investment, in additional to real estate investment, has offered a convenient and feasible alternative to bank deposits for the majority of Mainland investors. Finally, as China's trade surplus continues to rise, the opportunities for Mainlanders to retain their foreign currency proceeds outside the Mainland to avoid capital controls have increased. This in turn reflects increased ability of Mainlanders to arbitrage by purchasing the H-share of the same stock whenever they find the discount offered by the H-share attractive enough.

The rest of this paper is organised as follows. Section 2 examines the relationship between the returns of A- and H-shares in recent years. Section 3 examines the determinants of the price disparity between the dual-listed A- and H-shares, using a panel data regression model. Section 4 concludes.

2. PRELIMINARY ANALYSIS

Both the price and quantity data of A- and H-shares are monthly averages of daily data extracted from Bloomberg, covering the period from April 2000 to February 2007.[4] It is useful to note that this period saw significant growth in the market, with the number of dual-listed stocks more than doubling from 17 to 36 (Table 10.2) and, even after controlling for price increases, the size of the market capitalisation had expanded 16 times.[5] In Figure 10.1, we plot the indices of the market capitalisation of the dual-listed A- and H-shares over time, with all stock prices held constant at their February 2007 levels. As can be seen, in April 2000 the A- and H-share markets—controlled for price changes— were only about 6% as large as in February 2007. This is particularly important when comparing results with previous studies, because the A-H market today is quite different from what it used to be in the 1990s (covered by most other studies).

Figure 10.1

The Market Capitalisation (Feb 2007=100%)

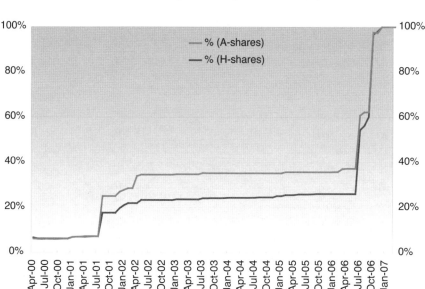

---

4. The earliest available record for all 17 stocks on Bloomberg is April 2000, although the history of dual-listed A- and H-shares dates as far back as 1993. There are two reasons for not covering the whole dual-listing history in this study. First, we want to maintain a higher degree of data consistency by using one data source. Second, and more importantly, the market in the 1990s was too small (compared to the market today) to have any useful policy relevance.

5. During the period from March to July 2007, the number of dual-listed stocks has increased to 39.

Table 10.2

The 36 Selected Companies Commonly Listed in Both Markets

No	Company	H Shares ticker	A Shares Ticker
1	Luoyang Glass	1108	600876
2	Nanjing Panda	553	600775
3	Northeast Electric	42	000585
4	Shandong Xinhua Pharmaceutical	719	000756
5	Sinopec Yizheng Chemical Fibre	1033	600871
6	Beijing North Star	588	601588
7	Beiren Printing Machinery	187	600860
8	Jingwei Textile Machinery	350	000666
9	China Eastern Airlines Corp	670	600115
10	Tianjin Capital Environmental Protection	1065	600874
11	Guangzhou Pharmaceutical	874	600332
12	Sinopec Shanghai Petrochemical	338	600688
13	Jiangxi Copper	358	600362
14	China Southern Airlines	1055	600029
15	Guangzhou Shipyard International	317	600685
16	China Petroleum & Chemical Corp	386	600028
17	Guangshen Railway	525	601333
18	Jiaoda Kunji High-Tech	300	600806
19	Dongfang Electrical Machinery	1072	600875
20	Air China	753	601111
21	Bank of China	3988	601988
22	Datang International Power Generation	991	601991
23	ZTE Corp	763	000063
24	Jiangsu Expressway	177	600377
25	Maanshan Iron & Steel	020	000000
26	Yanzhou Coal Mining	1171	600188
27	Industrial and Commercial Bank of China	1398	601398
28	Tsingtao Brewery	168	600600
29	Shenzhen Expressway	548	600548
30	Anhui Conch Cement	914	600585
31	Huadian Power International Corp	1071	600027
32	China Shipping Development	1138	600026
33	Anhui Expressway	995	600012
34	Angang Steel	347	000898
35	Huaneng Power International	902	600011
36	China Merchants Bank Co. Ltd.	3968	600036

Next, we compute the Divisia (1925) indices, correlations and variances of the A- and H-shares to provide a simple view of the relationship between their respective returns over time.[6] When applied in the current context, the Divisia price index is a market-capitalisation-weighted average of logarithmic price changes (returns). In the computation, share prices are adjusted for changes in the exchange rate. Figure 10.2 presents the scatter plot of the Divisia A- and H-share price indices where each point corresponds to a specific month. The dispersion of the Divisia A- relative to H-share price index and their deviations from the 45-degree line reflect the degree of segmentation between the two markets. There appears to be only a mild positive relationship between the returns of A- and H-shares. This is consistent with Figure 10.3 which shows that the two indices exhibit a slight tendency to move in tandem, especially from around 2003 Q3.

Figure 10.2
Scatter Plot of Divisia Indices (Monthly)

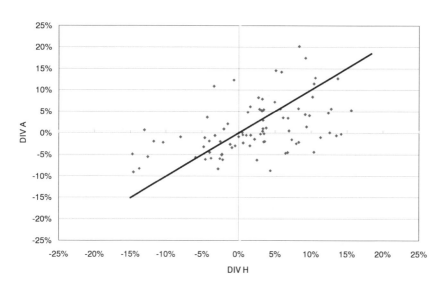

6. We employ the Divisia index instead of other more commonly used indices such as the Paasche, Laspeyre and Fisher indices, because its higher-order moments can capture the relationship among individual stock price changes while others cannot.

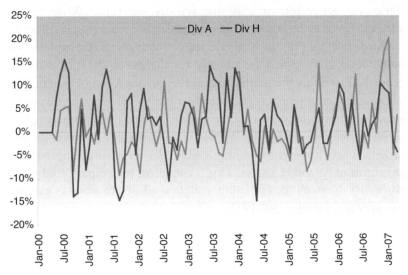

Figure 10.3
Divisia Indices (Monthly)

The Divisia A-H share correlation shows the co-movement between A- and H-shares. As can be seen in Figure 10.4, their relationship is found to be positively correlated in most of the period. It is also noted that the Divisia correlation averaged about 0.2 initially and then trended higher from around the beginning of 2003, reaching about 0.6 by the end of the period. Hence, gradual integration between the two markets seems to have taken place over the past four years. This result is consistent with the finding of Peng *et al.* (2007) that there was relative price convergence between the A- and H-shares of the dual-listed stocks.

The Divisia variance is the second-order moment of individual stock prices, which measures the extent to which the prices of individual stocks change disproportionately. In other words, it is a measure of relative price changes, not absolute price changes. When all prices change by the same proportion, it vanishes. Scatter plots of the monthly Divisia A- and H-share price variances for the past seven years are presented in Figure 10.5, with the upper panel including all observations and the lower panel excluding the outliers defined as larger than 0.01. In both cases, there are about two-thirds or 66% of observations lying above the 45-degree line. In other words, for the dual-listed stocks, A-shares tend to have a

Figure 10.4
Divisia Correlations (Monthly)

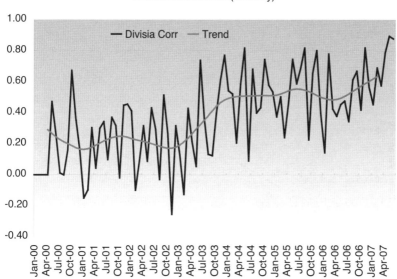

smaller Divisia variance than do H-shares, indicating that the prices of A-shares tend to move more in tandem, when compared with those of H-shares. There must exist some common forces that drive stock prices in the A-share market to go in one direction or the other, resulting in a smaller dispersion of price movements. What possibly are these common forces? The rest of the paper will shed some light on this question.

3. MODEL SPECIFICATION

To examine the relevance of the various possible factors leading to the price disparity, we employ a fixed effect panel data model in our estimation. Panel data model allows us to analyse the disparity for a large number of firms simultaneously using time series data, while a fixed effect structure can help control for unobservable firm-specific effects, so that differences across companies can be captured.[7]

---

7. See Domowitz (1997) and Hsiao (1996) for details.

Figure 10.5
Scatter Plot of Divisia Variances

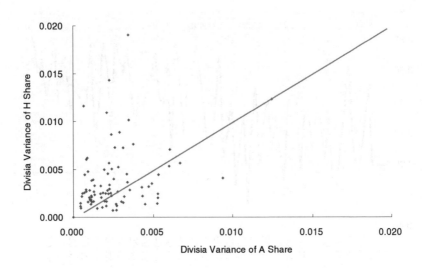

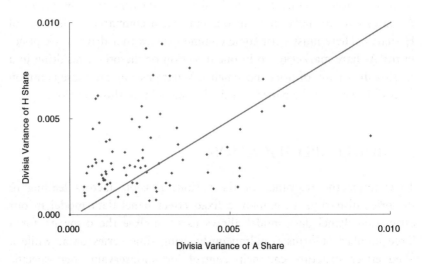

Specifically, the regression model is as follows:

$$PREM_{it} = \alpha_0 + \alpha_1 LQ_{it} + \alpha_2 SP_{it} + \alpha_3 RK_{it} + \alpha_4 INF_{it} + \alpha_5 MC_{it} \qquad (1)$$
$$+ \alpha_6 CUR_{it} + \alpha_7 M2_{it} + \alpha_8 TR_{it} + \alpha_9 PREM_{it-1} + \eta_i + \varepsilon_{it}$$

where subscripts i and t denote stock i and time t respectively. The dependent variable PREM represents the price disparity of stock i, defined as the price premium of stock i in the market of A-shares over the same stock in the market of H-shares at time t. LQ, SP, RK, INF, and MC denote respectively the five popular factors identified in previous studies, namely, liquidity, supply, risk, information asymmetry, and market conditions of the two markets (all in relative terms). To take into account the indirect impact of the macroeconomic imbalance, we introduce into the model three other variables CUR, M2 and TR which denote the 3-month renminbi non-deliverable forward (NDF) rate, money supply M2 of the Mainland, and the trade balance of the Mainland respectively.[8] How these variables can influence the A- and H-share prices and their disparity is discussed in detail in the context of the Gordon (1962) growth model in the Appendix 10.

The lagged price premium is included to reflect the trend of the price premium and filter out the autocorrelation (Domowitz, et al., 1997).[9] The coefficient vector $\alpha = (\alpha_0, \alpha_1, ..., \alpha_9)$ is fixed over time and across stocks by assumption.[10] The variables η_i are the individual effects capturing the

---

8. To avoid the problem of collinearity between levels of money supply of China and renminbi NDF rate which are shown to be monotonic increasing, the ratios of the current value over its lag X_t/X_{t-1} (i.e., with the variables in change form instead of level when taking logarithm) are considered in the estimation.

9. The correlation between the lagged dependent variable and the disturbance gives rise to the biased estimation of coefficients under ordinary least squares estimation. We employ a generalised method of moment (GMM) estimator to correct the standard errors for heteroskedasticity of unknown form in the time-varying error components and to permit efficient estimation.

10. A random effect model, which allows the individual specific effect to change over time, may provide a better explanatory power for the price premium over the fixed effect model. However, the Hausman test suggests that there is no significant difference between the two model specifications. Moreover, the number of parameters increases sharply when the random effect model is considered, which is especially unfavourable for the scarcity of data on the time dimension. In view of this, the fixed effect model is chosen.

Table 10.3

Description of the Dependent Variable and Explanatory Variables

Variable	Type of Variable / Factor	Description	Expected Effect
$PREM_t$	Dependent Variable	Natural logarithm of A-share price minus natural logarithm of H-share price of the same stock	
LQ	Liquidity	Monthly trading volume to the total number of shares outstanding in the A-share market over monthly trading volume to the total number of shares outstanding in the H-share market (in natural logarithm)	+
SP(1)	Supply (1)	Natural logarithm of number of free-floating shares in the A-share market over number of free-floating shares in the H-share market	-
SP(2)	Supply (2)	Natural logarithm of number of outstanding shares in the A-share market over number of outstanding shares in the H-share market	-
RK	Risk Level	Natural logarithm of 30-day annualised standard deviation of A-shares over 30-day annualised standard deviation of H-shares	+
INF(1)	Information Asymmetry (1)	Natural logarithm of total market capitalisation based on all free-floating shares listed in the A-share and H-share markets	-
INF(2)	Information Asymmetry (2)	Natural logarithm of total market capitalisation based on all outstanding shares listed in the A-share and H-share markets	-
MC	Market Conditions	Natural logarithm of Shanghai Stock Index over Hang Seng Index	+
CUR	Rate of renminbi Appreciation	Natural logarithm of 3-month nondeliverable forward contract of renminbi over its lag	-
M2	Growth of China's Money Supply	Natural logarithm of China's Money Supply (M2) over its lag	+
TR	Trade Balance	Natural logarithm of total export over total import in China	-
$PREM_{t-1}$	Lagged Term	The price premium in the previous month	+

unobserved idiosyncratic features of stock i and the variables ε_{it} are the disturbances.

Table 10.3 provides the data details of each explanatory variable used in the estimation. For each stock, the price premium *PREM* is measured by the logarithmic value of the average monthly A-share price P_A minus that of the average monthly H-share price, i.e., *PREM* = $\log(P_A)$ – $\log(P_H)$.[11] The liquidity factor *LQ* is proxied by the relative turnover rates of the two markets, where the turnover rate is defined as the monthly trading volume to the total number of shares outstanding in the markets.[12, 13] To reflect the relative supply of the two markets, two proxies, namely, (i) the ratio of the number of free-floating A-shares to the number of H-shares (denoted by SP(1)) and (ii) the ratio of the number of outstanding A-shares to the number of outstanding H-shares (denoted by SP(2)), are considered.[14] The ratio of the variances of returns is used to reflect the relative risk levels RK.[15] Information asymmetry is proxied by the relative market capitalisation of free-floating shares (denoted by INF(1)) and that of total outstanding shares (denoted INF(2)) of the two markets.[16] Some descriptive statistics of the variables are presented in Tables 10.4 and 10.5.

---

11. All A-share prices originally denominated in renminbi are converted to Hong Kong dollar.

12. Such measures are commonly used in the literature and they are more powerful in explaining price discounts than others in empirical analysis. See Ma (1996), Domowitz *et al.* (1997), and Wang *et al.* (2003). The bid-ask spread is also a natural proxy of liquidity (See Guo *et al.*, 2006). However, Amihud *et al.* (1986) found that assets return is an increasing and concave function of the spread. Therefore, some nonlinear properties should be imposed in the model when the bid-ask spread is used in the estimation.

13. A joint cross-correlation test is considered to examine the lead-lag relationship between the price premium and the turnover rate (i.e. the proxy of liquidity ratio). The joint cross-correlation test shows that the price premium leads the turnover rate significantly, while the turnover rate does not lead the price premium significantly. These results suggest that the issue of reverse causality (i.e. turnover rate leading price premium) is not significant in the analysis.

14. The free-floating H-shares is defined as the number of shares that are available to the public, while the free floating A-shares is defined as the number of current shares outstanding that are tradable or listed on the stock exchange.

15. They are the 30-day price volatility which equals the annualised standard deviation of relative price change of the 30 most recent trading days closing price. The volatility is the standard deviations of day-to-day logarithmic price changes.

16. Since larger firms have more information disclosure, the firm size proxied by the market value of total outstanding shares may reflect the availability of information. Chan and Kwok (2005) commented that the market capitalisation of total shares outstanding may also be a good indicator of the availability of information on the firm. However, their estimation results suggested that the market capitalisation of free-floating shares is a better indicator to reflect such factor.

Table 10.4
General Features of the Data[a]
(Sample Period: Oct 2005–Feb 2007; No. of Firm: 36; No. of Observations: 482)

	Mean	Median	Maximum	Minimum	Std. Dev.
PREM	1.6314	1.3090	5.2733	0.7702	0.7936
LQ (A-shares)	0.0062	0.0049	0.0421	0.0002	0.0056
LQ (H-shares)	0.0089	0.0069	0.1000	0.0003	0.0087
SP (1) (A-shares in mn)	541.8	217.8	7183.3	50.0	941.8
SP (1) (H-shares in mn)	2363.0	747.4	65553.4	62.1	7613.7
SP (2) (A-shares in mn)	8207.8	1433.2	250962.3	208.1	29879.8
SP (2) (H-shares in mn)	2920.8	747.5	83056.5	75.1	10954.1
Risk (A-shares, %)	41.3	38.6	172.9	15.3	15.3
Risk (H-shares, %)	40.1	36.9	150.6	0.0	16.1
INFO (1) (A-shares in HKD mn)	3581.0	1504.3	80663.8	124.4	7881.4
INFO (1) (H-shares in HKD mn)	10632.0	2806.3	309070.6	78.4	32404.8
INFO (2) (A-shares in HKD mn)	42833.4	8187.3	1395231.0	629.8	144623.1
INFO (2) (H-shares in HKD mn)	12906.8	2929.7	391593.3	78.4	44465.3
Shanghai Stock Index	1795.0	1689.4	3000.9	1157.8	575.3
Hang Seng Index	17144.1	16661.3	20106.4	14386.4	1811.6
Rate of renminbi Appreciation (%)	1.0030	1.0023	1.0088	0.9979	0.0026
Growth of China's Money Supply (%)	1.0139	1.0143	1.0273	1.0005	0.0079
Trade Balance[b]	1.2290	1.2163	1.4072	1.0469	0.0845

Notes:
a. All figures are not log-transformed in the table.
b. It is the ratio of export over import.

Table 10.5

General Features of the Data[a]

(Sample Period: Apr 2000–Feb 2007; No. of Firm: 36; No. of Observations: 2039)

	Mean	Median	Maximum	Minimum	Std. Dev.
PREM	3.7200	2.6771	26.9855	0.7702	3.6536
LQ (A-shares)	0.0036	0.0022	0.0421	0.0000	0.0041
LQ (H-shares)	0.0095	0.0067	0.1126	0.0002	0.0097
SP (2) (A-shares in mn)	4989.8	990.5	250962.3	208.1	18263.8
SP (2) (H-shares in mn)	1699.0	433.2	83056.5	75.1	6045.5
Risk (A-shares, %)	36.8	34.9	172.9	10.2	13.6
Risk (H-shares, %)	47.6	43.1	168.0	0.0	21.6
INFO (2) (A-shares in HKD mn)	24411.2	6970.4	1395231.0	513.2	83050.9
INFO (2) (H-shares in HKD mn)	5577.9	1357.7	391593.3	30.0	23434.2
Shanghai Stock Index	1675.0	1612.3	3000.9	1095.4	392.0
Hang Seng Index	13537.0	13516.9	20106.4	8634.5	2910.9
Rate of renminbi Appreciation (%)	1.0010	1.0005	1.0088	0.9938	0.0030
Growth of China's Money Supply (%)	1.0128	1.0130	1.0296	0.9979	0.0080
Trade Balance[b]	1.1253	1.1139	1.4072	0.8127	0.0967

Notes:

a. All figures are not log-transformed in the table.

b. It is the ratio of export over import.

4. EMPIRICAL RESULTS

Equation (1) is estimated by the generalised method of moments (GMM) so that it can avoid any bias when variables are endogenous.[17] Two regression models, Models A and B, are estimated. Model A is (1) using SP(1) and INF(1) as the supply and information asymmetry variables respectively and is estimated for the period from October 2005 to February 2007.[18] Model B is the same as Model A except that SP(2) and INF(2) are used as the supply and information asymmetry variables respectively. Given that more data are available for SP(2) and INF(2), Model B is estimated for a longer period from April 2000 to February 2007. Both models have their advantages because Model A contains variables that are arguably more able to capture the effects of supply and information asymmetry, while Model B covers a longer period.

The estimation results are reported in Table 10.6. The Portmanteau test statistics show that the residuals of the two models have insignificant serial correlation, suggesting that both models are adequately fitted.[19] The coefficients have same signs in both models, except that information asymmetry in Model B is found to be different from that in Model A. Our key findings for each variable are discussed below.

On the five popular factors identified from the literature

- The price premium is positively related to the relative liquidity of A-shares over H-shares (LQ). This finding suggests that a more liquid A-share (H-share) market tends to increase (reduce) the price premium and vice versa. This is consistent with the theoretical prediction—that investors tend to demand a smaller

---

17. In the estimation, we transform equation (1) into first differences with the "white period GMM weight" which provides correct estimates of the coefficient covariances in the presence of heteroskedasticity of unknown form.

18. Such information is only available since October 2005.

19. All residuals of Model A have insignificant correlations at a 0.05 level of significance. In Model B, all but two firms' residuals have insignificant correlations at a 0.05 level of significance. The two firms are found to have significant correlations among residuals because there were some violent fluctuations during early 2000. As the majority of the firms have already passed the Portmanteau test and the hypotheses for two firms are just marginally rejected, no dummy variable is introduced in the model.

Table 10.6

Determinants of Price Premium: GMM Estimates

Variable	Model A Oct 2005 – Feb 2007 Coeff.	Model B Apr 2000 – Feb 2007 Coeff.
LQ	0.0417***	0.0322***
SP(1)	-0.0779**	
SP(2)		-0.2081***
RK	0.0300**	0.0051
INF(1)	-0.1227***	
INF(2)		0.0728*
MC	0.3300***	0.3478***
CUR	-4.8083***	-1.8233***
M2	0.7166***	0.5178***
TR	-0.0164	-0.0008
PREM(t-1)	0.1911***	0.2931***
Portmanteau test statistics Q(6) for all stocks [2,3]	4.9, 4.5, 5.7, 5.0, 12.0, 1.5, 7.0, 3.8, 10.5, 4.3, 6.2, 7.2, 4.6, 3.9, 4.4, 4.8, (X), 4.0, 1.8, 6.4, 7.1, (X), 2.8, 2.4, 5.7, 5.9, 2.0, 3.2, 2.1, 7.5, 11.8, 7.9, 4.2, 4.5, 6.5, 2.5.	4.6, 5.2, 8.9, 5.1,10.6, 1.2, 4.4, 2.4, 9.3, 9.8, 9.9, 12.2, 1.9, 12.4, 3.3, 10.3, (X), 16.6, 5.9, 2.1, 6.2, (X), 5.3, 8.7, 4.9, 7.9, 2.0, 2.2, 2.2, 8.2, 7.0, 2.7, 2.5, 18.5, 9.5, 3.7.
No. of stocks	36	36
No. of obs.	482	2039

Notes:

1. ***, ** and * denote significance at the 1 percent, 5 percent and 10 percent levels respectively.

2. The Portmanteau test, Q(K), checks whether residuals of each firm are jointly zero correlated up to lag K. At 0.05 and 0.01 levels of significance, the critical values are 12.6 and 16.8 respectively. Their corresponding stocks (tickers) are: 1108, 553, 42, 719, 1033, 588, 187, 350, 670, 1065, 874, 338, 358, 1055, 317, 386, 525, 300, 1072, 753, 3988, 991, 763, 177, 323, 1171, 1398, 168, 548, 914, 1071, 1138, 995, 347, 902, 3968.

3. (X) denotes that the corresponding stocks are deleted due to missing information in the final estimation.

(larger) compensation for lower (higher) trading cost associated with a more (less) liquid market—as well as the findings in other empirical studies.[20]

- The price premium is found to be negatively associated with the relative supply of A-shares over H-shares (SP) in Model A. This result highlights the relative scarcity of A- over H-shares as an important factor in explaining the price premium, reflecting the lack of substitutes for stock investment on the Mainland.

- The price premium is positively related to the relative risk ratio (RK) in both models. This result supports the differential risk hypothesis, which postulates that the price premium can be explained by the relative riskiness of the assets because the A- and H- share investors have different risk profiles. Market commentaries often suggest that Mainland investors are more speculative, i.e., having a higher risk appetite or being less risk averse, and hence may be more willing to pay a higher price for an asset at the same level of risk. On the other hand, Hong Kong and international investors tend to be relatively more risk-averse. Our estimation finds the price premium to be larger for stocks with a higher price volatility in their A-shares than in their H-shares.

- Our results provide some but limited support for the information asymmetry (INF) hypothesis. This hypothesis states that price disparity can be explained by information asymmetry, which can be caused by factors such as availability of reliable information, speed of information flows, language barriers and different accounting standards. Information asymmetry may result in a certain group of investors being disadvantaged and thus less willing to pay. Many studies in the literature employ firm size as a proxy for asymmetric information because larger firms tend to have better information disclosure and attract more analysts

---

20. Chen *et al* (2001), Wang and Li (2003) and Chan and Kwok (2005) find a positive relationship between A-share price premium and relative trading volume/turnover rates of A- over H-shares. The results of Guo and Tang (2006) show a negative relationship between A-share price premium and the relative bid-ask spread of A-H shares – a more liquid market tends to have narrower spreads.

to study their stocks. In Model A, the results for the more recent period show that a larger firm tends to have a lower price disparity. However, Model B yields an opposite outcome. This may suggest that information asymmetry has become a relevant factor only recently, possibly attributable to the listing of some very large firms during 2006.

- Market conditions (MC) is found to be positively significant in both models. The stock market indices of the Mainland and Hong Kong are used as proxies for market conditions, to capture the effects of both market sentiment and general economic conditions, which in turn can have an impact on corporate performance.[21]

On the effects of the macroeconomic imbalance

- Renminbi revaluation or appreciation (CUR) has a negative relationship with the price premium. Appreciation or expected appreciation of the renminbi increases the value of renminbi-denominated assets in US dollars. Given current capital controls of the Mainland, H-shares remain the most direct and convenient way for foreign investors to acquire Mainland or renminbi-income-generated assets. Therefore, H-share prices should reflect the effect of renminbi appreciation on the firm's future earnings. The results suggest that an appreciation or expected appreciation of the currency induces H-share purchases, thus squeezing the price premium.[22]

- Money supply (M2) is found to be positively related to the price premium.[23] As the macroeconomic imbalance grows, money supply grows. The range of financial products available for

---

21. Based on historical data, the pairwise correlation between the changes in the H-share prices and the changes in the Heng Sang Index is 0.15, while that between the changes in the H-share prices and the changes in the Shanghai Stock Index is 0.21. These figures suggest that both markets' investment environment may somewhat affect the H-share prices. Better Hong Kong stock market conditions may stimulate market sentiment and provide more incentives for investors to buy discounted H-share stocks so that the price premium will narrow.

22. Note that the A-shares can only be traded by Mainland investors.

23. Bank deposits, including demand deposits, time deposits and saving deposits, were also considered in the initial estimations. All results were of similar flavour.

investment or savings is, however, very limited on the Mainland. With deposit rates kept very low for a long time, stocks have become an increasingly attractive investment option. The macroeconomic imbalance has thus indirectly contributed to the demand for local stocks, which have translated into higher A-share prices and large premiums over H-shares. Our results here simply confirm a widely-observed phenomenon.

- The trade balance (TR) is estimated to be negative, though the coefficients are insignificant. It is common knowledge that trade flows are often used to camouflage capital flows in the presence of capital controls. The trade surplus, which can capture the opportunities of Mainlanders to keep their foreign exchange earnings outside the country, is used here to proxy the ability of Mainland investors to arbitrage the price differentials of dual-listed A-H stocks in the H-share market. As a result, a rising trade surplus has the effect of lifting the price of H-shares, thus reducing the A-share price premium. The insignificant coefficient may, however, suggest that despite the large trade surplus the impact of Mainland investors on H-share prices remains limited.

- The coefficient of lagged price premium is estimated to be less than unity, indicating that share price differentials were partially adjusted over the period when other variables are kept constant.

5. FINAL REMARKS

Dual-listed A- and H-shares came into being as soon as the Mainland authorities allowed Mainland companies to be listed in the Hong Kong stock market in the early 1990s. For more than a decade there has existed a persistent premium of the A-share over the H-share for the same stock. Initially, dual-listed A- and H- shares were mostly small Mainland companies, but the last two years saw phenomenal growth of this market segment following the listing of some very large companies. As a result, the A-H share price disparity has attracted increasing attention and debates, not only among financial market participants, but also in policy circles.

This paper has examined the relevance of five micro factors identified from the literature to explain stock price disparity in determining the A-H share price premium. Consistent with most previous studies on the overseas emerging markets and the Chinese markets, our findings suggest that four of the five micro factors—namely, market liquidity, shares supply, risk level and market conditions—are important determinants of the premium. We have also studied the impact of the growing imbalance of the Mainland macroeconomy on the A-H share premium. Our results show that macroeconomic factors (renminbi appreciation expectations and monetary expansion) contributed to the A-H share price disparity through affecting the prices of A-shares, but their influence on the prices of the H-shares was insignificant. This finding is consistent with the earlier observation that the A-shares have a smaller Divisia variance than do the H-shares. Therefore, the common forces behind the implied more synchronised A-share price movements can possibly be attributed to these macroeconomic factors.[24]

On policy implications, the fact that the micro factors are found to be important determinants of the price premium implies that there exists significant room for improvements in price discovery and market efficiency. For instance, the A-share market liquidity, which averaged about only 40% of the H-share market liquidity in the period from April 2000 to February 2007, is bound to increase—thereby lowering the transaction cost—if arbitrage or participation by investors from the H-share market is allowed or relaxed. The finding that the macro factors are also found to have contributed to the price disparity suggests that any such mechanism or reform would be instrumental in alleviating the pressure on financial markets arising from the macroeconomic imbalance of the Mainland, making them less vulnerable to economic shocks.

Nonetheless, it is imperative to note that a mechanism or reform that allows investors of both or either of the markets to arbitrage the disparity will tend to equalise prices. This, in turn, means that a process

---

24. Note that this is not inconsistent with the finding of Miao and Peng (2007) that macroeconomic conditions are not significant factors explaining the relatively high volatility in the Mainland market. The Divisia variance measures the relative price changes, while volatility is a measure of absolute price changes. Theoretically, there can be extremely high volatility of share prices, but if these changes are of similar proportions, the resulting Divisia variance would remain small.

of risk sharing will necessarily take place between the two markets. To the H-share investor, therefore, the benefit is likely to come at the expense of greater market volatility, at least initially. Over the long term, however, a well-structured mechanism would probably be able to pull in additional liquidity and, other things being equal, a deeper overall market should be more conducive to financial stability.

Appendix 10

Price Disparity in the Gordon Growth Model

The disparity between the prices of the stocks dual-listed in the A- and H-shares markets can be considered in the context of the Gordon (1962) growth model. In the model, the intrinsic value of a common stock in perpetuity depends on the cash flow of dividends over the life of the stock. Based on information concerning the current and prospective profitability of the company, its fair market value is assessed by taking into account: (i) the constant growth rate of dividend per share, representing the growth of the earnings per share; and (ii) the discount rate, representing the appropriate risk-adjusted interest rate or the required return of investors on equity.[25]

Specifically, the prices of a dual-listed stock can be written as

$$P_A = \frac{E_0^A(1 + g_E)}{r_A - g_E} \qquad \text{(A1)}$$

and

$$P_H = \frac{E_0^H(1 + g_E)}{r_H - g_E} \qquad \text{(A2)}$$

where P_A and P_H, are the prices of the stock listed in the A- and H-share markets respectively; E_0^A and E_0^H are dividends denominated in the renminbi and Hong Kong dollar at the time zero respectively; g_E is the growth rate of dividend; and r_A and r_H are the required rates of return in the A- and H-shares markets respectively. Since E_0^H depend on E_0^A and the exchange rate of the Hong Kong dollar *vis-à-vis* the renminbi, equation (A2) can be expressed as:

$$P_H = \frac{E_0^A S_0(1 + g_E)(1 + g_s)}{(1 + r_H) - (1 + g_E)(1 + g_S)} \qquad \text{(A3)}$$

---

25. Specifically, the Gordon growth model can be represented by $D_0(1+g)/(r-g)$, where D_0, r and g are dividend at the initial period, required return rate of investors and the growth of dividend over the life of the selected firm respectively. In market equilibrium, the current market price will reflect the intrinsic value estimates of all market participants. If an individual investor whose estimate of price differs from the market price (P_A or P_H), in effect it must disagree with some or all of the market consensus estimates of D_0, g and/ or r. Note that the model assumes dividends to grow continuously at a constant rate over its life and assumes the growth rate to be less than the required rate on equity.

where S_0 and gs are the exchange rate of the Hong Kong dollar against the renminbi and the rate of renminbi appreciation respectively.[26] To compare the two prices, PA in equation (A1) is converted to

$$P_A^* = P_A S_0 = \frac{E_0^A S_0 (1 + g_E)}{r_A - g_E} \qquad (A4)$$

Using (A2) and (A4), the difference between the prices of the A- and H-share of a dual-listed stock, denominated in Hong Kong dollar, can be represented by:

$$\ln P_A^* - \ln P_H \approx \ln\left[\frac{r_H - g_E - g_s}{r_A - g_E}\right] \qquad (A5)$$

Under the theoretical framework of the Gordon growth model stated in equations from (A1) to (A5), the price disparity of the stock is reflected by (i) the different required rates of return of A- and H-shares investors; (ii) the appreciation of the renminbi; and (iii) the growth of dividends per share. Compared with our model specified in equation (1), the price disparity shown in equation (A5) suggests that:

- The micro and macro factors, including liquidity, supply, risk, information asymmetry, market conditions, money supply, and trade balance, can arguably influence the market consensus on the required rates of return in the two markets.

- Renminbi appreciation will result in a smaller price disparity, because a higher renminbi will, other things being equal, inflate the dividends denominated in Hong Kong dollars, hence lifting the price of the H-share.

- Given different required rates of return, A- and H-shareholders will respond differently to the same rate of growth of dividends of the same firm in perpetuity. However, all selected factors discussed in the paper are considered to have less impact on the payout policy and capital structure of the firm as long as dividend changes follow shifts in long-run sustainable earnings.

---

26. The prices of the H-shares specified in equation (A3) are assumed to increase with the renminbi appreciation in the long run. It is reflected by incorporating $S_0(1+g_s)$ into the equation (A2) to value the prices of stocks in perpetuity. Specifically, P_H can be represented by the sum to infinity:

$$\sum_{t=1}^{\infty} E_0^A S_0 (1+g_E)^t (1+g_s)^t / (1+r_H)^t$$

REFERENCES

Amihud, Y. and Mendelson, H., 1986, "Asset Pricing Aivd the Bid-ask Spread," *Journal of Financial Economics* 17, 223–249.

Bailey, W., 1994, "Risk and Return on China's New Stock Markets: Some Preliminary Evidence," *Pacific-Basin Finance Journal* 2, 243–260.

Chakravarty, S., Sarkar, A. and Wu, L., 1998, "Information Asymmetry, Market Segmentation and the Pricing of Cross-listed Shares: Theory and Evidence from Chinese A and B Shares," *Journal of International Financial Markets, Institutions and Money* 8, 325–356.

Chan, K. L. and Kwok, K. H., 2005, "Market Segmentation and Share Price Premium: Evidence from Chinese Stock Markets," *Journal of Emerging Market Finance* 4:1.

Chen, G. M., Lee, B. and Rui, O., 2001, "Foreign Ownership Restrictions and Market Segmentation in China's Stock Markets," *Journal of Financial Research* 24, 133–155.

Divisia, F., 1925, "L'Indice Monétaire et la Théorie de la Monnaie," *Revue d' Economie Politique* 39, 980–1008.

Domowitz, I, J. Glen and A. Madhavan, 1997, "Market Segmentation and Stock Prices: Evidence from an Emerging Market," *Journal of Finance* 52, 1059–1085.

Fung, H., Lee, W. and Leung, W. K., 2000, Segmentation of the A- and B-share Chinese Equity Markets," *Journal of Financial Research* 23, 179–195.

Gordon, Myron J., 1962. *The Investment, Financing, and Valuation of the Corporation.* Homewood, Ill.: R.D. Irwin.

Guo, L., and Tang, L., 2006, "Cost of Capital and Liquidity of Cross-Listed Chinese Companies," presented at Financial Management Association, Salt Lake City, Utah.

Hsiao, C., 1986, *Analysis of Panel Data*, Cambridge University Press, Cambridge.

Miao, H. and Peng, W., 2007, "Why A-share Market Volatility is High?, *China Economic Issues*, June, 6/07.

Ma, X., 1996, "Capital Controls, Market Segmentation and Stock Prices: Evidence from the Chinese Stock Market," *Pacific-Basin Finance Journal* 4, 219–239.

Ng, L. and Wu, F., 2007, "The Trading Behavior of Institutions and Individuals in Chinese Equity Markets," *Journal of Banking and Finance*, forthcoming.

Peng, W., Miao, H. and Chow, N., 2007, "Price Convergence between Dual-listed A and H Shares," *China Economic Issues*, July, 6/07.

Su, D. and Fleisher, B. M., 1999, "Why Does Return Volatility Differ in Chinese Stock Markets?" *Pacific-Basin Finance Journal* 7, 557–586.

Sun, Q. and Tong, W. H. S., 2000, "The Effect of Market Segmentation on Stock Prices: The China Syndrome," *Journal of Banking & Finance* 24, 1875–1902.

Wang, S. Y. and Li, J., 2003, "Location of Trade, Ownership Restriction, and Market Illiquidity: Examining Chinese A- and H-Shares," *Journal of Banking and Finance*, Forthcoming.

Chapter 11

Price Convergence between Dual-listed A and H Shares

Wensheng PENG
Hui MIAO
Nathan CHOW

1. INTRODUCTION

Dual-listed Mainland China shares now account for about 10% of tradable Mainland stock market capitalisation and 11% of Hong Kong stock market capitalisation. As more Mainland China companies choose to adopt the dual-listing model, this type of stocks is likely to command an increasing share of the markets. One somewhat disconcerting feature is large persistent price differentials observed. As of early June 2007, for dual-listed companies, A-shares enjoyed a premium over their H-share counterparts ranging from 10% to 260%, with a market capitalisation-weighted average of over 50%.

Such large price gaps for the two types of shares that enjoy the same voting rights and dividend payments highlight the segmentation of the two capital markets within China, and raise questions about the efficiency of price discovery and resource allocation in these markets. Calls have been made in both Hong Kong and the Mainland for measures to strengthen the linkages between the two markets, with a view to reducing the price gaps and developing an integrated financial market to help sustain the rapid economic growth in China (Yam, 2007a&b, and Fan 2007).

There are research efforts in understanding factors contributing to the price gaps (Chan and Kwok, 2005). Restrictions on foreign investor access to A-shares and Mainland investor access to H-shares, coupled with the relatively small supply of A-shares, are often found to be the main reasons explaining the price differentials. Almost all dual-listed Mainland companies have issued many more H-shares than A-shares, and Mainland investors by and large have no access to H-shares. The resulting differential demand and the scarcity of those stocks lead to the A-share premium.

Instead of investigating the causes, this Chapter studies the issue from a new perspective by considering the impact of the price gaps on A and H share price dynamics. With the dual-listed companies accounting for an increasing market share, it is important to understand and monitor the interactions between A and H share prices and their potential impact on the wider Mainland and Hong Kong stock markets. Are there signs of price convergence between A and H shares due to arbitrage activities through formal and informal channels? Do price premiums of A-shares over H-shares act as a constraining force on increase of A-share prices and likewise a pulling force on H-share prices? Or as some have argued, the segmentation of the markets has been exploited by some traders with an effect of exacerbating market volatility? This Chapter attempts to shed light on these questions by studying the price dynamics of 39 dual-listed companies using the panel data regression technique.

The rest of the Chapter is organised as follows. Section 2 provides some stylised facts on price movements of the dual-listed stocks and articulates various hypotheses on the dynamic relationship between the A and H shares of dual-listed companies. Section 3 presents the econometric models used to investigate the impact of price gaps on stock price dynamics and provides the empirical results. Section 4 concludes with remarks on policy implications.

2. STYLISED FACTS AND COMPETING HYPOTHESES

2.1 Data and stylised facts

As of early June 2007, there were 44 A and H dual-listed stocks, and our study covers 39 of these companies.[1] The data used in this study was obtained from Bloomberg. The sample consists of daily observations on closing prices of the 39 dual-listed firms from 22 July, 2005 to 8 June, 2007, with total panel data observations of 13,837. The panel dataset is imbalanced as dates of the initial public offering (IPO) of these companies were different. The selection of July 2005 as the starting point of the sample period is based on the following considerations. The reform of the renminbi exchange rate regime on 21 July 2005 and the share desegregation reform initiated in mid-2005, are considered to be major structural changes affecting investor confidence and the development of the Mainland stock market.[2] Furthermore, some large

---

1. H-shares of two companies have been suspended for trading since June 2005 and October 2006, and as a result, the A and H share price differentials are now exceedingly large. Three other companies had their A-share IPOs only in May 2007. Including these stocks in the empirical study would distort the results.

2. In particular, the share desegregation reform cleared investors' concern about the overhang of the large number of nontradable shares held by the government. The reform also helps to align the interests of majority and minority share holders, and thus alleviates concerns on corporate governance.

financial firms have been listed only since 2005, and the imbalance of the panel would be a greater concern if the starting point was selected to be a much earlier date. For comparison purpose, A-share prices were converted in Hong Kong dollar terms using the spot exchange rate between the renminbi and the Hong Kong dollar.

The dual-listed companies are from diverse industry sectors, and there is a wide cross-sectional variation in the A-share price premium as shown in Appendix 11. Table 11.1 presents some stylised facts about the 39 dual-listed stocks. These stocks represent a significant proportion of trading activities in both Mainland and Hong Kong markets. During the sample period, the dual-listed stocks accounted for 13% and 18% respectively of the Mainland and Hong Kong stock market turnover. On a weighted-average basis (using market capitalisations as weights), the A-share prices of dual-listed companies rose by 161% during the sample period, compared to 71% for relevant H-shares. Reflecting this, dual-listed A-shares are valued much higher than their H-share counterparts with a weighted average P/E of 47 compared to 27. In the meantime, A-share prices were almost twice more volatile than the corresponding H-share prices.[3]

Table 11.1

Performance of Dual-listed Stocks Relative to Market Index

(Weighted by Market Capitalisation)

	Dual-Listed A-shares	CSI 300 Index	Dual-Listed H-shares	HSI Index
Turnover (% of total market volume)	13	–	18	–
Market Capitalisation (% of total market cap.)	10	–	11	–
P/E ratio	48	45	29	16
Price appreciation (%)	161	365	71	41
Volatility (%)	24	51	14	12

Note: P/E, price appreciation and volatility are calculated on a weighted average basis, using market capitalisation of individual companies as weight.

Source: Bloomberg and authors' estimate, sample period from July 22, 2005 to June 8, 2007

---

3. Hui and Peng (2007) argue that factors including the structure of the investor base, sectoral concentration of the listed companies and trading mechanism explain the relatively high volatility in A-share prices.

A-shares of dual-listed comapnies on average underperformed the overall A-share market but was also less volatile (as compared with the CSI 300 index). In contrast, H-shares of dual-listed companies on average outperformed the Hang Seng index and were more volatile. Specifically, almost all dual-listed H-shares outperformed the Hang Seng Index in terms of price increase, while about 75% of the dual-listed A-shares underperformed the CSI 300 index. Therefore, these dual-listed stocks are somewhat "special" when measured against the peers in their respective home markets. A natural question is how price movements of dual-listed A and H shares may interact with each other.

2.2   Arbitrage and price convergence hypothesis

A and H shares of dual-listed companies are of the same voting rights and dividend payments. However, foreigners can not legally purchase A-shares outside the qualified foreign institutional investor (QFII) schemes, and formal channels of overseas portfolio investment by domestic residents are restricted to qualified domestic institutional investor (QDII) schemes. This type of ownership restriction is common in emerging markets, and generally leads to market segmentation and price differentials.

Until the recent liberalisation of the scope of QDII investment, private portfolio investment flows through the formal channels between the Mainland and Hong Kong were quite limited. However, there are other channels through which A and H share prices can be related, and interactions may limit the size of the price gaps. There are reports of Mainland and Hong Kong investors shifting funds through informal channels to trade H and A shares. The size of such trading is difficult to gauge, and A and H shares of dual-listed companies are not fungible, thus any arbitrage involved is partial and incomplete. Nevertheless, such activities should help limit the price differentials at the margin. Furthermore, for long-term value investors on the Mainland, the H-share valuation, which is determined in an open international market, would serve as an important benchmark and influence their investment decisions. These arguments support a general convergence hypothesis under which price gaps between A and H shares induce trading activities that buy relatively low-valued shares and sell high-valued shares of the same company, leading to a long-run trend of price convergence.

Figure 11.1

Relative Performance of Dual-listed Stocks against Market Indice

(Annualised Return, Sample Period: 7/2005–5/2007)

Dual-listed A-shares over CSI 300 index

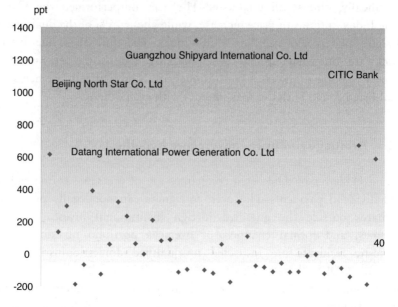

Dual-listed H-shares over HSI

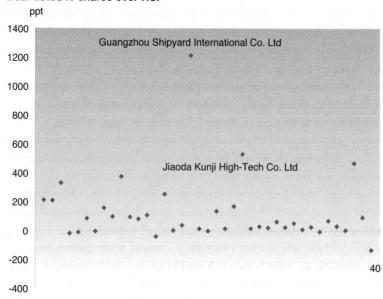

Source: Bloomberg and authors' estimate

2.3   Differential demand, information asymmetry and price divergence hypothesis

An alternative hypothesis stresses the differential demand for A and H shares due to capital account controls, and a divergence A and H share prices. Under this hypothesis, a given price gap would not have significant impact on the dynamics of the A and H share prices of dual-listed companies. Furthermore, there are reports that the segmentation of the two markets and differential demand have been exploited by some for hedging and speculative trading, which work against the force of arbitrage activities.

First, as stock index future trading is not allowed on the Mainland, the H-share index can be used as a proxy for hedging. Specifically, investors who have access to both markets can buy A-shares and sell the H-shares index futures at the same time to hedge against the downside risk. Other things being equal, this would raise the price differentials. The key to the success of this strategy is strong correlation between high frequency changes of A-share and H-share prices of dual-listed companies.

Another trading strategy that could cause price divergence takes advantage of the difference in price elasticity of Mainland and international investors. The demand by Mainland investors is less price elastic than the international investor demand, partly because of the scarcity of A-shares. The reported trading strategy is to acquire H-shares of a dual-listed company first (with limited impact on prices owing to the market depth), and use a relatively small order to push up A-share prices (as A-share market is shallower). It is hoped that the increase of A-share prices and the resulting wider price gap over corresponding H-shares would induce buying interest from international investors in the respective H-shares. The trading profits arise mainly from the H-share position, but A-share prices probably need to rise by much more than corresponding H-share prices in order to achieve the pulling effect.

Information asymmetry between local and overseas investors might also play a role. For large companies, there are much research and analysis of their business prospects and valuation, and international investors are unlikely to be disadvantaged. However, it is argued that domestic investors are better informed about the business prospects of the relatively small dual-listed Mainland companies. In this case, movements of A-share prices would lead those of corresponding H-share prices, with persistent price gaps as information asymmetry is resolved slowly. This argument of information asymmetry suggests that the above-noted speculation trading strategy has a higher chance of success in the case of shares of relatively small capitalisations. This is because for the small companies, the signalling effect of A-share price movements to H-share price is stronger as foreign investors have limited independent information.

Both the convergence and divergence hypotheses suggest that under the current restrictions on capital account transactions, the large price differentials between A and H shares would induce cross-border fund flows through informal channels. While some of these trading activities are for arbitrage purposes, the persistently large price gaps in recent periods raise questions about the significance of this force. Some participants take advantage of the segmentation of the A and H share markets and adopt trading strategies that may exacerbate volatility in both markets. This would not facilitate healthy development of the capital market of China as a whole. It is thus useful to assess the significance of these competing hypotheses in practice, and this is the task of the next section.

3. EMPIRICAL ANALYSIS

Two types of empirical tests are conducted. One is to test for unit roots in A and H share price differentials. The non-existence of a unit root suggests that the price differentials are stationary, and that A and H share prices have a trend of convergence. The estimated coefficient would have implications on the speed of convergence. A regression is also run to test whether A and H share price gaps have significant impact on price changes of A and H shares respectively, after controlling for changes in the overall market conditions.

3.1   Panel unit root test

As the univariate unit-root test often fails to reject the null of a unit root when it is in fact false, due to its low power, one way that researchers have confronted this problem is to exploit the cross sectional dimension of data. Panel data can dramatically increase the power of the unit-root test, and in contrast to the univariate case, the test statistic in a panel context is asymptotically normal. In this study, the following equation is estimated on panel data of price gaps of the A and H shares of 39 dual-listed companies.

$$\Delta q_{i,t} = \alpha_i + \beta q_{i,t-1} + \sum_{n=1}^{N} \varphi_n \Delta q_{i,t-n} + \varepsilon_{i,t} \tag{1}$$

Where $q_{i,t}$, is the logarithm of the A-H-share price differential for dual-listed stock i at time t , and Δ is the first difference operator. The length of lags N, used to account for possible serial correlation in the error term as in a univariate augmented Dickey-Fuller test, can be determined by Campbell and Perron (1991)'s top-down t-test approach, which involves initially specifying a sufficiently long length of lags to the extent permitted by data and then sequentially eliminating the lags that are not significant. Central to the test of convergence is the estimated value of β. If $\beta \geq 0$, the price gap $q_{i,t}$ is non-stationary, implying persistent or explosive price divergence. A negative value of β suggests price convergence, and its magnitude indicates the speed of convergence. Specifically, the half-life of a shock to the price differential is computed as $-\ln(2)/\ln(1+\beta)$. The estimated value of α_i can be used to test the hypothesis of long-run price equalisation. A value of α_i not significantly different from zero suggests that the price gap has a zero mean and A and H share prices of dual-listed stock i will eventually be equalised. On the other hand, a value of αi being significantly positive suggests that the A-share price of dual-listed stock i will be persistently higher than its corresponding H-share price. Thus, the case of $\beta < 0$ and $\alpha = 0$ can be called absolute price convergence (i.e. long-term price equalisation), while the case of $\beta < 0$ and $\alpha > 0$ can be termed relative price convergence (where price differentials will not diverge persistently from a certain level α).

Using the critical values established by Levin and Lin (1992), the null hypothesis of a unit root for price differentials ($\beta=0$) is rejected (Table 11.2). The estimate of α is positive and significantly different from zero, however. This suggests that price differentials are stationary around a non-zero mean. In other words, a shock that raises the price differential

Table 11.2
Price Gap and Rate of Relative Price Convergence
(Sample Period 25/07/2005–08/06/2007)

	All firms	H-share index constituents	Non - H-share index constituents
α	0.770*	0.329*	1.204*
	(10.972)	(6.384)	(8.553)
β	-0.017*	-0.015*	-0.018*
	(-10.702)	(-6.132)	(-8.479)
φ_1	-0.011	-0.069*	0.022**
	(-1.336)	(-5.769)	(1.989)
φ_2	-0.043*	-0.041*	-0.047*
	(-5.475)	(-3.665)	(-4.290)
Half-life (days)	40	47	37
Adjusted R^2	0.008	0.011	0.010
D-W statistaics	1.999	2.002	1.997
Number of observations	15148	7057	8091

Note: t-values are in ( ), ** and * indicate that coefficients are significant at the 5% and 1% levels respectively.

Source: Authors' estimate

will gradually die out and A and H share prices converge to a long-term average gap. The estimate of β suggests that a divergence from the long-term average price gap would dissipate by one half in about 40 trading days.

Unit root test is also conducted by dividing the sample into H-share index constituent stocks and non-constituent stocks. The index constituent stocks are generally of relatively large capitalisation and their price dynamics may be different from that of stocks of small capitalisation. The large-cap stocks are generally less subject to information asymmetry issue noted above, and the long-term valuations of H and A shares are likely to be closer to each other than in the case of small-cap stocks. Two observations are made. First, the estimate of α is much smaller for the index component stocks than for non-component stocks, consistent with the observation that the A and H share price gaps of large-cap stocks are generally smaller than those of small-cap stocks. Specifically, the average price gap for the index constituent stocks is estimated to be 33%, while that for the non-constituent stocks is 120%.

Second, the estimate of β suggests that the speed of convergence following a shock to the long-term average is faster in the case of non-index constituent stocks than the constituent stocks. Specifically, half of the impact of a shock to the price gap will die out in 37 trading days for the non-index component stocks, and in 47 trading days for the component stocks. This may reflect the fact that small-cap stocks generally have larger price gaps which tend to induce stronger force of arbitrage activities.

3.2 Impact of price gaps on A and H share price dynamics

To examine how a given price differential may affect price dynamics of A and H shares respectively, the following regression model is employed.

$$\Delta p_{i,t} = \alpha_i + \beta q_{i,t-1} + \gamma index_t + \varepsilon_{i,t} \qquad (2)$$

Where $p_{i,t}$ is the logarithm of daily closing price of dual-listed A-share (or H-share) at time t. $q_{i,t}$ is the daily A and H share price differential of stock i at time t as defined above. The lagged $q_{i,t}$ is included to examine the impact of the price gap yesterday on A and H share price movements today. Under the convergence hypothesis, the estimate of β should be negative for A-share price and positive for H-share price, as the A-share premium would act as a constraining force on A-share price and pulling force on H-share prices so that the price gap would be stationary. A and H share price changes are affected by the overall market developments as well. To control for this, the daily percentage changes of CSI 300 index and Hang Seng index are included in the A-share and H-share equations respectively (computed as log differences of the index and denoted as $index_t$). α_i is the individual effect and ε_t is the disturbance term.

The panel data regression is employed. Besides increasing the degree of freedom, the panel data technique reduces potential collinearity between the explanatory variables and improves efficiency of estimation. The estimation is based on the two-factor fixed effects model with both individual and time-specific effects. Individual effects take into account the specificity of individual firms reflected in its price premium, while time effects consider the overall market effect on all stocks.

Table 11.3

Price Gap and A- and H- Share Price Dynamics (Linear Model)

	Full sample (22/07/2005–08/06/2007)		Sub-sample (22/07/2005–29/12/2006)		Sub-sample (05/01/2007–08/06/2007)	
	A	H	A	H	A	H
α	0.457*	-0.268*	0.528*	-0.260*	1.415*	-0.302
	(7.595)	(-4.684)	(7.241)	(-3.805)	(6.867)	(-1.570)
β	-0.012*	0.009*	-0.016*	0.007*	-0.027*	0.013*
	(-8.599)	(6.804)	(-8.438)	(4.144)	(-6.814)	(3.487)
γ	0.947*	0.819*	0.964*	0.730*	0.916*	0.972*
	(68.630)	(49.999)	(49.619)	(40.458)	(41.189)	(27.957)
Adjusted R²	0.260	0.157	0.213	0.143	0.323	0.182
D-W statistaics	1.757	1.838	1.874	1.935	1.583	1.738
Number of observations	13824	13837	10107	10060	3717	3777

Note: t-values are in ( ), * indicates that coefficients are significant at 1% level.

Source: Authors' estimate

Equation (2) is first estimated for the whole sample from July 2005 to June 2007. The estimated β for A- and H-shares are of the expected signs and statistically significant, consistent with the general arbitrage hypothesis (Table 11.3). That is, the A-share price premium tends to reduce A-share price, but raise the corresponding H-share price, after controlling for the effect of the overall market conditions.

It is observed that the price gaps increased sharply in the first half of 2007, reflecting the rally in the A-share market. To examine whether there is a notable change in the relationship, the sample period is split into two: one is from 22 July 2005 to the end of 2006, and the other is from the beginning of 2007 to 8 June 2007. The results presented in the last two columns of Table 11.3 suggest that the pushing down and pulling up effects on A and H share prices respectively of a given price gap increased in the first half of 2007 as the price gaps rose to a high level. Taking the estimates literally, a price gap of 10% today would reduce A-share price by 0.16% the next trading day during the period up to the end of 2006, but by 0.27% in the first half of 2007. Likewise, the same size of the price gap would increase the H-share price by 0.07% in the first part of the sample period, and by 0.13% in the first half of 2007.

Table 11.4

Price Gap and A- and H- Share Price Dynamics (Nonlinear Model)

(Sample Period 22/07/2005–08/06/2007)

	A	H	H
α	0.559*	-0.176*	-0.196
	(8.912)	(-2.935)	(-4.828)
β_1	-0.023*	-0.001	–
	(-9.512)	(-0.445)	–
β_2	1.2E-04*	1.0E-04*	9.3E-05
	(5.652)	(5.120)	(8.509)
γ	0.947*	0.819*	0.819
	(68.705)	(50.018)	(50.018)
Adjusted R^2	0.262	0.158	0.158
D-W statistaics	1.757	1.838	1.838
Number of observations	13824	13837	13837

Note: t-values are in ( ), * indicates that coefficients are significant at 1% level.

Source: Authors' estimate

This suggests that there is probably a nonlinear effect whereby a larger price gap would induce more arbitrage activities through either formal or informal channels.

To capture the possible nonlinear effect, a term of the squared price gap is added in the regression:

$$\Delta p_{i,t} = \alpha_i + \beta_1 q_{i,t-1} + \beta_2 q_{i,t-1}^2 + \gamma index_t + \varepsilon_{i,t} \quad (3)$$

For the equation of A-share price, the size of the estimated coefficient on the squared price gap is small but statistically significant (Table 11.4). This suggests that an A-share price premium would reduce the A-share price at an increasing rate as the premium itself increases up to a threshold. This is consistent with the convergence hypothesis, and suggests that a larger price gap would induce greater arbitrage activities. However, beyond the threshold, the impact would start to decline. Based on the estimates of β_1 and β_2, Figure 11.2 plots the predicted nonlinear relationship between A-share price premium and A-share price growth rate. The threshold of the price gap that represents the turning point in

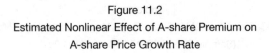

Figure 11.2
Estimated Nonlinear Effect of A-share Premium on
A-share Price Growth Rate

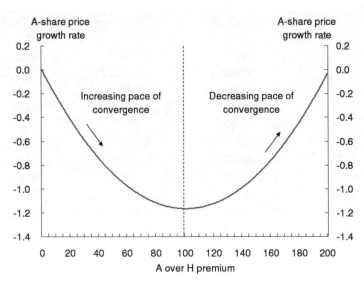

the nonlinear relationship is estimated at just above 100%.[4] Take the estimate literally, the first 20% price gap would reduce A-share price by 0.4% in the next trading day, compared with 1.17% in the case of 100% price gap, and 0.03% in the case of 200% price gap.

How to explain the puzzle of the nonlinear relationship? An examination of the data show that of the 39 stocks in the sample, 13 had a price gap exceeding 100% as of early May 2007, and only three of these were H-share index constituents. Our interpretation is that these mostly small cap stocks are more subject to speculative and other forces that work against the arbitrage force. As noted earlier, one possibility is the trading strategy which aims at driving up the A-share price to enlarge the A and H share price gap with a view to inducing a rise in H-share price and benefiting from the earlier acquired H-share position. This pushing-up effect on the A-share price tends to offset the

---

4. The slope of $q_{i,t-1}$ equation (3) can be obtained by taking the first derivative of $\Delta p_{i,t}$ with respect to $q_{i,t-1}$ $(\frac{\partial \Delta p_{i,t-1}}{\partial q_{i,t-1}} = \beta_1 + 2\beta_2 q_{i,t-1})$. The turning point is the level of $q_{i,t-1}$ that gives rise to $\beta_1 + 2\beta_2 q_{i,t-1}$.

Figure 11.3

Estimated Nonlinear Effect of A-share Premium on H-share Price Growth

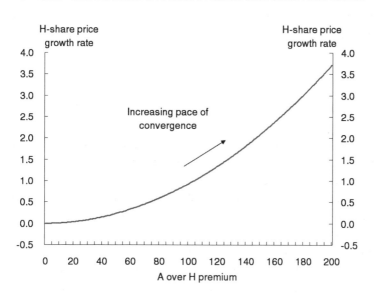

normal arbitrage that may be induced by the enlarged price gap. The relatively small supply of A-shares for the small cap companies makes it easier for speculators to move A-share prices. In addition, as the small cap companies are more subject to information asymmetry with the local investors enjoying an advantage, the signalling effect of the run-up in A-share prices to H-shares is stronger than in the case of large-cap companies.

For the equation on H-share price growth rate, the lagged price gap becomes insignificant after adding the squared price gap. The equation is re-estimated after dropping the insignificant variable and the results are presented in the last column of Table 11.4. The estimates suggest that as the A-share price premium increases, a given change in the price gap would have an increasing pulling up effect on H-share price. Specifically, the first 20% price gap would increase H-share price by 0.04%, compared with 0.93% when the price gap is 100% (Figure 11.3). This is consistent with the general convergence hypothesis where a larger price gap represents greater profit opportunity, inducing more arbitrage activities. However, this result also supports the speculative trading

311

strategy noted above. At high levels of A-share price premium (which are associated mostly with small-cap stocks), there are increasing pulling-up effect on the H-share price and decreasing pushing-down effect on the corresponding A-share price, benefiting the traders taking long positions in both shares.

4. CONCLUSION AND POLICY IMPLICATIONS

To our knowledge, this research is the first attempt to use econometric tools to document price convergence of dual-listed A- and H-shares and the impact of the price gaps on A and H share price dynamics. Based on the panel data of 39 dual-listed companies in Mainland and Hong Kong, this Chapter investigates the time series properties of the dual-listed A and H share price gaps, and their impact on the dynamics of A and H share prices in their respective markets. The panel unit root tests indicate that the A-H-share price differentials are stationary around a positive constant. This suggests relative price convergence (differentials do not persistently deviate from a certain level), but not absolute price convergence (no long-term price equalisation). Our estimates suggest that the simple average of the price gaps was 77% during the sample period of July 2005 to June 2007, and the time for a divergence from this gap to dissipate by one half is estimated at around 40 trading days.

Panel data regressions are also run to examine the impact of such price gaps on the dynamics of A and H share prices, using two-factor fixed-effect panel data models. The linear model estimates suggest that the well-documented A-share premium tends to reduce A-share price and raise the H-share price growth rate after controlling for changes in overall market conditions. This is consistent with the convergence hypothesis under which A-share price premium would increase the demand for H-shares and decrease the demand for A-shares, other things being equal. The estimates of the nonlinear suggest that the relationship is more complicated than what the linear model can capture. Specifically, below the threshold of a 100% price gap, an increase in the gap would have an increasing dampening effect on A-share prices, but beyond the threshold, the dampening effect would diminish. The pulling-up impact on H-share prices is also nonlinear, with an increasing force as the gap widens. This suggests that at high levels of the price gaps which are usually associated with small-cap stocks, the positive effect on H-share prices tends to be large while the negative effect on A-share prices tends to be small. This seems to provide evidence supportive of a reported speculative trading strategy that takes advantage of market segmentation and information asymmetry.

The findings have implications for policy thinking and discussion on the relationship between the Mainland and Hong Kong stock markets. First, there is evidence supporting the existence of investment activities that arbitrage on the price gaps. Owing to the restrictions on cross-border capital flows in and out of the Mainland, much of such arbitrage activities probably go through the informal channels. As the number of dual-listed companies increases over time, the size of such illicit capital flows would rise, complicating the authorities' analysis of fund flows and monitoring of associated risks.

Second, the segmentation of the markets with only partial and incomplete arbitrage seems to induce speculative activities that take advantage of the imbalanced supply of A and H shares of the dual-listed companies and information asymmetry between Mainland and international investors, particularly in relation to small-cap companies. Such activities work against the force of arbitrage and may increase volatility in both A and H share prices. Again, this concern will increase as the number of dual-listed companies rises. This would inhibit efficient price discovery, and also add to market volatility on both sides.

Our results support the case for furthering market integration between the Mainland and Hong Kong. By enhancing the linkages between dual-listed A- and H-shares through expansion of QDII/QFII schemes and other means of increasing convertibility between A and H shares including Exchange Traded Funds (ETF), the investors' access to both markets will be improved, enhancing the price convergence process. This would deter illicit cross border capital flows and speculation and manipulation of stock prices that add to market volatility, and help to promote the healthy development of the financial market of the whole country.

Appendix 11

A-share Price Premium of Dual-listed Stocks and Stock Ownership

		Ratio of outstanding A/H shares to total outstanding shares (%)		Share prices		Premiums (%)
		A	H	A	H	A over H
1	* Air China Ltd	9.5	36.0	10.8	6.0	79.7
2	* Angang Steel Co. Ltd	15.9	15.0	18.7	16.1	16.2
3	* Anhui Conch Cement Co. Ltd	16.8	27.7	56.2	43.9	28.0
4	Anhui Expressway Co. Ltd	18.1	29.7	9.3	6.8	37.8
5	* Bank of China Ltd	2.1	29.9	5.8	3.8	52.7
6	Beijing North Star co. Ltd	28.2	21.0	15.4	6.0	159.5
7	Beiren Printing Machinery Holdings Ltd	28.5	23.7	11.3	4.0	182.2
8	China Eastern Airlines Corporation Ltd	8.1	32.2	9.8	3.7	162.4
9	* China Life Insurance Co. Ltd	3.2	26.3	37.8	24.2	56.3
10	* China Merchants Bank Co. Ltd	32.0	18.1	22.2	20.2	10.0
11	* China Petroleum & Chemical Corporation	4.1	19.4	15.2	8.7	73.8
12	* China Shipping Development Co. Ltd	13.6	39.0	22.3	15.3	45.7
13	China Southern Airlines Co. Ltd	22.9	26.8	9.7	4.6	110.8
14	* Datang International Power Generation Co. Ltd	5.2	27.3	24.1	10.2	136.8
15	Dongfang Electrical Machinery Co. Ltd	16.9	37.8	53.4	34.5	54.7
16	* Guangshen Railway Co. Ltd	25.6	20.2	9.4	6.5	44.3
17	Guangzhou Pharmaceutical Co. Ltd	20.1	27.1	14.2	8.0	77.2
18	Guangzhou Shipyard International Co. Ltd	32.5	31.8	43.9	37.5	17.0
19	Huadian Power International Corporation Ltd.	12.3	23.8	11.3	4.1	175.3
20	* Huaneng Power International, Inc.	5.4	25.3	14.4	8.0	79.2
21	* Industrial and Commercial Bank of China Ltd	2.7	24.9	5.6	4.1	36.7
22	* Jiangsu Expressway Co. Ltd	6.0	24.3	9.4	7.5	25.7
23	* Jiangxi Copper Co. Ltd	9.8	47.9	26.0	12.5	107.8
24	Jiaoda Kunji High-Tech Co. Ltd	25.3	28.8	19.4	12.8	51.5
25	Jingwei Textile Machinery Co. Ltd	37.6	29.9	10.8	5.6	95.4
26	* Maanshan Iron & Steel Co. Ltd	12.5	26.8	9.1	6.1	49.5
27	Nanjing Panda Electronic Co. Ltd	12.0	36.9	11.2	4.1	175.6
28	Northeast Electric Development Co. Ltd	20.6	29.5	8.3	3.1	166.6
29	Shandong Xinhua Pharmaceutical Co. Ltd	26.1	32.8	9.2	3.2	185.3
30	Shenzhen Expressway Co. Ltd	10.0	34.3	10.0	6.2	62.3
31	* Sinopec Shanghai Petrochemical Co. Ltd	10.0	32.4	14.2	5.2	176.0
32	Sinopec Yizheng Chemical Fibre Co. Ltd	5.0	35.0	13.8	3.8	262.8
33	Tianjin Capital Environmental Protection co. Ltd	22.8	24.5	9.2	4.8	90.2
34	* Tsingtao Brewery Co. Ltd	18.0	50.1	25.7	19.2	34.1
35	* Yanzhou Coal Mining Co. Ltd	7.3	39.8	15.7	10.1	56.3
36	* ZTE Corporation	50.8	16.7	54.2	37.5	44.5
37	* PING AN	7.8	34.8	62.2	45.3	37.4
38	CHONGQING IRON	16.2	31.0	8.2	3.6	127.8
39	CITIC BANK	5.9	31.8	10.9	5.9	83.4
	Average	16.1	29.5	–	–	88.9

Figures as of 13th May 2007

*H-share index constituents

REFERENCE

Campbell, John. Y. and Pierre Perron, 1991, "Pitfalls and Opportunities: What Macroeconomists Should Know about Unit Roots," in O.J. Blanchard and S. Fisher (eds.) *NBER Macroeconomics Annual*, Vol. 6, MIT Press, Cambridge, Massachusetts.

Chan Kalok and John K. H. Kwok, 2005, "Market Segmentation and Share Price Premium: Evidence from Chinese Stock Markets," *Journal of Emerging Market Finance*, 4:1, pp. 43–61.

Fang Xinghai, 2007, "Linking A and H shares," *Caijing*, 10 January, 2007.

Hui Miao and Wensheng Peng, 2007, "Why A Share Market Volatility is High?" *China Economic Issues*, June 2007.

Levin, Andrew and Chien-Fu Lin, 1992, "Unit Root Tests in Panel Data: Asymptotic and Finite-Sample Properties," mimeo, University of California, San Diego.

Yam, Joseph, Linking the Mainland's and Hong Kong's Financial Markets," *Viewpoint*, Hong Kong Monetary Authority, January 2007.

Yam, Joseph, "Linking the Mainland's and Hong Kong's Financial Markets (II)," *Viewpoint*, Hong Kong Monetary Authority, February 2007.